MODERN NATIONALISM

Dr John Hutchinson is Senior Lecturer in the Faculty of Humanities at Griffith University, Brisbane. He has degrees in History and Sociology and is the author of *The Dynamics of Cultural Nationalism* (1987). He is currently co-editing with Anthony Smith a reader on Nationalism and working on a study of historical sociological approaches to the analysis of world history.

D1634809

N 0080064 3

FONTANA MOVEMENTS AND IDEAS
Series Editor: Justin Wintle

titles available:

JOHN HUTCHINSON

MODERN NATIONALISM

FontanaPress
An Imprint of HarperCollins*Publishers*

Fontana Press
An Imprint of HarperCollins*Publishers*
77–85 Fulham Palace Road,
Hammersmith, London W6 8JB

A Fontana Press Original 1994

1 3 5 7 9 8 6 4 2

ISBN 0 586 09056 9

Photoset in Linotron Baskerville by
Rowland Phototypesetting Ltd, Bury St Edmunds, Suffolk

Printed in Great Britain by
HarperCollinsManufacturing Glasgow

To Colin and Jane Crisp

CONTENTS

ACKNOWLEDGEMENTS

After finishing what has sometimes seemed to be a never-ending task, it is a special pleasure to record my appreciation to those who made this book possible.

To begin with, let me thank the Faculty of Humanities, Griffith University, for financing a period of six months research leave in 1990 to initiate this book, and the Department of Sociology at the London School of Economics which gave me visitor status during this time.

Several friends and colleagues commented usefully on earlier versions of these chapters, but I would like to mention, in particular, Linda Weiss who from the very beginning provided encouragement that was sustained from afar to the end. I am also grateful to Margaret Quinn for her able work as a research assistant; to Diana Solano for compiling the index with her customary perfectionism; and to Janice Mitchell for last minute secretarial assistance.

Two of the chapters are based on previously published material: Chapter 2 on 'Moral Innovators and the Politics of Regeneration: the Distinctive Role of Cultural Nationalists in Nation-building', *International Journal of Comparative Sociology*, xxxiii (1–2), 1992, pp. 101–17; and chapter 6 on 'State Festivals, Foundation Myths and Cultural Politics in Immigrant Nations', in *Celebrations of the Nation*, ed. T. Bennett et al., Sydney: Allen & Unwin, 1992. I am grateful for permission to reprint some of the material in this book.

This study was composed while I was carrying a heavy administrative load at my university. I would like to acknowledge the patience of Justin Wintle, my series editor, despite all the delays and his helpful criticisms.

To my father and mother I offer heartfelt thanks for putting up (without too many complaints) with occasional periods of Trappist silence. In spite of all appearances to the contrary, I have never forgotten how much I owe them.

Finally, I would like to express my deep gratitude to Colin and Jane Crisp for their kindness and friendship over twenty years. At a late stage in this project their support was invaluable and allowed this book to be completed. This book is dedicated to them.

INTRODUCTION

Over the past twenty or so years, there has been a remarkable revival of interest in nationalism among historians, social scientists and cultural critics who have produced a steady stream of novel and provocative books and articles on the topic. Observing this, the distinguished historian, Eric Hobsbawm, suggests in a recent book that it is a sign that nationalism is now past its peak.[1] Like Hegel, whom he cites, Hobsbawm believes that wisdom comes at the dusk of a phenomenon.

This author is not so sure. We appear rather to be in the midst of a major revival of nationalism. The skeleton has escaped from the cupboard. Just as nationalism has come alive again as a political issue and confronts us all with acute practical dilemmas, so too it is an object of controversy among scholars who disagree, often fiercely, about its past, present and future. This book will explore some of these important debates about modern nationalism and the modern nation.

To do this I have organized this volume into six chapters. The first two address more general theoretical issues and introduce the ideas of many of the leading contributors to the theory and comparative analysis of nationalism. They are followed by four chapters that use a variety of theoretical perspectives to reflect on a series of contemporary challenges to nationalism and the nation-state as classically defined.

Chapter 1 analyses what is becoming the most contested issue in the recent literature: the question of whether the nation is a peculiarly modern social formation or is embedded in history. This has all sorts of implications for our relationship to the past, our conceptions of modernity and the relationship of nationalism with respect to it, and our understanding of the varieties of nation-states and of their viability in the long run. We will see that many of the issues raised here run through the rest of the book, including the important question of whether the long-term political stability of states is dependent on their being built on the history and culture of a dominant ethnic population.

Chapter 2 examines and contests one of the underlying assumptions in much recent scholarship: that nationalism is essentially a political project directed to the achievement of an independent state. I argue that there are also cultural nationalisms the aims of which are the construction of distinctive collective identities rooted in history that can direct the modernization process. Although these identities may be mythical, I maintain that they have had just as significant a part as political nationalism in the making of modern societies.

Chapter 3 studies the contemporary religious revival to explore the complex relations between nationalism and religion in the modern world. Nationalism is often regarded as a successor ideology to religion in providing the equivalent legitimating basis for modern societies that religious belief systems furnished for premodern formations. But in many parts of the world nationalism has emerged sometimes in alliance, sometimes in competition with religious movements, and there are those who regard the current Islamic revival centred in the Middle East as providing a radical challenge to the nation-state. Exploring these issues raises question marks against those accounts that too easily correlate nationalism with the project of modernization.

Chapter 4 focuses on the recent collapse of the Soviet Union to understand the relationship between nationalism and one of its great competitors this century: the secular salvation ideology of communism, that predicted the eventual demise of the nation. After outlining the nationalities policies of the Soviet Union and providing an explanation for its collapse, I examine the larger implications of these events. Do they represent the fall of the last empire in the modern world, or the failure of the communist modernization project, or, yet again, the potential risks faced by all modern states with multi-ethnic populations? The discussion highlights the role played by cultural nationalism in the collapse, and the ambiguous relationship between the state and its Russian ethnic core.

Whereas during the 1980s in Eastern Europe the national model seemed to be triumphant, in Western Europe many observers asked if the classical model of the European nation-state was increasingly obsolete. Chapter 5 reviews this issue, examining threats to the European nation-states from three levels: from the supranationalist movement to create the European Community; from the eruption of autonomist campaigns of ethnic minorities within the nation-state; and finally, from the challenge of large immigrant communities that undermine nationalist assumptions about cultural homogeneity.

Finally, chapter 6 assesses arguments that one can find in the New World multi-ethnic societies of the USA, Australia, and Canada the post-national multicultural future of humanity. But do these societies represent a genuine alternative, or are these claims just another form of nationalism postulated by relatively 'young' societies seeking to differentiate themselves from prestigious 'Old World' states? The chapter discusses these questions through a study of recent commemorative festivals of their founding moments. After exploring the use by the state of such festivals to accelerate the processes of nation-building, it analyses the self-images and the competitive cultural politics to which they gave rise.

The reader will find recurring themes and arguments running through these chapters, though they take different forms. One debate, in particular, stands out: between, on the one side, those who regard nationalism and the nation as peculiarly modern, essentially political, an invented phenomenon, and one which is likely to fade with internationalization; and, on the other side, those who argue that both nationalism and the nation are embedded in history, have as their central concern the problem of identity, are a directive force resistant to easy manipulation, and are here to stay as permanent features of our modern world.

My own position is that although the processes of internationalization are continuously altering the character of nations, both nations and nationalism are more resilient than some would allow. Indeed, it is the uncertainties and disruptions created by the impact of modernization on established meaning systems and organizational structures that cause nationalism to be a recurring phenomenon, offering new pathways towards social progress. It is, however, dangerous to romanticize nationalism, though it does have its positive side. For we will see that there are deep tensions within most modern societies between the exclusive cultural claims of the nation and the universalistic and egalitarian expectations engendered by such institutions as citizenship. These tensions are particularly evident and troublesome in multi-ethnic states where nationalism, as we shall note in the case of the USSR, can be a major threat to cohesion and can lead to terrible violence and suffering.

To these problems there are no easy answers. Nevertheless it is important to understand the mainsprings of nationalism and how it operates in different contexts. This book does not pretend to offer the comprehensive analysis necessary for a full understanding. But I hope that it throws a little light at times on the central issues and that it will encourage readers to turn to the rich and nuanced scholarship of the authors presented in these pages whose texts I have been compelled occasionally to simplify but not, I hope, unduly distort.

1

How Modern is the Nation?

Fact of History or Modern Myth?

Today the nation is the dominant form of political organization over much of the world. Accompanying this is a pervasive acceptance of the assumption of nationalism that nations are facts of nature that have differentiated humanity into distinctive cultural communities, each of which has its own territorial habitat and capacities for self-government. Most states justify their independent status by claiming to embody the political aspirations of a nationality; and the world forum of states is called the United Nations.

Many historians date the rise of nations to the time of the French Revolution which, in supplanting dynastic loyalties with the idea of popular sovereignty, transformed passive subjects into active and self-governing citizens. The success of the French republic as the first nation-state made it a model for other political communities in Europe and Latin America. Since then nation-states have formed in discontinuous bursts. As they did so, units smaller than the nation (the principality, the city-state) have been swallowed up and larger units (non-national empires) have crumbled. Major landmarks have included the unification of the German and Italian peoples through war into nation-states in the 1860s and 1870s; the formation of many new nation-states in Eastern Europe and the Balkans as a consequence of the collapse of the historic Habsburg and Ottoman Empires at the end of the First World War; the emergence in Africa and Asia of independent states that accompanied the decolonization of the European powers after the Second World War; and, recently, the rise of a dozen or so would-be nation-states from the ashes of the Soviet Union. The process of nation-formation is by no means completed, as the current struggles in the Balkans, Western Europe and India indicate.

Although at first glance the nation seems a thoroughly modern institution, it is deeply ambiguous. On the one hand, the nation is the political site of modernity for much of humanity: through national citizenship one secures access to a general and technical education, employment, political office, and the ability to participate in scientific progress. On the other hand, contemporary nations legitimize themselves by claiming descent from ancient communities, and the nation-building project is formulated by nationalists in terms of 'revival'. Everywhere (although to differing degrees) the formation of nations has been accompanied by the revival of 'historic' names, symbols, languages, heroes, and cultural practices.

When then did nations come into being and what is their relation to the state and to modernity? To what extent can they be regarded as the invention of modern socio-political groups seeking to harness social change, and to what extent were they shaped by premodern ethnic sentiments and structures? These are the questions that will be addressed in this chapter.

As we will discover, they are still the subject of lively debates between those we might characterize as modernists and ethnicists. These controversies are of great interest, for they raise important questions about the nature of social identities, of modernity, and of our relationship to the past. The debates also highlight how important disagreements are derived from different models of historical and sociological explanation. On a practical level the debates have policy implications, for they reveal differences about the extent to which national conflicts can or cannot be managed.

Before analysing the major points of contention, let me review the different schools of interpretation. As we shall see, they tend to operate with different definitions of the nation.

Primordialists, Modernists, Ethnicists

The study of nationalism has been distorted by the close relationship between the rise of modern historiography in the nineteenth century and the emergence of nationalism. Major historians such as Frantisek Palacky, Eoin MacNeill and Nicolae Iorga were important figures in their respective (Czech, Irish and Rumanian) national movements. They presented the past as the story of nations engaged in a perpetual process of self-realization. These nations were primordial entities embedded in human nature and history that were objectively identifiable through their distinctive way of life (e.g. through language, history, education, religion), their attachment to a territorial homeland, and their striving for political autonomy.

Although the development of history as a 'scientific' profession led to the discrediting of this overtly ideological view of the past, until the Second World War (and even after), many of these primordialist assumptions continued to shape the work of distinguished European historians. Hugh Seton-Watson perceived the gradual elaboration in Europe of a sense of nationality from the time of the barbarian invasions in late antiquity, if not before in classical antiquity itself.[1] Walker Connor cites Marc Bloch's claim that a national consciousness was already highly developed in England, France and Germany by the year 1100, and also repeats Johan Huizinga's perception that national consciousness was evolving throughout the medieval period.[2] These historians recognized that before the eighteenth century nationality was still subordinate to religious and dynastic principles and often smothered by them, and that nationalism, as we know it, came into being with the diffusion of ideas of popular sovereignty that identify the mass of the people as the source of power and value. None the less, their contention is that nations existed well before the modern era of nationalism.

Since the 1960s this stance has been discredited by such writers as Karl Deutsch, Ernest Gellner, E. J. Hobsbawm and Benedict Anderson, who argue that the nation is a peculiarly modern institution and accuse their precursors of projecting current conceptions anachronistically back into the ancient and medieval periods.[3] Hobsbawm argues that before the nineteenth century the term 'nation' in European cultures had no political connotations, and linguistic continuities do not support the primordialist case on the grounds that there is no conception before the eighteenth century that sharing a common language had any social or political implications.[4] Walker Connor notes that many peoples are ethnically quite distinct from their alleged ancestors. For example, modern Greeks are descended not, as they claim, from the ancient Hellenes but from Slavs who from the sixth century AD migrated in large numbers to mainland Greece.[5]

Since the rise of the nation as the global political norm has occurred only in the last two centuries, it should be understood in terms of the great revolutions – industrial, democratic, rationalist – that are synonymous with the rise of modernity. There are, as we shall see, notable differences between the above-mentioned writers. But together they identify five important points of discontinuity between nations and earlier forms of communities.

Firstly, nations differ from their cultural predecessors as embodying a new rationalist political vision of humanity emerging in the late eighteenth century. Previously societies had been governed by a religious view of the world, which portrayed the monarch or ruler as the representative of God on earth, and the population as his subjects, owing him reverence. But out of the Enlightenment came a view of nations as composed of individuals who because of their rationality are equally endowed with the capacity and drive for self-government. The nation, in short, can be understood only by reference to its goal, a *nation-state* whose legitimacy in turn rests on the will of 'the people' constituted as the body of citizens.[6] This implies the enfranchisement of the masses, which occurred only in the nineteenth and twentieth centuries.

Secondly, nations tend to differ territorially from previous political units in their size and degree of consolidation.[7] Modernists explain this by referring to the new scale of organization brought about by the rise of the modern bureaucratic state and the market economy, which have eroded regional and local loyalties and produced wider networks of interaction.

Thirdly, nations, when they form nation-states are strikingly different from earlier units in being based on the principle that political and ethnic boundaries should be congruent.[8] Although reality often diverges from this norm, what is striking is the states' concern for ethnic homogeneity, vigorously promoted through the construction of official languages, the educational curriculum, and the expulsion or 'cleansing' of minorities. It was only during the nineteenth and twentieth centuries that ethnic minorities came to be perceived as a threat to the integrity of the territorial state. Indeed, according to W. H. McNeill, before the eighteenth century polyethnicity was the norm of advanced societies, and different ethnic populations lived in stable relations with each other in imperial units.[9] Claims of ancestral affinity with earlier political units are thus fictive.

Fourthly, modern nations are artefacts of print capitalism whose new genres – the newspaper and the novel – make the nation imaginable.[10] The nation is an anonymous, socially differentiated and large-scale collectivity, unified by a 'high' literate and scientific culture based on a single and distinctive vernacular language. By contrast, premodern societies were localized, small-scale kinship groups marked by high rates of illiteracy and by cultural heterogeneity. Their cultural specialists (the clergy) were seldom tied to the political unit or to vernacular folk societies but rather to a transnational Church and a sacred language (Latin in Europe, Arabic in the Islamic world); and the social and economic elites were often linguistically distinct from those below. No unified national consciousness was possible.[11]

Fifthly, nations are industrial societies with a high degree of economic integration throughout the territory. By providing large-scale ascending career pathways, they become the institutional nexus for an emerging urban middle-class society imbued with the ethos of continuous social mobility. It is above all these middle-class groups who identify with the interests of the nation-state and who, forming political, social and economic organizations, serve to integrate the apathetic masses into the new political order. By contrast, there was no such integrating national class in premodern agrarian societies whose economy was essentially static and localized. They were marked by an ideology of inequality which justified a battle for extraction waged by lords on the peasantry and resulted in a high degree of social stratification. While it is true that some aristocracies developed a type of national consciousness (as a warrior stratum in conflict with their rivals), they would and did reject the notion that they had a shared identity with and obligation to the mass of the people.[12]

Modernists, therefore, reject the notion that nations are primordial entities with distinctive cultural attributes that shape the development of modern societies. It is rather the case, Gellner claims, that modernization has given rise to nationalism, and nationalist elites have invented nations. Modernists then disavow *objective* in favour of *subjective* definitions of the nation. As Deutsch demonstrates, no single criterion (language, geography, and so forth) fits all cases, and indeed, the national symbols of individual countries shift over time.[13] What is crucial is the self-awareness of a population that it constitutes a nation. Of course, Gellner and Hobsbawm are aware that without some public commitment to a set of common symbols and values it is unlikely that a group can long persist, but the distinctive histories and cultures that nations proffer are mythic constructs of parvenu social formations to justify their prestige and political existence in the modern world.

Even a hard-nosed modernist such as Gellner, however, concedes the existence of some nations (e.g. England) in Western Europe before the modern era, but he maintains that their existence in agrarian countries was merely accidental. It is since the nineteenth century that the nation has become the global norm and it is this fact, together with the embracing of the nation-state model by states in Africa and Asia which have no correspondence to any previous cultural or political units, that refutes the primordialist case. The interesting problem, Gellner suggests, is to explain why what was a contingent has now become a necessary phenomenon, and this can be done only by reference to modern factors.[14]

As we shall see, modernists differ over several matters, including periodization (dating the rise of nations and the modern), models of explanation (whether the nation and nationalism developed out of a conjunction of separate developments or as a necessary consequence of a single modernization process), and in their selection of causal factors: for Anderson it is print capitalism, for Gellner industrialization, for Breuilly the development of the modern state.[15] But they agree that nationalism is not an outgrowth of already existing nations; rather it is the case that nationalist elites have invented nations.

ETHNICIST APPROACHES

Interpretations, however, of the nation as a modern artefact have been challenged recently by two scholars, John Armstrong and Anthony Smith, who, while rejecting primordialism, and accepting that modern nations have certain distinctive features, including the integration of 'the masses' through citizenship rights, argue that the formation of nations needs to be examined in *la longue durée*.[16] This leads them to contextualize the emergence of nations within the larger phenomenon of ethnicity which shaped them. By ethnicity they mean different things, with Armstrong adhering to the boundary approach of Fredrik Barth,[17] and Smith to the importance of intrinsic meanings given by myths, symbols, and cultural practices, a divergence to which we will return later. But each rejects as the core of nationality the political definition focusing on citizenship which is preferred by modernists. The nation is thus an ethno-cultural community shaped by shared myths of origins, a sense of common history and way of life, and particular ideas of space, that endows its members with identity and purpose.

Armstrong's work is not easy to summarize, but he suggests two different patterns of political community in Europe and the Middle East. In Europe, ethnic identity crystallized round the experience of sedentarism which led to the principle of territoriality and to the city as the centre of social life. In the Middle East, ethnicity formed round nomadism which led to the genealogical principle and, in contrast to Europe, to a nostalgia for a lost world of the desert.[18]

Smith's approach is more far-ranging. He agrees that a distinction can be made between post-eighteenth-century nationalism and nations, on the one hand, and earlier ethnic sentiments and ethnic communities (which he calls *ethnie*), on the other. Nationalism has a polycentric and dynamic vision of humanity as divided by nature into distinctive communities each with its special role to play in human progress, and the modern nation as a named population has a set of distinctive features: possession of a consolidated territory, common myths and history, a mass public culture, an integrated economy, common legal rights and responsibilities, and, above all, a claim to sovereignty.[19]

In contrast, earlier *ethnie* were xenophobic; most were scattered with no political consciousness, and even those ethnic polities, closest to the modern nation-state – of the Egyptians, Greeks and Jews – were economically localized, legally and religiously stratified with different laws and religious practices applying to different classes, and with their educated class divided. Nationalism in the modern sense emerged in conjunction with the rise of a new secular, educated, and mobile middle stratum (the humanist intellectuals and an intelligentsia) which, forming in the cities as a consequence of the intellectual, political and commercial–industrial revolutions, challenged the religio-dynastic order and sought to establish a distinctive legal-rational state based on equal citizenship rights.

Nevertheless, Smith maintains against the modernists that the differences between modern nations and *ethnie* are of degree rather than kind, that the historical record shows the existence of many more such ethnic polities than are generally recognized, and that such ethnic identities are durable over time despite destructive conquests and waves of immigration.[20] He argues, therefore, that the rise of modern nationalism should be explained in terms of a larger cycle of ethnic resurgence and decline in history, and that modern nationalism has been shaped by premodern ethnic identities. He lists several factors, including the experience of settlement in a territory after a period of migration, as contributing to the rise of ethnic identities. But he places particular importance on the role of recurring interstate wars between neighbouring populations. Out of these form collective identifications with territorial boundaries; ethnic stereotypes crystallize as a result of state-organized propaganda dichotomizing 'us' and 'them'; and, from episodes of collective triumph and disaster, legends arise that transmit the idea of the nation as a distinctive community of heroes knit by sacrifice and valour. These identities once formed are often diffused by powerful political and cultural institutions to become firmly rooted in the social order.[21] Indeed, the modern nation is in large part built on premodern *ethnie*, which he divides into two types: lateral or aristocratic, which develop round a centralized state and have only a limited reach into the general population; and vertical or demotic, usually subject to rule by others and sustained by religion, whose values and institutions pervade and unify the population.[22]

Smith argues that these two ethnic structures interact with the processes of state modernization, economic revolution, and cultural transformation to construct political communities. The first pattern operated for England, France and Spain, which then became models for other countries. In the case of the second, with the state depicted as the enemy of the 'subject' *ethnie*, the process of transformation was slower, for religion, the other major social institution, had a vested interest in sustaining its view of the community. The key role in the rise of nationalism in such populations was played by the secular intelligentsia, who, influenced by neo-classical and romantic cults of nature and history, sought to reinterpret this religio-ethnic identity and to harness it for the purposes of group mobilization against the state.[23] In either case, however, the pre-existing ethnic profile served to shape the contours of the modern nation-state. Smith concedes that such nation-states may be a minority, since many do not possess such ethnic pasts, but he argues that these two forms have provided models for African and Asian leaders who since 1945 have sought to 'invent' a nation to correspond to the novel political structures they have inherited from European powers. In these and other cases, he observes that populations without a clear ethnic core community find it difficult to build a cohesive political order.[24]

The Issues

It is clear from this discussion that there is a good deal of common ground between modernists and ethnicists. The latter would accept that post-eighteenth-century nations differ significantly from earlier forms of community in several respects, including their political conception of human identity, the democratic character of their societies and the intensity of social and economic interactions. But there is dispute about three major issues: firstly, about the degree of overlap between modern nations and earlier ethnic formations; secondly, about conceptions of modernity and premodernity and the idea of *a* transition; and thirdly, about the extent to which nations are to be seen as inventions or reconstructions shaped by earlier ethnic sentiments.

It is to these topics that we will now turn. As we shall see, it would be silly to construct a series of intellectual exchanges into a simple battle between two camps. Once we begin to examine the individual positions in any detail, we find that the reality is much more complex. There are as many differences within the modernist stance as there are between ethnicists, and apparent protagonists share many points of agreement. The outcome of this analysis will be to suggest that this is not a simple debate about dates and evidence, that the problem addressed is one of rich ambiguity and one's response is dependent in part on one's definitions of key concepts and preferred model of historical explanation. None the less, the answer has implications for how one perceives the future of the nation, whether it should be regarded as a product of special and historically contingent factors or as rooted in recurring processes in world history.

THE NATION AND ETHNIC COMMUNITIES

A major divide between the two camps is over the degree to which the modern nation should be understood as akin to earlier ethnic communities. How constitutive of the modern nation are such institutions as legal citizenship rights and the consequent unitary and mass character of the political formation? To Hobsbawm, Gellner and even Connor, this mass, integrated, and political character is all important and continuities with earlier ethnic communities are fictive. But to Armstrong and Smith, these emphases are problematic and obscure the modern nations' affinities or, sometimes, direct lineages with the culture and politics of premodern communities. Let us examine these propositions in turn.

1 National identity and the masses

For modernists one of the core ideas of nationalism is the doctrine of popular sovereignty, and the essence of the nation is its equation with the masses or the people as a whole. But there is little or no evidence that the masses before the nineteenth century were aware of a national identity. A number of distinguished historians including Marc Bloch and Johan Huizinga, and more recently Hugh Seton-Watson and Bernard Guenée, might trace the formation of a popular national consciousness in the European Middle Ages, but Walker Connor accuses them of relying on the evidence of a few members of the political and intellectual elite.[25] Scholars, he argues, should be more cautious in evaluating the written documents of premodern societies where literacy was confined to privileged status groups. Nor can one cite the existence of distinctive languages or other objective cultural traits as indicators of national identity: it is *awareness* of having a common culture or origins that constitutes nationality. Real evidence of popular attitudes is only available in the last two centuries, and even that indicates a pervasive allegiance to locality for much of the nineteenth century. Here Connor cites the responses given by immigrants between 1840 and 1915 at the time of their arrival in the United States. Drawn largely from rural and poorly educated backgrounds, few respondents if any defined themselves by national rather than village or regional origins. He also refers to Eugene Weber's celebrated study of late nineteenth-century France, which shows that most men and women in the countryside and small towns were profoundly local or regional in their outlook, in their use of dialects, and in their economic and social transactions. It took a revolution in transport, integrating the regions for the first time with each other rather than with the centre, the introduction of mass education and conscription to result in a nationalization of French life.[26]

Connor assembles a powerful case, but there are several possible rejoinders. Firstly, given the paucity of surviving evidence of mass consciousness of preliterate societies, any argument one way or the other is going to be difficult to maintain. None the less, if used with caution, linguistic usage, folklore and archaeological data may, in many contexts, hint at the existence of a popular ethnic consciousness. One might note Hobsbawm's admission of the existence of a popular identity of belonging to 'Holy Russia' developed in conflict with the Muslim Turk as expressed in Cossack epic tales in the early seventeenth century.[27] The persistence of indigenous languages and myths among Anglo-Saxons despite invasion and conquest by the Normans suggests such a thing. Although Connor correctly rejects any automatic association between language use and ethnic identity, he himself points to the resistance of Neapolitians and Calabrians to Mussolini's attempts to impose the Italian language as evidence of the strength of local identities in Italy.[28]

Secondly, he tends to see the concept of identity in either/or terms so that if individuals acknowledge locality they cannot be national, whereas in reality people's identities are multiple. The question then is not 'are individuals *at any one time* national in their orientation?', but rather 'do national identities become primary under certain circumstances in premodern societies?' – a point to which I shall return.

Thirdly, the definition of nations in terms of mass consciousness invites the question, as Connor himself recognizes, of how many people are required to bring the nation into being. Recognizing the difficulties, he falls back on a formulation that suggests that nations exist when significant groups are mobilized into collective action by national appeals. But by shifting the question away from numbers to social effectiveness, he blurs the distinction between elite and mass nations. Certainly, it is useful to bear in mind when explaining social behaviour that elite attitudes are not necessarily those of the larger population, but this does not mean nationalism had not an important determining influence on societies in spite of this. It seems anachronistic to insist on the importance of mass consciousness when, until recently, small elites set the political and social agendas. Arguably, it would be more sensible to focus not on when nations fully form but when ethnic principles regulate social and political life. After all, most modernists indicate the salience of nationalism as a hegemonic *ideology* in nineteenth-century West European states. And if we date the effective emergence of nations to when the political elites of the community are driven by national principles, then this opens the door to considering many premodern communities as nations, although, of course, differing in important respects (notably, in their non-democratic character) from their successors.

2 The nation as an integrated community

Modernists could respond by arguing that the nation is not just a mass phenomenon but a unitary community overriding the claims of all other groups over its members, whom it integrates through novel legal, cultural and economic institutions. In the words of Rupert Emerson, 'the nation is the largest community which, when the chips are down, effectively commands men's loyalty, overriding the claims of both lesser communities within it and those which cut across it or potentially enfold it within a still greater society'.[29]

Modernists agree that central to the nation are the ideas of unmediated and equal membership deriving from the Enlightenment and embodied first in the French republic, notably through citizenship rights. However, they differ in attributing the relevant causal factors. Gellner points to the role of universal educational systems and the new socio-economic mobility produced by the flourishing industrial capitalist economy of the late eighteenth and nineteenth centuries which broke down localism and created an anonymous society of interchangeable individuals. Anderson argues that the modern nation differs from its precursors in being an imagined community, which was made possible by the rise of the new cultural forms of the eighteenth-century newspaper and novel (which in turn developed out of a new print culture that had been emerging since the fifteenth century).

Nevertheless they are in accord in contrasting the modern nation with the stratified societies of the past. One might occasionally trace a national consciousness among the elites of earlier agrarian societies, but, it is argued, this was secondary to religious, regional and class loyalties. Prior to the eighteenth century, religion not ethnicity was the primary regulator of social, economic and even political life in most countries, and legitimated an ethos of inequality. In such countries as Italy, Turkey, China, and India, nationalists have regarded themselves as at war with religion to achieve national unity. Even in those premodern societies (for example, early modern France) which possessed some national consciousness, regional laws, customs and cultures weakened national integrity. In considering the enserfed societies characteristic of the medieval West, and Eastern Europe up to the nineteenth century, Connor argues that a sense of common nationhood was not compatible with cross-cutting class cleavages as deep and unremitting as that between slave and landowner.[30] He exemplifies the profound social chasms that existed in such societies by citing the statement made about a Croat magnate that he would sooner have regarded his horse than his peasant as a member of the Croat nation.[31]

When then can one say that a unitary national community comes into existence? Connor suggests one criterion of nation-formation for societies avowedly wedded to the idea of popular sovereignty is the willingness of ruling elites to subordinate their class interests to their national allegiance by admitting the masses to the democratic franchise. By this test he argues even countries like nineteenth-century England could not be regarded as constituting a nation. But this formal definition violates his stress on the subjective character of the nation (as a self-aware ethnic group), and in practice it means that nations only come into being in the mid to late twentieth century (when women were given the vote). Connor, for all his provocative brilliance, has produced a *reductio ad absurdum* of the modernist position. For his stipulative criteria threaten to banish nations from history altogether in spite of the fact that it is the historical efficacy of nationalism in the first place that has inspired the debate about the origins of nations.

There are, in fact, dangers in insisting on a black-and-white contrast between post- and pre-eighteenth-century societies. Certainly, national identity is now embedded institutionally in the life of modern societies, and prescribes as never in the past all groups to obey the national summons. As Anderson remarks, the experience of the two World Wars this century demonstrates that countless millions are prepared to fight and die for the nation, whereas in the past the only comparable institution to inspire mass sacrifice was that of religion, most notably in the Crusades.[32] None the less, many modernists, including Hobsbawm[33] and Hroch,[34] point to the strong challenge posed to national identities by class loyalties, particularly where – as in the case of Slovaks, Lithuanians, and Flemish – the latter had formed first. Ideological and class cleavages impeded French national defence in the Second World War, when French Communists under instructions from the USSR refused to mobilize behind the French state.

In short, the nation is continually challenged by other loyalties in the modern world. On the other hand, one should also note that in the premodern period religious beliefs and institutions, although at times subverting a sense of ethnic differences in communities, have often consolidated and perpetuated them. This is particularly true of groups living for centuries on either side of the boundaries between warring religious oecumene. The case of the Russians identifying themselves by the seventeenth century with Orthodoxy against the Muslim Turk has already been mentioned. But the tendencies of religious systems to schism and develop local practices has led to conflicts within Christianity and Islam which has contributed to the crystallization of national consciousness. Religio-dynastic wars in sixteenth- and seventeenth-century Europe formed the modern English and Dutch identities as Protestant nations.

This analysis suggests that neither since nor before the eighteenth century can the nation be represented as a unitary and bounded totality, but rather as one identification amongst many that competes for the loyalty of its purported members who belong to kinship, economic, cultural, political and other networks. At particular times other allegiances may override the nation, so that to the extent that the nation is dominant this is a *recurring* not a once-and-for-all phenomenon. As Connor wisely observes, nation-formation should be seen as a process rather than as an event.[35] The question then arises: are there factors common to many periods of history that generate a primary loyalty to an ethnic community? This question will be addressed in a later section.

3 The nation as political community

The third argument for the discontinuity between modern nations and earlier ethnic communities rests on the distinctive political character of the former. Modern nationalism puts forward a theory of political legitimacy whereby the political and ethnic boundaries must coincide and state institutions must represent ethnic values.[36] The nations that result are markedly different from their precursors, which were primarily cultural entities and lacked any drive to achieve political sovereignty. Even the ancient Greeks – often claimed to have a national consciousness because of their common language, religious cosmology and practices, and cultural institutions such as the Olympic games, and their self-differentiation from outsiders (equated with barbarians by Herodotus) – lacked a sense of political unity, divided as they were into city-states, some of which were at times willing to ally with Persian invaders against their Greek rivals. Until the modern period most states were relatively decentralized, weak, and, according to McNeill, polyethnic. It is only with new rationalist conceptions of humanity and the development of citizenship that the formation of autonomous national states became possible. Nationalism can be understood only by reference to its goal, a nation-state, and this emerged with the French Revolution and refers to a body of citizens who declare their sovereignty by association in a state and whose loyalty to the nation must override all allegiances.[37] Any parallels between such states and earlier ethnic communities are accidental and insignificant in comparison with this decisive difference.

This focus, however, on state and citizenship as the core of nationality is one-sided and West Eurocentric, and is indicative of a widespread tendency, observed by Walker Connor, to conflate the terms *nation* and *state*, as is evinced in naming the leading world organization the United Nations when its membership is composed not of nations but of states. The term *nation*, Connor argues, should refer to a politicized and self-aware ethnic community which (as in the examples of Wales and Slovakia) does not necessarily have to possess a state of its own, and *state* to a centralized politico-territorial unit.[38] But more than this we can say (and this will be elaborated in the next chapter) that there are in fact two conceptions of the nation. The first is civic, focusing on the achievement of an autonomous state of equal citizens, a concept which emerged first in Western Europe, and the second is ethnic, associated with Central and Eastern Europe, where the nation was initially conceived of as a historical and cultural individuality which must be preserved or revived. This cultural nationalism too has a politics but it is communitarian. Statehood in this latter version, if desired at all, is a secondary feature of the nation.

Smith argues that these two modern conceptions are based on two earlier types of *ethnie*; the elite or aristocratic *ethnie* which identifies with the honour of a given territorial state and whose strength lay in its lateral reach rather than its social depth; and the demotic *ethnie* sustained usually by distinctive religious institutions which penetrated across status groups. France would be an example of the former, the Armenians and the Irish an example of the latter. For the modern French, national identity was created from above through reshaping (republicanizing) the French state, which was regarded as the primary institution of the nation and the means by which it was to be built and integrated. By contrast, the struggle for nationality in Eastern Europe and Ireland came from below, as secular intellectuals challenged the Church for dominance of the nation.[39]

In practice and over time, in modern nation-building processes one finds both concepts being employed as necessary for the viability of nations in the modern world. Hence, during the latter part of the nineteenth century, Czech, Ukrainian and other nationalists in Eastern Europe became increasingly concerned with independent statehood as a means of preserving the cultural nation. But it is also the case that in Western Europe relatively advanced states became increasingly ethnicized, claiming descent from ancient founders or heroes. One observes this in the powerful French and German states, where in the late nineteenth century at times of class conflict there developed a statue mania celebrating figures such as Arminius, who rallied the ancient Germans against the Roman legions, and Joan of Arc, defender of France against the English.[40]

This drive to establish the state on ancient ethnic foundations is, according to Smith, not just decorative: the cultivation of an alleged unique past may serve as a set of regenerative rites at times of crisis (e.g. war and class conflict) with the aim of galvanizing demoralized populations. Nations require more than citizenship to bind their members in solidarity, as is demonstrated by the endemic instability of what may be called the contemporary *state-nations* of the African continent, whose elites are motivated by a project of nation-formation that has yet to be realized but where the common ethnic bases of European states are as yet lacking. Indeed, Smith maintains that because of the decline of religion as a social cement, modern societies require even more than their precursors the ethnic heroes and potent myths to provide meaning and purpose in a world disenchanted with old salvation stories. For these myths and memories provide a kind of immortality by identifying individuals and groups with a society which has existed from time immemorial and which, through the memories and examples of each generation's sacrifices and achievements, will extend indefinitely into the future. They thereby supply a means of overcoming death.[41]

Of course, modernists who pour scorn on these pretensions to ethnic continuities argue that this changed function of ethnicity is precisely the point. It is anachronistic to assume that casual cultural resemblances indicate any real equivalence between premodern and modern ethnic communities. This question of the fictiveness of the ethnographic claims of nationalists will be addressed in the final section of this chapter. But even were this to be the case, the ethnicists' analysis does suggest that it is worth considering the rise of the nation in terms of the wider phenomenon of ethnicity in history. This would then shift the focus from looking at specific post-eighteenth-century factors to recurring processes in world history.

The Nation and Models of Modernity

For modernists such as Gellner this is anathema; he argues that although it may be possible that nations existed in ancient times, they were aberrant forms; but since they have become the political norm, it is to modern factors that one must look to explain them. Indeed, Gellner, like many social scientists, regards the nation as the product of a transition between premodern and modern societies. While this statement might seem at first sight unproblematic, it raises questions about what one means by modernity and transition. Once again, answering these questions involves more than attributing dates: it means choosing between different models. As we shall see, the idea that nationalism and the nation are correlatives of modernization is full of pitfalls.

GELLNER'S MODEL

In the writings of the most radical of the modernists, Ernest Gellner, the transition is conceived as a step-like leap from one plateau to another, from agro-literate societies which are regulated by structure to industrial societies whose mode of integration is by culture.[42] The former are highly stratified, immobile, and compatible with a high degree of ethnic and linguistic diversity: people's identities are given and reproduced by invariant roles in a generally localized community in which there is little need for a trans-stratum medium of communication. By contrast, the latter are egalitarian, mobile and culturally homogeneous: their identities are generated within a standardized high culture that is maintained by a territorial state. Nationalism is produced by the transition to industrialism, and nationality and industrial society are indivisible in the long run, with the possible exception of Islamic societies.[43]

What made nationalism so necessary was the shift to a complex and continuously changing division of labour which broke down older stratifications and the fixed specialisms attached to them. This resulted in a fluid, interchangeable and increasingly urbanized society of strangers, one integrated by routinized interest rather than by magic or ritual. The new social system required for its maintenance that its population have a generic training which would allow them to respond to occupational change, together with an expertise in specialist techniques. This in turn entailed the creation of a standard literary language making possible precise communication between strangers. Such training functions could no longer be executed by the family. Only a standardized educational system would suffice, and this could only be financed by a state capable of extracting resources over a relatively large territory. The central demands of nationalism and the characteristics of the modern nation – ethnic homogeneity, an extensive territory, universal education in a single language, an autonomous and efficient state – are all explained by reference to the imperatives of industrialization.

It is the nature of the industrialization process that accounts for the transition resulting in a plurality of nation-states rather than one world state. As Gellner argues, industrialization proceeds unevenly, emerging in particular centres and hence causing competition for resources and significant movements of population. Where there are no significant cultural differences between competitors, the outcome is class conflict. But linguistic, religious and racial differences are often used as mechanisms of exclusion to curtail competition. Whereas in pre-industrial societies inequality is the norm, the new mobile society generates egalitarian ideas that make such arbitrary exclusion intolerable. As a consequence, aggrieved groups try to form their own ethno-political units as the means by which they can participate in the new industrial world.

Most analysts would agree that Gellner's model of the transition and his ideal-typical contrast between the premodern and modern industrial societies is extremely illuminating. But there would be disagreements about his conception of post-eighteenth-century societies and the teleological overtones of his account of the relationship between nations and this 'modernity'; about his depiction of the formation of modern and national societies in terms of a single and revolutionary transition; and about his corresponding neglect of the extent to which recurring processes in world history contribute to the formation of nations.

Is the rise of nations and nationalism essentially linked to the inception of an unprecedented social formation, governed by a disenchanted instrumental rationality which is exemplified in capitalist relations of production and exchange, a scientific mode of cognition, and the bureaucratic state? Hobsbawm and Gellner would have us believe so. Hobsbawm relates the formation of nations to the requirements of capitalism for large-scale and centralized territorial and political units which will provide the necessary legal framework and market outlets. Gellner argues that it is the need of industrialization for cultural homogeneity that generates nationalism. Nationalism in turn invents a nation-state which will establish the general education system to sustain the basis of a productive society.

Neither scholar, however, provides a convincing causal account of these connections. Hobsbawm does not explain why nation-states in Europe, emerging in the late eighteenth century, pre-dated the development of an industrial capitalism which became a significant presence in many West European countries only by the 1830s. Gellner's difficulties are not just that in many contexts (e.g. Eastern Europe) nationalism predates industrialism, but that there appears to be no causal link between early industrialization and mass education. Britain, the pioneer industrializer, did not develop such a system until the 1870s. Critics such as Smith argue that the rise of the modernizing bureaucratic state is a more convincing precondition than industrialization for the rise of modern nationalism.[44] Gellner and Hobsbawm could and do respond by maintaining that capitalism (in Hobsbawm's case) or industrialization (in Gellner's) cannot be reduced to a single variable but rather must include such factors as the Enlightenment, bureaucratic rationalization and so forth which cumulatively produce the nation.

Yet in stretching concepts such as industrialization in this way, they reduce the explanatory utility of their model and are open to the charge that such elasticity operates as an immunizing strategy against criticism. Moreover, it gives their interpretations an immanentist and teleological cast, in which nationalism is explained as a function of modernization – defined in terms of an emancipatory project – that was unanticipated by nationalists themselves. One implication is that nationalism and the nation are transitory phenomena. Thus Gellner argues that once industrialization is achieved, the intensity of nationalism declines: cultural differentiae cease to be important when groups find themselves belonging to the same social world of economic growth, social mobility and so forth.[45] Hobsbawm goes further, and maintains that nations will disappear as political units as industrialization becomes increasingly international and global: they only had a transitional role in the breaking down of localism.[46] Gellner therefore has difficulty in explaining the revival of a ferocious terrorist nationalism within the contemporary heartlands of Europe, among the relatively prosperous Basques and Catalans against the Spanish state. Hobsbawm, when analysing the resurgence of secessionist nationalism in the contemporary period (for example, Quebecois nationalism in Canada), has no plausible response except to denounce this as a temporary irrationalist reaction to the complexities of modernity.[47]

This highlights two major weakness in their accounts. First of all, they fail to understand that nationalism arises not just as a means to achieve modernity, but rather to (re)create a sense of distinctive identity and autonomy that will enable populations to survive in a modern world in which unpredictable change is the norm. A second and related criticism can be made of their conception of modern history as embodying a transition from the passions to the interests. To assume that the progress of industrial society will result in the triumphant formation of societies integrated by reason and socio-economic progress is curious in a century tainted by global wars unprecedented in their destruction and by the mass murders and genocidal frenzies of Hitler and Stalin. It is this enhancement of threat produced by modernization that helps explain the spread and deepening of ethnic politics, manifested in modern nationalism.

A further set of criticisms concerns the idea of recent history as shaped by a single decisive transition.[48] Disagreements about whether significant processes or outcomes should be explained by revolutionary or evolutionary models are pervasive in historical inquiry. In the light of the extraordinary upheavals that shook Europe from the late eighteenth century onwards – the waves of political revolutions, the industrial 'take-off' of Western Europe, the decline of religious authority before the challenge of science, it is not surprising that Gellner, Hobsbawm and others should adopt a revolutionary model of modernization to explain the proliferation of nationalism and the nation since the nineteenth century.

As we have observed, however, Gellner admits that his theory is unable to deal with the much more evolutionary formation from the thirteenth century onwards of national states in Western Europe (e.g. of England, France, Holland and Spain) analysed by Charles Tilly and others.[49] It should be said that not all modernists commit themselves to a 'revolutionary' model. Anderson and McNeill, adopting a more historically grounded approach, indicate that the causal sequence which resulted in the proliferation of nations in the late eighteenth century took place over an extended span. Among the crucial factors adduced by Anderson is the emergence of print cultures in the fifteenth century which, together with the decline of religion, made possible the linkage of anonymous individuals into imagined national communities, sharing the same homogeneous time and space.[50] McNeill looks to the gradual growth of centralized states and an urban economy in the early modern period and the military innovations of the seventeenth century, and acknowledges the growth of an English and French national consciousness arising out of the Hundred Years War.[51] In this these modernists differ little from three writers whom Yoshino calls historicists: Charles Tilly, Gianfranco Poggi, and John Breuilly. While admitting the distinctiveness of post-eighteenth-century nations, they connect the rise of the national community to the development of a competitive interstate system from the thirteenth century onwards.[52] But the further back the origins of the modern are set and the more modernization is traced as a long-term process composed of discrete factors, the hazier the notion of a divide between the pre-modern and the modern becomes, and the more difficult it is to maintain that post-eighteenth-century nationalisms are funda-mentally different from earlier ethnic outbreaks in history.

For such reasons, Smith and others argue it makes sense to consider post-eighteenth-century nationalism and nation-building in *la longue durée*: in other words, to understand their emergence in terms of a wider theory of ethnic formation that refers to factors that may be common to the premodern and the modern periods. One of the major factors that Smith identifies as important for the crystallization of ethnic communities is, as we have already noted, the experience of interstate warfare, a form of which, long predating the formation of a European system, can be found in the ancient world.[53] War does not in itself create ethnic or national identities, for to cohere a threatened population must have some pre-existing common cultural traits (often provided by religion) round which it can be mobilized. But it is notable how populations such as the Armenians and Georgians on shifting frontiers between warring Islamic and Christian states have retained an ethnic identity tied to religion into the modern period. Although the development of a global society of competing states is relatively recent, Smith argues that recurrently in history such competitive systems have emerged in particular areas of the world at which times ethnicity has become increasingly salient as a regulative cultural and political principle in a manner analogous to nationalism in the modern world.

This stress on the role of war is consistent with Smith's funda-mental explanation of the recurring salience of ethnicity in his-tory: the identification by individuals with a community linked to immemorial origins which has survived both triumphs and disasters is a means of overcoming death. In the premodern era, ethnic identities were usually secondary to religion, which prof-fered answers to the problems of evil and suffering. But with secularization the modern ethnic ideology of nationalism now has become a surrogate religion and the primary basis of identity for the community.[54]

Smith's focus on war is a valuable corrective to any simple

correlation of ethnic politics with modernization, *per se*, and his arguments gain some confirmation from an examination of modern French nationalism, which has been a fluctuating force in which war or state rivalries have played a more important role than socio-economic transformations. For if one accepts the usual ascription of the origins of the modern French nation to the introduction of universal citizenship rights during the French Revolution, it is then a curious fact that over eighty years later, during which time such processes as industrialization, urbanization, and secularization had greatly advanced, a sense of nationalism appeared to have attenuated with regional identities prevailing over much of the countryside. It is likely that institutions such as the *levée en masse* and the experience of nearly twenty years of continuous war against the European powers during which about a million Frenchmen died were the formative factors in engendering a popular nationalism. As Weber demonstrates, a further surge of nationalism occurred in the period 1870–1914, marked by a growing sense of military rivalry with the newly ascendent German state, which led to large-scale military conscription and the development of a mass education system. This culminated in the hostilities of 1914 that introduced a new form of war, a total war of peoples (whose only precursor in Europe was the period of the Revolutionary and Napoleonic wars), and which, according to Weber, brought a mass democratic nation into being.[55]

There are, of course, many qualifications that could and should be introduced into this discussion to avoid oversimplifying the relationship between war and nationalism. War is by no means the only generator of nationalism, as will become clear in later chapters, and as Michael Howard has reminded us there are many different types of interstate war. In the nuclear era, he suggests, the nexus between war and nationalism has been broken, since hostilities are likely to be brief and bloody and can now be conducted almost autonomously by political elites and their technical specialists without the necessity to secure mass participation over an extended time.[56] It could be said that the many regional interstate wars in the Middle East and South Asia since the Second World War indicate that Howard is being premature. But even if Howard is correct, what this discussion demonstrates is that nationalism is not a correlative of modernization and that though the intensive and extensive communication networks created by the modern bureaucratic and industrialization process make possible modern national identities, they do not explain their rise. For nationalism is a recurring phenomenon, whereas modernization has become a continuous presence in many post-eighteenth-century societies. One has to look to specific factors to account for the periodic resurgence of nationalism, some of which are also present in the premodern period.

Ethnicity and the Making of the Modern Nation

The analyses presented to date support the case that the rise of the modern nation should be understood as part of the wider phenomena of ethnicity in history. But what of the most interesting issue in the debate, namely the relationship between ethnicity and the making of modern national societies? Are, as Smith maintains, successful modern nations substantially built on the framework of pre-existing ethnic cultures? Or, as modernists tend to maintain, is their ethnic character *invented* to serve the community-building goals of interest groups engaged in a competition for power that arises out of the modernization processes? Are national identities instruments or can they be directors of social change?

The point here is that one cannot deduce from the prior existence of *ethnie* that they necessarily have any causal status in the formation of modern national societies. To do so without empirical examination is to make uncritical assumptions about continuities between premodern ethnic and modern national identities and to fall into the *post hoc ergo propter hoc* fallacy. Indeed, modernists, in observing that modern nations differ radically from earlier societies in their territorial, demographic, socio-economic and political structures, deny also any substantive similarities in the content of ethnic identities between premodern and modern communities.

They attempt to show that national cultures are composites,

often selected from alien and previously marginal populations; they are peculiarly modern, produced by novel processes, institutions and ideas, and adopted by new social groups (e.g. professional middle classes); and they are accepted by populations not because of their continuities with a cherished heritage, but because they meet contemporary needs. To modernists, then, ethnicity is essentially a fluctuating instrument which is constructed and reconstructed to serve changing social interests, and they tend to reverse the causal relationship and explain the formation of national identities by reference to the novel requirements of post-eighteenth-century societies.

Modernists like Hobsbawm tend to adopt a position that is in sympathy with Fredrik Barth's boundary approach to ethnic groups.[57] Barth treats ethnic groups as groups of self-ascription, which develop identities through dichotomization with others. Their cultural symbols operate to mark the boundaries of interaction between 'us' and 'them' and are subject to change. This emphasis on the processual rather than the objective dimensions of nationality leads to the conclusion that there is no necessary relationship to earlier ethnic loyalties in cultural content, territorial forms, or social bases. Cultural symbols are proposed, according to this argument, not to express a commitment to fundamental values, but rather to effect a differentiation of the group from others. In this context they have a functional rather than an essential significance: they act as border guards, preserving a sense of difference, and hence can and do change without affecting the integrity of the group. The fact of their fluctuation over time suggests they have little ideological content and, by extension, little formative power.

These positions are rejected by Smith, who argues that the (re)turn to a golden past by nationalists is motivated not just by ambition but by a quest for identity and direction at times of moral and social crisis created by the erosion of established belief systems and social structures by modernization. He agrees that there is often a considerable degree of invention in this process and that the mythic pasts thus created legitimate the drive for power and status of novel social strata – above all the intelligentsia or professional middle classes – who are the core constituency of nationalism. None the less, since nationalism is a multi-class movement with a limited range of symbolic repertoires, its themes must have a general resonance and cannot be explained in socially reductive terms. And to be accepted as an authentic conception of the past and thereby to be socially effective, any reworkings cannot fall too far outside existing historical understandings of the collective past. Because of this the national past is not a *tabula rasa* to be continually reinvented; earlier ethnic identities can have a directive role. Indeed, the type and strength of such identities are important for explaining the eventual shape of the modern nation.[58]

There would appear to be two main issues here. One is the extent to which the turn to the past should be seen in terms of manipulation and invention or of a search for identity and rediscovery followed by regeneration. The second is the model of ethnicity used and its implications for nation-building. Is an ethnic group to be seen as an organization concerned with the maintenance of boundaries against outsiders in terms of which its cultural content is incidental and fluctuating over time and determined by the needs of external differentiation? Or is its history and culture the core of an ethnicity determining its relations with others and its trajectory through time?

THE INVENTION THESIS

One of the most succinct formulations of the invention thesis is provided by Ernest Gellner: 'Nationalism is not the awakening of nations to self-consciousness: it invents nations where they do not exist.'[59] Elsewhere he writes, 'The cultural shreds and patches used by nationalism are often arbitrary historical inventions. Any old shred and patch would have served as well.'[60]

But the term *invention* with reference to nations is used in several different senses by scholars. It has the connotations of novelty, manipulation, and, at extremes, deliberate fabrication and even forgery, as in Trevor-Roper's account of the formation of the modern Scottish nationality based on a distinct Highland tradition.[61] This, he argues, was a retrospective invention because the Highlanders as an ethnic offshoot of Ireland were regarded before the eighteenth century as an alien and barbarous people by most Scots. The formation of the new Scottish identity was in large part the result of the usurpation of Irish history and culture by two men called Macpherson, one of whom (James) fabricated an ancient Scottish epic by Ossian out of Irish literary materials, while the other (the Reverend John) provided an accompanying history.

Other historians are sceptical of forgery interpretations,[62] but even if Trevor-Roper is right in this case, to propose as a general proposition that national cultures are forgeries or fabrications is untenable because it implies there is an authentic original which has been copied. There is also the problem of explaining why these forgeries are accepted as plausible by the larger society. In Trevor-Roper's analysis nationalism has an unexplained and mysterious power to sweep away pre-existing values and practices and reshape the environment to its will.

Recognizing the need to qualify such a bald constructivism, Hobsbawm suggests a more sophisticated formulation when, in a recent study, he argues that nations are

> dual phenomena, constructed essentially from above, but which cannot be understood unless also analysed from below, that is in terms of the assumptions, hopes, needs, longings and interests of ordinary people, which are not necessarily national and still less nationalist.[63]

In Hobsbawm's account national cultures are inventions in both their content and form. Firstly, they form out of a creative process of selection and composition of the past, and although it is claimed they express continuities with ancient values and institutions, they evoke entirely novel meanings. Secondly, the symbols take on a different significance through the modern ritual and institutional forms (for example, popular festivals, monument building, and mass educational systems) through which they are communicated that arise with industrialization and the state centralization. Social change has undermined established ideologies and institutions, and in this context traditions have no directive power over the present: the invented tradition that is the nation is rather *politically* shaped in terms of the present needs and interests of (particular) social groups.[64]

As a Marxist, Hobsbawm links the political *invention* of the nation to the needs of capitalism and of a rising bourgeoisie seeking hegemony and coming into competition with old established groups and religious belief-systems. He qualifies, however, such a reductionist approach in two ways. Firstly, he observes that, once created, the national model is also capable of being used selectively by traditional elites, for example, the Prussian monarchy and land-owning aristocracy in the new post-1871 Germany, who, realizing the necessity of finding new legitimations in a secular democratic age, sought to incorporate the masses by claiming a role as the permanent guardians of national continuity. Secondly, he notes that a particular national definition cannot simply be imposed; any such attempt engenders conflict with the conceptions of other social groups.

By acknowledging, however, the capacity of premodern social groups to shape national politics, Hobsbawm weakens the instrumentalist position. Paul Brass limits it still further by distinguishing between national projects where the movement draws upon an old and rich ethnic heritage with a persisting core and those which create their cultures after-the-fact.[65] In the former case, the existence of such heritages, particularly where they are attached to traditional institutions (the rabbinate, in the case of the Jews) and social structures, offers strong incentives and constraints in group mobilization by indicating what types of appeals and symbols are likely to be effective. None the less, he argues that even in these cases there is never a unanimity about what constitutes the central values of the community, and that the leaders of national movements select from traditional cultures only those elements that will unite the group and promote its interests as the leaders define them. Moreover, the process of modernization leads to elite differentiation and competition and to conflicting definitions of tradition. For this reason, Brass argues:

the study of ethnicity is in large part the study of politically induced change. More precisely, it is the study of the processes by which elites and counter-elites within ethnic groups select aspects of the group's culture, attach new value and meaning to them, and use them as symbols to mobilize the group, to defend its interests, and to compete with other groups. In this process, those elites have an advantage whose leaders can operate most skilfully in relation both to the deeply felt primordial attachments of group members and the shifting relationships of politics.[66]

Brass defends this instrumentalist approach in a notable debate with Francis Robinson about the importance to be assigned elite manipulation for political purposes rather than Muslim values and institutions in explaining the separation of the Hindu and Muslim peoples of the Indian subcontinent into the 'nation-states' of India and Pakistan.[67] Both writers agree that a crucial factor in destabilizing the balance between Hindu and Muslim populations was the expanding role of the British colonial administration in nineteenth-century India. By interfering with the religious jurisdictions of both groups and by creating a new English-educated Hindu and Muslim class, it politicized the two populations. Robinson argues that the historic religious differences between the two communities on such matters as idol worship and the cow predisposed them to separatism as they became mobilized. Brass, by contrast, proposes that separation occurred rather because a section of the Muslim elite, fearing that Muslims would lose their former privileges as the dominant community in a future post-independent India in which Hindus would be the majority, chose to differentiate their population historically and culturally from Hindus.

Brass supports his position thesis by arguing that the ritual and religious practices of each community did not exclude acknowledgement of the rights of the other, and that there was no unified Muslim community or set of symbols beyond a commitment to religious practices. The momentum for separatism built up not so much from inevitable Hindu and Muslim antagonisms, for there was room for compromise on fundamental issues, but from elite diversification and consequent intra-elite competition in the Muslim population between the landlords and government officials who traditionally enjoyed a privileged status, the *ulama*, and an emerging secular professional class. Muslim separatism was a relatively late development linked to the growing strength of the third group, who feared that Muslims would be politically marginalized in a Hindu-dominated India.

The strength of religio-cultural sentiments among the masses, according to Brass, limited the field of manoeuvre for leaders, but because of the lack of homogeneity of the population, elite groups had a certain autonomy in selecting values and symbols as part of the process of defining and mobilizing a political community. He argues that different symbols and issues were employed, depending on context, by these groups who were competing both for power within their community and to achieve a secure position for Western-educated co-religionists in the struggle with Hindus for employment in the new state sectors. To explain, in short, the eventual *novel* shape of modern nations one has to look to politics rather than to alleged continuities in core values.

Such positions have been attacked by Francis Robinson, who argues that even a sophisticated instrumentalism gives elites an undue autonomy from their communal traditions and is reductive of their motives by characterizing them only in terms of power. Demanding a recognition of the fundamental role of Islam in motivating political action, he explains the drift of Muslims to political separatism by reference to the tendency, visible over centuries, of Muslims to organize in politics on the basis of their faith. Political structures played an important part in determining the trajectory of their politics: the move to separatism became the popular option once the measures of the British government, in devolving positions and power to Hindus, threatened the Muslim way of life. But the driving force was a desire to live within an Islamic society regulated by the *shari'at* (historic Islamic legal code), which the political setting merely channelled in a particular way.

In support of his argument for the importance of belief-systems in shaping human action, Robinson states that, in acknowledging the constraining power of communal sentiments, Brass is unaware he has made an important concession. Adopting an argument of Quentin Skinner, Robinson suggests that individuals, in justifying their actions, are limited by the range of concepts in existence in the community, and more particularly by the statements they have earlier made to legitimate their actions. Because of these appeals to 'primordial' sentiments, they find themselves forced to modify subsequent actions to be consistent with these statements. In this way, ideological attachments come to shape policies even in the least case situations when the political elites do not necessarily share them.[68]

Robinson, however, suggests there is also a strong case to be made for the directive power of ideas and sentiments on nationalists. It is implausible to portray elites as governed only by the drive for power, as if they lived outside the cultural framework of their society of origin. Although nationalist leaders were secular and Western-educated and clashed with traditional religious elites and their conceptions, the ideas of Muslim or Hindu community, which they had internalized as part of their socialization, were likely to – and did – inform their ultimate goals even if they had in some measure abandoned them.

Robinson makes a cogent case, but it requires qualification on two grounds. Firstly, it underplays the extent to which the secular middle classes, as a result of their socialization through secular educational institutions, meritocratic career structures, and political parties, are inspired by the *ideal* of modernization. What unites them is often the dream of leading their people to participate in the great international centres as equals in a global drive to achieve human progress, and a corresponding sense of revulsion against the restrictions of the traditional order and the privileged status of its guardians. In pursuit of their ideal of political autonomy, they may well employ traditional sentiments in a manipulative sense. Secondly, as Michels reminds us, the power of party bureaucratic machines in the modern era permits leaders to enjoy a relative autonomy from their base, and their capacity to deploy this depends on the existing structure of power.[69] In a competitive political environment this autonomy will not be long lasting, but where the nationalist organization operates as the umbrella political organization, or where nationalists after independence establish a one-party state, this is not the case.

None the less, over time this autonomy is limited since, as Smith demonstrates, the modernists are only one of three responses to the impact of modernization on traditional belief-systems and social structures and they have to compete with those whom he calls neo-traditionalists and reformists.[70] All three groups consist of individuals socialized in both traditionalist and modern scientific cognitive and organizational systems and who feel a need to resolve the tension between them. According to Smith, each project is driven to legitimate itself by reference to an ethnic past, and this commitment to a common national tradition can act as an integrating force and lead to a return to tradition (albeit now ethnicized) on the part of modernists. This thesis is complex and will be examined in greater detail in chapter 3. It is enough to say at this point that for Smith the search into history is motivated not just by a drive for power, but for signs and meaning at a time of crisis, and that the pasts constructed by nationalists, while containing a good deal of manipulation, are credible and potent as a political force only in so far as they are compatible with earlier ways of conceiving the collective past.

This thesis does not in itself have much to say about the resonance of the past. Here, Smith concedes one of Brass's points: that societies differ according to the richness of their collective traditions and also to the extent they have been carried down by powerful institutions.[71] In certain contexts, would-be nationalists have to concoct a common past out of fragmentary memories or conflictual traditions, but in these contexts the sense of nationality is weak. In other contexts, the traditions are strong but guarded jealously by powerful social institutions such as churches and aristocracies which are often able to channel and co-opt the nationalist movement. The process of nation-building in either case is complex and sometimes drawn out.

If this is so, then the premodern structure of ethnic groups should have an important bearing on how the modern nation does form. In investigating this, as we have already noted, Smith identifies two important types of ethnic community: first, vertical and demotic, which occurs usually where religion and ethnicity are fused (as in the case of the Jews and Irish); and, second, lateral, usually confined to a warrior aristocracy (as in medieval France). The former, identifying the *ethnie* with a special religious aura, create the framework of small nations, endowing them with a sense of mission. The latter usually give basis to the modern great powers whose identity is focused on the prestige of a centralized state and memories of military greatness. As we have noted earlier, this gives rise to different routes to nation-building. In the case of the former, the process is more 'bottom-up' and a leading part is played by nationalist intelligentsia, whereas in the latter the process is 'top-down', emanating from the political centre. It is notable that this model is compatible with the findings of Eugene Weber that local rather than national consciousness was dominant even in nineteenth-century France, before the latter was institutionalized by mass schooling, mass conscription, and regional economic integration.

We can see from this that Smith provides a radically different theory of ethnicity to that of Barth. Against those who suggest that ethnic symbols are pliable and work primarily as differentiators, he argues ethnic identities change more slowly than is assumed and may express deeply held values and meanings of the group. He agrees that symbols of group identity may evolve and are reconstructed according to changes in the experience of the group, but that the cultural genres and forms (e.g. artistic, religious, military and administrative practices) of groups are much more long lasting, and have been sustained in many cases by founded religions, which by codifying ideas and practices in writing, give a relative fixity to traditions.[72]

Of course, not all modern nations can establish themselves on a firm ethnic base, and many form only out of prolonged processes of differentiation, which include cultural clashes and wars in the post-eighteenth-century period. In highly regionalized states like

Italy, it may be unclear where the ethnic core lies, something that has encouraged the recent rise of regional Leagues in the North against Southern 'domination'.[73] In much of contemporary Africa it is modern (European) political and cultural forms that create a unifying base for state elites, for whom the (multi-) ethnicity of their populations is only a source of division. But even in these unpropitious circumstances, these states use the rhetoric of nationalism to integrate their diverse population, although they are inspired by civic rather than ethnic models: they seek in other words to build the state to invent the nation. In doing so, African leaders look to the Western European experience for models of nation-building, promoting the unification of their territories through communication systems, state schools, and economic development. Apart from the difficulty of trying to achieve in a few generations what was accomplished (with less than complete success) by European states over centuries, one of the difficulties they face is that the African state, unlike its European forebears, is an exotic institution. These fragile states do achieve a measure of viability by virtue of their recognition as nation-states (for example, through membership of bodies such as the United Nations) and by the interstate system which discourages potential ethnic secessionist or irredentist challenges.[74] Moreover, state leaders have buttressed their authority by tapping Pan-African sentiment through their highly visible campaigns against the Afrikaner South African state, until very recently, the remaining symbol of European colonialism in Africa. But bedevilled by endemic and systemic conflict, they do not refute Smith's argument that where there has been no strong ethnic core political identity, it has not been easy to construct a stable nation-state.

CONCLUDING REMARKS

In a single chapter it is hard to do justice to the wide range of issues raised in these debates, let alone the subtleties of individual positions which frequently overlap the main divisions that have been identified here. But we may conclude by making three points.

Firstly, the contestations arise in part from a lack of clarity about the concept of nation which is a result of the protean character of the phenomenon itself. They demonstrate also the importance of defining terms in order to explore empirical complexities rather than to pre-empt argument. One of the valuable contributions of the modernists has been to expose the anachronistic Eurocentric and national assumptions of much scholarship about the human past, that are to be explained by the fact that the professionalization of history took place within emerging European nation-states. By exploding the primordialist account and by highlighting that the proliferation of self-professed nation-states is recent and global, modernists have encouraged a closer world-comparative inquiry into what constitutes a nation and also into the causes of nations, and their relationship to social and political development.

Secondly the limitation of many of the modernists is their correlation between the nation and the modern and their conception of a modernity, discontinuous with the past, which entails the corresponding assumption that nationalist claims to continuities must be mythical. As we have observed, a politicized ethnicity is neither entirely absent before the eighteenth century nor all-pervasive after it, but may be one of many identities that individuals might simultaneously adopt. There is a reluctance, therefore, to recognize that there may be *recurring* factors in the relationships between populations (e.g. military and cultural conflict) that may embed ethnicity as a political and cultural force in human history.

Finally, the discussion suggests that although modern nations are distinctive in certain respects, their configuration and cohesion is heavily determined by the routes taken by nation-builders. This varies according to whether or not the state can be used for the task and the presence or absence of pre-existing ethnic structures. Hence, nation-building is not simply an outcome, but can be a moulder of modernization. Agency, therefore, has to be built into the study of nation-formation.

With this in mind, the next chapter will examine two distinctive types of nationalist project: cultural and political nationalism.

Later chapters, however, will show that whatever model is adopted it is no simple task for nationalists to construct (let alone invent) the nation.

Is Nationalism Statist?

The Nation as a Cultural Project

Revolutionary France has long provided us with the image of the first modern nation-state based on the transformation of subjects into citizens. Born out of a revolt in the name of the people against an archaic but oppressive monarchical state, it resulted in the abolition of the monarchy and feudal privileges, the destruction of clerical power, the elimination of provincial rights, and an attack on regional cultures. Instead a new centralized state formed, guaranteeing through written constitutions and legal codes the rights of man, subordinating religious belief to allegiance to the polity, imposing uniform laws and linguistic practices throughout the territory, and offering through its extension of education and the introduction of competitive examinations for public positions the prospect of social mobility by merit, all with the aim of creating a unitary democratic political community.

With this transformation came a new iconography and set of rituals. The emblems of monarchical rule sanctified by religious rites and arcane aristocratic codes were replaced by a national flag (the tricolour), a stirring national anthem (the Marseillaise), and great open-air festivals of public dedication (oath-taking) to and commemoration of the nation, which were marked by mass participation.[1] A new political religion was being formed in which the people, now deified, worshipped themselves.

This model of a dynamic and mobile political community has had a huge world-wide impact through conquest or emulation. In Western Europe where territorial states enclose relatively homogeneous ethnic populations, nationalism by placing sovereignty in the nation has only upset the internal distribution of power, as there has been a struggle to make the political institutions representative of the people as a whole. But else-where in Europe where the boundaries of ethnic groups and states are misaligned, the impact of this model has on occasion resulted in profound territorial conflicts as nationalists have struggled to unify the nation, divided as in the German and Italian territories between many little states, or to secede from multinational empires (e.g. the Austro-Hungarian) whose elites excluded from power the representatives of the nation or who discriminated against its culture.

In short, the spread of nationalism has been accompanied by the proliferation of centralized states, each claiming legitimacy by virtue of its basis on the popular will. As these nation-states have formed, each in turn has sought international standing by virtue of its possession of the attributes of statehood, diplomatic missions, a military establishment, a strong economy integrated on national lines and so forth.

Because of this, commentators have tended to regard modern nationalism as a theory of political legitimacy: that a state is legitimate when its political and ethnic boundaries coincide and when its ruler is co-cultural with its population.[2] The overriding aim of nationalists therefore is that each nation should have a state of its own.

I propose to argue that it is misleading to interpret nationalism as *just* a political movement, and that there is a distinct species of nationalism, called cultural nationalism, which in many contexts has preceded and accompanied the formation of nation-states in the form of major historical, artistic and linguistic revivals. These movements have usually been small in scale, con-fined to coteries of intellectuals, cultural societies idealizing ancient heritage and rural harmonies, yet on occasion they have provided an umbrella for significant social and political move-ments that have helped shape the nation-state.

Why then has comparatively little attention been given them? There are three major reasons. First, there has been a tendency to regard cultural nationalism as just a cover for political nation-alism when normal political activity is not possible. Second, even where scholars have noted their presence, they have tended to regard these movements as essentially regressive products of otherworldly romantics, belonging to declining or oppositionist social groups, which have little capacity to direct social change. Third, as a corollary of this they have been portrayed as a transient phenomenon, destined to disappear with full modernization.

I, however, will argue that there are two distinctive and sometimes competing types of nationalism: a political nationalism that has as its aim autonomous state institutions; and a cultural nationalism that seeks a moral regeneration of the community. Although the latter looks backward, it is not regressive; rather it puts forward a mobile view of history that evokes a golden age of achievement as a critique of the present, with the hope of propelling the community to ever higher stages of development. Indeed, at times of crisis generated by the modernization process, cultural nationalists play the role of moral innovators proposing alternative indigenous models of progress.

By comparison with political nationalist movements, those of the cultural nationalist variety are relatively small in numbers and must give way to state-oriented movements since their models can only be implemented through the state. Nevertheless, they perform vital integrative functions, and, if transient, cultural nationalism is also a recurring force since the political dispensation is regularly shaken by the unpredictable challenges of modernization. Unless we take this aspect of nationalism seriously we cannot offer adequate accounts of its dynamism in the modern world, which is founded on its attempt to preserve a sense of identity by reforming a valued heritage that can orient economic, social and political development.

Two Types of Nationalism

How, then, does cultural nationalism differ from political nationalism? In practice, of course, it is often difficult to distinguish between cultural and political nationalists, for both put forward what, since the eighteenth century, has been in many contexts a revolutionary doctrine: that sovereignty is located ultimately in the people, and that the world is divided into distinctive peoples, each with unique homelands. Cultural interests have often provided a useful cloak for the political struggles of rising social groups hostile to the established polity. In Africa, cultural fora such as the Nkrumah's Nzima Literary Society provided outlets for a small educated stratum of civil servants, excluded from formal political activity by the British authorities.[3] Similar societies provided an equivalent function for early nineteenth-century Czechs, Slovaks and Slovenes, who, because they lacked a native nobility, had no political status within the Habsburg Empire,[4] and for nineteenth-century Ukrainians, divided between two states.[5] In other cases cultural and political nationalists might share the same organization: in the 1840s, Young Ireland were members of Daniel O'Connell's Repeal movement. Individuals, such as the Chinese intellectual Liang Ch'i Ch'ao, might combine in their person the attributes of the two nationalisms.[6]

This is one of the reasons that has led some to conclude that it does not make much sense to differentiate the cultural and the political. One influential interpreter, Elie Kedourie, proposes an essentially political definition of nationalism. Nationalism, he argues, is a doctrine formulated by new secular intellectuals, hostile to the traditional dynastic and religious order and concerned with individual and collective autonomy, that has as its primary aim the integration of the people in an independent state.[7] He notes that there are two quite different varieties of nationalist doctrine: the first (republican), deriving from Kant and associated with political nationalism, that conceives of the political community as a body of individuals who have signified their will regarding the manner of their government; and the second (organic), deriving from Herder, that perceives the nation as a natural solidarity endowed with unique cultural characteristics. But in practice, he argues, the two conceptions converge. Although the first is explicitly concerned with integration within a state through citizenship rights, Kant also argued that nature, by dividing individuals culturally through differentiae such as language, had ordained diversity and competition between political groups. Likewise, Herder's injunctions on the need to defend the cultural uniqueness of the nation led to the conclusion that each nation must have a protective state of its own.[8] Hence, in its 'mature' formulation by Fichte, nationalism became a statist doctrine that prescribed that individuals could find autonomy only by a total integration within their natural polities, which in turn were defined in terms of their distinctive cultural attributes.

The problem with this account is that although, as we have noted, the two nationalisms do often converge in movements of new secular groups subversive of the traditional order, it radically underplays the very distinctive conceptions of cultural and political nationalism which often find expression in quite different organizations and political strategies.

Thus behind the political nationalist focus on citizenship rights is the belief in reason as the ethical basis of the community, which is often inspired by the polis of classical antiquity. Of course, this is a cosmopolitan conception that logically looks forward to a common humanity transcending traditional differences. Indeed, many notable political nationalists began as enthusiasts of universalist ideologies: Daniel O'Connell as a liberal, Nehru as a socialist, each having broken with the traditions of their societies. However, as they come to realize that the world is divided into a multiplicity of political communities each with their embedded cultural biases, they are driven to achieve their vision of a just society within their homelands. To mobilize a political constituency on behalf of this goal, they may appeal to ethnic sentiments and in the process become 're-traditionalized', but their objectives are essentially modernist: to secure a representative state for their community so that it might participate as an equal in the developing world civilization.[9]

This objective can lead to a wholesale rejection of 'tradition' (often identified with the religious heritage) as an oppressive encumbrance. For example, in order to create a secular 'European' Turkish nation from the ruins of the Ottoman Empire, Kemal Atatürk decided on the necessity of a complete break with the Islamic Ottoman heritage. This entailed using the state to force through against powerful opposition a shifting of the capital from Istanbul to Ankara (chief city of the Turkish heartlands in Anatolia); the overthrow of the Sultanate and the Islamic

Caliphanate, regarded as preeminent by Muslims world-wide; the abolition of polygamy; and the change of the language from an Arabic to a Roman script.[10]

In contrast, for cultural nationalists the state is, at best, accidental, and is frequently regarded with suspicion as a product of an over-rationalist ethos that seeks to impose a mechanical uniformity on living cultures.[11] Rejecting the ideal of uniform citizenship rights as the basis of solidarity, cultural nationalists perceive the nation as a differentiated community, united not by reason or law, but by passionate sentiments rooted in nature and history.[12] According to this organic conception found, for example, in Herder, humanity, like nature, is infused with a creative force that endows all things with an individuality.[13] Nations are primordial expressions of this spirit; like families, they are natural solidarities. Thus the Slovak poet, Kollar, contrasted the formal allegiance due his state with the instinctual loyalty he offered his cultural nation.[14]

Cultural nationalists demand that the natural divisions within the nation – sexual, occupational, religious and regional – be respected, because the impulse to diversity is the dynamo of national creativity.[15] The core of a nation is its unique and differentiated civilization, which is the outgrowth of the strivings of countless generations settled in unique homelands, each one of which has added its contribution to the common heritage. Thus nations are not just political units, but creative personalities continually evolving in time, and it is to history their members must return to discover the triumphs and tragedies that have formed them and the lessons they may draw for the future.

Not surprisingly, the leading proponents of cultural nationalism are not politicians or legislators, but, initially, historical scholars and artists, who form academic and cultural societies, designed to recover this creative force in all its dimensions, to evoke a love of this common heritage and culture in the members of the nation, and thereby fashion the future according to the spirit of the past.

The nationalist historians – Palacky of the Czechs, Iorga of the Rumanians, Hrushevsky of the Ukrainians, MacNeill of the

Irish – are not just scholars but encyclopaedic 'myth-making' intellectuals who combine a romantic search for meaning with a scientific zeal to establish on authoritative foundations the nation's honour as a distinctive people with a high civilization and the laws of its development. These histories typically present a set of mythic patterns: a migration story, the time of settlement, a golden age of cultural splendour, the fall into a dark age, then a period of regeneration, perhaps beginning in the present.[16] Since such histories have rarely been documented by premodern political and religious elites, this quest has resulted in an explosion of research in the genetic sciences – archaeology, folklore, philology, topography – in order to recover the civilization of the people from the cultural substratum.

But, if it is through the historian one recovers the national destiny, it is the artist who dramatizes the rediscovered myths and legends, projecting them to a wider audience. In many respects the artist is for cultural nationalists the paradigmatic figure of the national community, for, unlike the great religions, the nationalist cosmology sets up no prophets to be imitated nor, indeed, any authoritative class of interpreters. The source of creativity is placed not in an eternal supramundane order but in the continually evolving people itself.[17] Every true member of the nation is thus an artist-creator, and the great artists are those who create out of the collective experience of the people as preserved in its historical legends and who reshape their lessons for the present.[18]

Kollar, epic poet of the Slavs, Lonnrot, creator of the Finnish epic, *Kalevala*, the poet Mickiewicz, author of the *Book of the Polish Nation* and of the *Polish Pilgrimage*, became 'fathers' of their respective nations, celebrating the separate origins, unique cosmology, and integration of national life, and providing a pantheon of exemplary heroes and villains who furnished a repertoire of role models for their contemporaries.

These intellectuals then promote a wide-ranging renascence in order to inspire a rising educated generation to reject the ossifications of the present, and to recreate the idea of the nation as the animating force in the lives of the people. But it is only when it is adopted by journalists and pamphleteers who translate the cultural into more concrete economic, social, and political programmes that it becomes a significant movement.

The Politics of Cultural Nationalism

Cultural nationalism thus does tend to develop from a cultural to a political movement, but its goals and techniques differ from those of political nationalism. As I mentioned earlier, the objective of the latter is to achieve an autonomous state based on common citizenship that will enable the community to participate as an equal in the modern world. When not driven underground, political nationalists tend, as in the cases of the Indian Congress and the Irish Parliamentary Party, to organize on legal-rational lines, forming centralized apparatuses that pose as a counter-state to the existing state and seek to mobilize the various interests of the nation to a unitary end.

Cultural nationalists are suspicious of such a centralist politics. Their aim is rather the moral regeneration of the 'way of life' of a unique historical community. Since this is an essentially spontaneous social order, it cannot be constructed like a state from above, but rather, they believe, can only be resuscitated from the bottom up in a manner that pays respect to the 'natural' diversities (regional, occupational, religious, and so forth) within the nation. They are above all educational movements, and they seek to rebind the different constituents to a presumed common essence, forming decentralized clusters of historical and language societies, dramatic groups, publishing centres, agricultural centres and political parties in order to do so. Evoking the name of the nation, engaging in invidious comparison with the culture of others, organizing collective 'pilgrimages' to sacred national sites: these are some of the techniques by which a national identity is constructed.[19]

It is therefore misleading to narrow cultural nationalism to a linguistic movement. Nationalists seek to revive all distinguishing facets of national life, and, as Brass has argued, they choose multiple symbols and seek to make them congruent;[20] for what lics behind their activities is an attempt to recreate the nation as total personality as a basis for the regeneration of the present.

It is, of course, the case that cultural nationalists are not hostile by definition to independent statehood – for example, their organizations offered a platform for political revolution in the uprisings of 1848 in the Habsburg territories.[21] But here, cultural activities became a cloak for anti-state organization where formal politics was blocked. Young Ireland, it is true, joined O'Connell's campaign for an independent Irish parliament, but as a means of securing an audience for their revivalist ideals. They retained their separate journal and sought to transform his organization, formed for electoral mobilization, into 'the schoolmaster of Ireland', through such initiatives as the provision of local reading rooms that would educate a patriotic elite.[22]

In 'normal' circumstances cultural nationalism takes the form of small-scale grass roots self-help movements, unlike political nationalist movements, which may, like the Indian Congress, transform themselves from elite urban-based to mass movements by generating grievances against the existing state among different, even competing groups. But because the state is the major locus of power through its coercive, financial and educational institutions, the communitarian goals and strategies of cultural nationalism fail. Often unable to reach beyond the educated strata, cultural nationalism is forced to adopt state-oriented techniques by which to institutionalize its ideals in the social order. Nevertheless, it is still often of political importance. Relatively well-financed revivals, such as the Greek and Magyar movements of the early nineteenth century, have provided some alternative channels of social mobility for a disaffected intelligentsia, forming them into a counter-culture against the existing regime.[23] At times of crisis for the state, when traditional leaders are also discredited, this intelligentsia, socialized to sacrifice themselves for the nation, have served as a focus of opposition for other discontented groups and as a revolutionary vanguard against the state.

Regressive and Progressive Nationalisms?

Many would agree that cultural nationalism can make an important contribution to nation-building by giving dispersed populations, often with a shadowy sense of identity, a degree of
corporate consciousness and cohesion. But, even so, there is the
tendency of scholars as different as Hans Kohn and Ernest
Gellner to regard it as a reactionary phenomenon, a construct of
secular intellectuals in backward societies, who, when faced with
the challenge of more scientifically advanced cultures, compen-
sate for feelings of inadequacy by retreating into a visionary
golden age in order to claim descent from a once great organic
community. These activities are somehow functional for the formation of nations, but, by themselves, cannot shape their paths
to socio-political modernization.[24]

I shall argue that cultural nationalism must be given a much
more dynamic role than this in determining the modernization
process (by which I mean those changes that occur in economic,
cultural, social and political institutions when scientific principles
are applied to solve the problems of social and natural life). Arising out of a transnational secular culture that perceives the world
in polycentric and interactive terms, cultural nationalists, I maintain, act as moral innovators who establish ideological movements at times of social crisis in order to transform existing belief
systems from within and thereby enable socio-political development on indigenous lines.

THE REGRESSIVE THESIS

According to Kohn's famous typology, there are two forms of
nationalism – political and rational, cultural and mystical – and
the emergence of one or other as dominant is determined by the
level of development of the community.[25]

First to appear was political nationalism in the 'West' (defined
by Kohn as England, France, Netherlands, Switzerland, USA,
and the British Dominions) in populations which possessed a
secular urban vernacular culture dating back to the Renaissance,
and distinct ethno-political boundaries. When nationalism

formed, all that was required was the transformation of the existing order into a people's state, where practical and constitutional objectives would be articulated by an expanding middle class.

When nationalism arose later in the 'East' (defined as Central and Eastern Europe and Asia), it was in imitative response to the rationalist culture of the 'West'. These territories were agrarian peasant societies, with only a tiny middle class, dominated by a reactionary aristocracy, and where, frequently, there was a lack of congruence between ethnic and political boundaries. Unable, therefore, to identify with a concrete territorial polity, and aware of their backwardness compared to the 'West', nationalists turned to myths and legends to conjure an ideal nation that possessed an ancient historic mission and unique cultural attributes. Against the rationalist citizenship models of the 'West', they celebrated the superior organic bonds between peasant, land and community as the mode of national integration.[26]

This was a cultural nationalism led by historians and poets who operated as an educational force, inspiring in a nascent public opinion a sense of loyalty to the national model, which furnished a matrix for later political nationalist movements. None the less, it was essentially a backward-looking phenomenon, incapable of directing social change.[27]

Gellner presents a paradoxical relationship between cultural nationalism and modernization. Revivalism is the product of intellectuals in backward societies who, under pressure from an exotic scientific-industrial culture with which they feel unable to compete, sentimentalize the integrated world of the native folk community whose culture they try to resurrect. In symbolically contesting the 'invasion' of an alien social order, they often serve as precursors to a nationalist seizure of the state, but their effects are almost precisely the opposite of what they intend. Instead of the recreation of a 'folk museum', what emerges is a new scientific high culture using native idioms.[28]

Such analyses do usefully highlight one central point: these historico-cultural revivals do represent a defensive riposte by educated elites to the impact of exogenous modernization, especially, in so far as it is mediated by that major demon of cultural nationalists, the bureaucratic state. But it is wrong to characterize the return to the past as necessarily the search for a prelapsarian community, free from all the dilemmas of modernity. For, as we have noted, cultural nationalists present the nation as a creative high civilization that, evolving in interaction with other cultures through cycles of achievement, decay and regeneration, has to be continuously renovated in terms of the needs of each generation.

True, cultural nationalists evoke a golden age, but this exemplifies an extraordinary integration of the different spheres of social life, including the religious and secular. In the nineteenth century, Indian nationalists celebrated Aryan India as the linguistic, religious, mathematical and philosophical mother civilization of humanity.[29] Irish nationalists recalled an early medieval Ireland which, as a centre of both religious and classical learning, had played a formative part in the rise of Christian Europe after the fall of the Roman Empire.

Cultural nationalists evoke such heroic ages as a critique of present degeneration, for decay and external dependence comes from an ossification of tradition in the hands of the established leaders. The means to regeneration is for the young to reject the old and look back for guidance to the golden age, to recreate authentic values for the future. History, cultural nationalists thus argue, teaches not tradition but a modernization from within: to combine the sense of distinctiveness given by indigenous traditions with the progress provided by modern science through a regeneration of indigenous cultures and institutions.

Typical of cultural nationalist enterprises is the Ukrainian Shevchenko Scientific Society, which, in the nineteenth century, promoted in association with other agencies the raising of the Ukrainian language from a peasant vernacular to the obligatory medium for scientific and academic discourse, technical education, reading libraries and scientific agriculture.[30] Cultural nationalism, moreover, frequently emerges in close conjunction with circles of religious and social reform, with the Bernacacina movement in the Slovak territories,[31] and with the Arya Samaj in India,[32] which sought to reconcile traditional values with the modern scientific culture through a laicization of teachings, the support of secular improvement, and so forth.

Rather than being a regressive force, cultural nationalists explicitly advocate progress through struggle. Conflict, they believe, is an inevitable symptom of the anomie that results when tradition has ossified, but it is also the means by which the nation is regenerated.[33] Indeed, cultural nationalism regularly crystallizes into historico-cultural societies at times of social discord between traditionalists and modernists, generated by the impact of external models of modernization on the established status order. When given socio-political articulation by modernist journalists, it regularly finds its cadres among rising educated youth, impatient with the passivity and obscurantism of traditionalists, and frustrated by their sense of inferiority to advanced metropolitan cultures. Adopting revivalism, they work to restore their country to its imagined former standing as a nation embodying a higher integration of the traditional and the modern by reconstructing sophisticated scientific, economic, social and political structures on the ethnic remains of the past.

CULTURAL NATIONALISTS AS MORAL INNOVATORS

For these reasons cultural nationalists should be regarded as moral innovators who, at times of crisis when society is polarized between traditionalist and modernist groups, construct new matrices of collective identity and directions for collective action. By education rather than by machine politics, they aspire to redirect these groups away from mutual conflict and instead unite them in the task of creating an integrated, distinctive and sovereign community, capable of competing in the modern world.

They innovate by introducing a new ideology of the nation in which the accepted meanings of 'tradition' and 'modern' are transformed. The 'modern' (or, as it is frequently designated, the 'West') is particularized to adherents as a local manifestation of a universal drive for progress to be found in all peoples. 'Tradition' is undermined in the eyes of its followers by demonstrating it to be the outcome of a mobile society whose achievements sprang from an interaction with other cultures. For both traditionalists and modernists, it is argued, the true matrix is the nation in whose drive for realization all must find their individual and collective identities.

There have been many strategies for achieving this. A favourite one for outflanking traditionalists is to resurrect a forgotten golden age anterior to the accepted model past as the authentic tradition. We see this employed by Swami Vivekananda, whose neo-Vedantic movement formed in the 1880s in the aftermath of the demoralizing controversy that engulfed secular liberal Indians and orthodox Hindus concerning the British adminis- tration's proposal (supported by the former) to outlaw the traditional custom of child marriage.[34] Rejecting both sides, Vivekananda, engaged to reform Indian abuses – polytheism, the inequality of women, caste discriminations – on native Hindu lines.[35] He tried to undercut the appeal of Hindu traditionalists by depicting as the authentic India a dynamic Aryan founding civilization that had educated the other world centres of learning (Persia and Greece), and that rejected any inherent barriers between the sexes, between castes, and between secular and religious branches of knowledge. The religious taboos on contact with aliens and the caste laws imposed by the Brahmin priests he criticized as a degeneration from this democratic civilization. To learn from foreign cultures entailed no break with Indian custom. This was merely a way of recovering skills and knowledge once in Indian possession.[36]

In analogous vein, revivalists would try to sap an uncritical dependence on the West on the part of modernists. The Chinese scholar Liang Ch'i Ch'ao tried several techniques, which included citing Western critics against the West. China, he argued, was a formative civilization when the West was in darkness, hence the West was once no better than the Chinese were now, and what- ever was to be found of value in the West had been taken from China.

At another time, he suggested from his readings of European history that it was futile to take over Western values blindly, for Western progress had emerged out of its own unique path of glory and decay. Elaborating on this theme later, he, like the

African intellectual, Edward Blyden, argued that, according to Western intellectuals themselves, the hegemony of the West was passing, for it had over-developed the material at the expense of the spiritual and was now faced with internal dissolution. The future lay with those who, like the Chinese (or, in Blyden's case, the Africans), had retained their ancient religious and aesthetic traditions and were set to lift humanity to a new plane where the moral and the material would be combined. To be progressive, therefore, was to be native: the West was a fading civilization.[37]

Cultural nationalists thus disavow an uncritical rejection of scientific modernity and, at the same time, the assimilation of the community to any universal model of development. Liang deconstructed the West from an imposing monolith into a collection of nation-states pursuing quite different economic and political policies.[38] Each nation, they believe, has its own path to follow, and they appeal to the intelligentsia to borrow from other cultures, but in order to regenerate rather than to efface indigenous institutions.

This polycentric and dynamic vision of the native community is the product of secular intellectuals, exposed to contact with the metropolitan centres of the West and often participants in the transnational cultural networks emerging since the eighteenth century. Many cultural nationalisms in peripheral societies have been indebted to the investigations of their metropolitan counterparts, who, like the British Orientalists in Bengal, unearthed a forgotten high civilization, organized a chaos of events into periodic sequences analogous to those of Europe, and established Indian-language printing presses,[39] or, like the German Celtic scholars, published the first major philological studies of the Irish language. Such investigations not only furnished the skeleton of a national history for societies otherwise poor in modern academic resources, they also often served to legitimate the national struggle in the eyes of insecure native intellectuals who, looking to prestigious foreign centres, discovered their ancestors transformed from the status of primitive barbarians to that of the progenitors of modern progress.

In late nineteenth-century Ireland cultural nationalists were able to legitimate their drive against 'official' opposition to raising the status of Irish – then just a peasant vernacular – in the educational system by directly mobilizing international support. When Irish was ridiculed by the prestigious Anglo-Irish Protestant scholars of Trinity College, Dublin, who regarded the campaign as a threat to British hegemony in Ireland, the nationalists were able to turn the tables on their opponents, depicting them as provincial bigots by securing testimonials from international Celtic scholars to the centrality of Celtic Ireland in European culture.[40]

Although cultural nationalists found this transnational culture a powerful resource, one has to explain their emergence by reference to a drive, generated by an *internal* crisis, to integrate the traditional and the modern. Their constituency has usually been small, having its core in those doubly socialized in the customary and the modern secular cultures. But for that reason they have often been of importance in being able to mobilize influential groups across the tradition-modern spectrum, the secular middle classes, and the liberal and conservative clergy.

They have helped to create the basis for collective progress in three ways. First, by highlighting the dynamic aspects of the native past, they have enabled modernizing groups to harness traditional symbols to their purposes. Second, by stressing the indigenous sources of Western progress, they have provided a powerful critique of attempts to impose a single model of development on world societies. Finally, by reconciling for a time potentially antagonistic groups, they have provided a stable platform for social initiatives.

Cultural Nationalism as a Recurring Movement

It may be admitted that cultural nationalism opens up possibilities for political development on communitarian lines by renovating decaying indigenous symbols, but this may also suggest that cultural nationalism is only a transient force, doomed to disappear once societies overcome the customary restraints on their march to secular modernity.

This is another common assumption to be found in the literature, and one advanced by Kohn in his interpretation referred to above. He argues that cultural nationalism becomes an important presence in areas such as Eastern Europe, where the misalignment of ethnic and political boundaries and socio-economic backwardness make a democratic state-directed politics impossible. But with the emergence of a reform-minded middle class in 1848 forming the basis of such a politics, cultural nationalism is superseded by a rational political nationalism.[41]

This, although accurate in some respects, does not tell the whole story. Cultural nationalism is, indeed, a transient phenomenon, regularly giving way to a political nationalism. But Kohn has failed to give sufficient weight to the fact that it is also a recurring force, often re-emerging in modern societies to have a long-term effect on the distribution of social power. Like political nationalism, it arises in response to a deep-seated conflict of identities, generated by the continual challenge to the established status order by externally inspired modernizing pressures as mediated by the bureaucratic state.[42] Kohn's weakness is his failure to acknowledge that there is no fixed resolution to this conflict.

We should view cultural and political nationalism as complementary and competing responses – communitarian and state-oriented – to this problem, which often form in alternation, each eliciting the other. Gaining their first constituency among a disaffected educated middle class who find their mobility 'blocked', these two movements thus channel disaffected groups into different nationalist strategies against the existing state. The effect of this alternation, as we shall see, can be to reinforce rather than attenuate (religio-)traditionalist sentiments.

I have already made the point that, although both are modernizing movements, cultural and political nationalism have different concepts of the nation, of national integration, and modes of organization. Cultural nationalists celebrate the differentiated character of the community. Rejecting legal-rational concepts of integration, they seek to unite the competing groups by inculcating a common pride in the distinctiveness of the nation, and to modernize by building on the unique traditions of the society. By contrast, political nationalists espouse an essentially rationalist approach, seeking to override traditional differences in favour of a homogeneous community integrated through possession of a common state that guarantees equal citizenship rights. Although they are constrained to realize this vision within their historic ethnic community, they use ethnic sentiments instrumentally in order to unite diverse groups against the existing polity to win a representative national state.

We also noted that cultural nationalism, unlike political nationalism which frequently expands into a centralized mass organization, is normally a decentralized educational movement, and that its communitarian strategies fail against the power of an interventionist modernizing state. Cultural nationalism is forced to shift into a state-directed politics to embed its programme in the social order, and it thereby paves the way for its supersession by political nationalism.

Although cultural nationalism elicits a formally organized political nationalism, more capable of mustering diverse groups to gain state power, political nationalism in its turn regularly reignites a cultural nationalism. For, periodically, conflicts break out between the competing constituencies of political nationalism (for example, traditionalist clerics and secular middle classes) over the definition of the unitary end (an autonomous state) which is its ultimate goal. As a result of the bitter struggle, cultural nationalism crystallizes from a loose set of intellectuals to an integrative movement with distinctive institutions.

At this stage, despite being weakened by defections, political nationalism still remains the dominant partner. But what may undermine it is its tendency, as a large-scale formal organization, to ossify into oligarchy despite its democratic pretensions. This is particularly visible in the case of political nationalism because of its proclivity to set up, as a counter to the state, a unitary organization that seeks to subordinate all intermediate groups to its claim to be the single voice of the nation. Hence, as it ossifies, it increasingly exercises a stifling effect on all national forces.

At times of crisis, when established political leaders have become remote from their constituents and are seen to be impotent against an alien threat, this can be the cue for a reversion to the communitarian strategies of cultural nationalism by a new generation of secular political intellectuals, who translate the cultural platform of the scholars into concrete socio-political programmes. Appealing through journals, first to an emerging but discontented intelligentsia, who find their aspirations to secular power, career, and status apparently blocked both by the state and the exclusionary practices of 'ageing' nationalist oligarchs, these intellectuals seek to reinvigorate the nation by mobilizing all competing groups in grass-roots economic, social and political campaigns.[43]

Let me briefly illustrate this alternating sequence by examining the historical patterns of modern Ireland, a country conquered in the seventeenth century by Britain, which imposed an English Protestant aristocracy on the native Catholic people. Here, as I have argued in a large-scale study, three major cultural nationalist movements have formed since the eighteenth century, each of which turned to Ireland's pre-conquest Gaelic past in order to differentiate Ireland from England, unite its different social and religious groups, and provide models for national development.[44] As we shall see, each revival developed in interaction with political nationalism in three phases: *gestation*, *crystallization* into historico-cultural societies, and *socio-political articulation*, with the third revival having a decisive impact on the formation of the Irish nation-state.

We see the first revival emerging among tiny circles of historians in conjunction with the rise of the Patriot movement of the 1760s. This campaign, based on the 'settler' Protestant minority, sought to secure the legislative independence of the Irish parliament from Britain in order to guarantee equal rights with their British kinsmen. The aims of the historians, although influenced by neo-classicism, were not political but integrative, and they promoted the establishment of an academy that, in reviving memories of an ancient Gaelic pagan civilization, would provide native enlightenment models round which indigenous Catholics and settler Protestants could unite.

Overshadowed by the Patriots, these proposals had little

impact until the partial achievement of the Patriots' goal in 1782, which set off a conflict between conservative Anglican gentry who wished to preserve their privileges, and middle-class radicals who wished a more democratic franchise that would include Catholics.

In this atmosphere of discord, the Royal Irish Academy was established in 1785 to unite the Irish of all persuasions in the scholarly analysis of Irish history and culture. The impact of the RIA was limited, but revivalist themes influenced sections of a younger generation of nationalist intellectuals, frustrated at evidence of the growing failure of the 1782 settlement to rein back British power and to achieve radical democratic aspirations. In 1791 the Society of United Irishmen was founded to promote a secular liberal (and, later, republican) ideology, and they gained support from a growing professional stratum of Catholic and Dissenting lawyers and doctors in the cities who felt excluded from power. Although not initially revolutionary in its aims, when repressed by the British government the Society was driven into an ill-fated revolt in 1798 that heightened sectarian passions and was ruthlessly crushed.[45]

The results of this revolt were the further incorporation of Ireland into the British political system by the Act of Union, which abolished its independent parliament, and the conversion to British loyalties of Irish Protestants, alarmed at the sectarian hatreds released by the national revolt. But by 1816, a second revival had begun to form under the leadership of George Petrie, the artist and antiquarian, who assembled a group of Protestant and Catholic historians, poets and painters. Evoking early medieval Ireland as a time of Christian idealism and artistic splendour, they sought to unite the increasingly antagonistic religio-political communities in a romantic vision of Ireland as a small-scale landed and spiritual society, superior to and quite distinct from the utilitarian and industrial England.

This emerged in response to rising ethnic sentiments within the Catholic community, inspired by Daniel O'Connell. O'Connell was a political nationalist, whose long-term goal was the return of an Irish parliament based on the will of the (Catholic) majority, but whose first campaign between *c.*1805 and 1829 was for Catholic Emancipation (the opening of public office to Catholics), round which he mobilized the Catholic middle classes and peasantry. Heavily involved in British radical causes, he was a liberal utilitarian who wished for political autonomy as a means of guaranteeing British liberties for Catholics, but his effect was to identify Irish nationalism with native Catholic grievances.[46]

In an era dominated by O'Connell, cultural nationalism had little impact until it crystallized in the 1830s into scholarly societies and journals which sought to chart new directions for a society in disarray. The context was the increasing strife within Protestant Ireland at Britain's concession of Catholic Emancipation in 1829, and the conflicts within O'Connell's ranks between nationalist radicals and conservative Catholic clergy, following his announcement of a new campaign for Repeal (of the Union). Petrie's crusade, while it did engender a wide-ranging revival of interest in Celtic culture in sections of the Protestant and Catholic professional strata,[47] failed in its larger regenerative ambitions.

By the late 1830s, however, there was a growing disillusionment with O'Connell who, in order to secure remedies for Catholics, had compromised with the British Whig government with disappointing results. To segments of a younger Catholic intelligentsia, it seemed that the Repeal movement had ossified into an oligarchy of O'Connell's cronies and become detached from its base in the peasantry. The result was the emergence of a new group of modernist Protestant and Catholic journalists, known as Young Ireland, whose vehicle was the journal, the *Nation*. Rejecting what they saw as the assimilationist and sectarian aspects of O'Connell's nationalism, they harnessed Petrie's conservative populist ideas to Prussian models of development with the aim of constructing an independent, self-sufficient rural Celtic nation that would save a spiritual people from the materialist embrace of liberal industrial England.[48]

Although Young Ireland, as a rival to O'Connell, at first sought support from patriotic Protestant elites, in 1842 it was forced to join the large-scale Repeal movement in order to gain access to a wider audience for the *Nation*. Using the organization in order to promote communal self-help (as mentioned earlier), Young Ireland gained. a limited audience among radicalized Catholic lawyers and journalists. Subsequently, however, the Repeal campaign was stalled by the British government, and tensions developed with O'Connell over the issues of sectarianism and physical force which led Young Ireland to secede to form an independent organization in 1847. This adopted an increasingly radical populism to achieve support among the peasantry, but with little success. By this stage a disastrous series of famines had derailed the whole nationalist enterprise, and when, in despair, Young Ireland mounted a revolt in 1848, it was easily crushed.[49] So ended the second revival.

The destructive effects of the famines generated a bitterness that led to a revolutionary nationalist movement, the Fenians, who rose in ill-fated revolt in 1867. But the third phase emerged during the late 1870s in response to a new wave of interventionist reforms by the British state in the fields of religious and land rights, education, local government, the civil service, and social welfare, that were designed to assimilate Ireland to Britain by addressing the grievances of the native majority. Against this a new cultural nationalism emerged, the dominant wing of which, looking back to a Gaelic golden age of Christian and secular learning in the early medieval period, differentiated Ireland as a decentralized Irish-speaking rural and spiritual civilization from power-hungry imperial and industrial Britain.

As before, however, this was overshadowed by a new political nationalist organization, the Irish Parliamentary Party. Although its outstanding leader, Charles Stewart Parnell, was a Protestant landlord, it followed the O'Connellite mould. Its cadres were Catholic lawyers and journalists who, constructing a highly disciplined party machine, tapped the land grievances of the peasantry and the religious interests of the Catholic Church in order to win a Home Rule parliament. Like its predecessor, although it succeeded in exciting ethnocentric Catholic passions, its political models came from British liberalism.

Until the 1890s cultural nationalism was confined to a few

historians, folklorists and artists, whereas the Irish Parliamentary Party had become a mass organization, returning a majority of Irish MPs, and effectively creating a state within a state in Ireland. None the less, cultural nationalism crystallized in 1893 into a significant cultural organization, the Gaelic League, set up to unite all groups within a revived Irish-speaking culture.[50] The catalyst was the involvement of Parnell in a scandal that led in the 1890s to the alienation of the Catholic Church from the party and to near civil war within nationalist Ireland between secularists and clericalists. Although the regenerative themes of the Gaelic revival, evoking a golden age of religious and political harmony and achievement, attracted the sympathy of reform-minded clergy, their impact was limited until *c.*1900. At this point the revival was adopted by a notable set of journalists, including Arthur Griffith and D. P. Moran. Reacting against the demoralization of national life, they used the revival's communitarian vision as a model for a socio-political programme that would construct a dynamic modern Gaelic economic and social system. Their first constituency was the upcoming generation of educated Catholics who had emerged from new schools and university colleges with expectations of social and political advance, but who were undergoing a crisis of vocation and function as a result of finding their aspirations checked by overcompetition in the professions and civil service. At the same time, the paths to power in the Home Rule party were blocked by an ageing nationalist oligarchy, who appeared increasingly remote from the social issues of the new urban Ireland and absorbed into a British political system that in 1900 returned a Conservative government opposed to Home Rule.

A reformulated integrative vision offered this educated stratum a vocation as political leaders of a grass-roots modernizing campaign. Mobilizing in addition both reform and neo-traditionalist wings of the Catholic clergy, which was now seeking a renewed role in politics, the journalists made the Gaelic League the hub of a loosely related set of activities – industrial associations, agricultural co-operatives, temperance associations, athletic clubs, religious crusades against immoral (English) literature, and political parties – which attempted to embed a distinctive Gaelic identity in everyday secular and religious life.[51]

Between 1900 and 1906 the Gaelic League became a significant social movement, but after 1909 its communitarian politics went into decline. Among the factors in this decay were the elections of 1906 and 1910 which returned Liberal governments committed to Home Rule, bringing about a revival of the Home Rule party; and the release of census data which demonstrated a further decline in Irish-speakers. Increasingly, cultural nationalists were driven to religious traditionalism as a shield against secular English values, and to a state-oriented politics, with most favouring an alliance with Home Rulers.

The revival, however, had formed a powerful counter-culture to established values that could offer a platform for revolutionary politics, should parliamentary nationalism falter. When the Home Rulers committed Ireland to the British cause in the First World War without achieving Home Rule, the result was in an increasing militancy that culminated in the 1916 rebellion. Although this rising was crushed, British threats of coercion gave legitimacy to a guerrilla war of liberation directed by the revivalist elite who, with the tacit and sometimes open support of the Catholic clergy, overthrew the Home Rule party in elections and eventually won in 1921 an independent, if partitioned, Irish state.[52]

The ideals of the third revival provided the official ideology of the new state, and, up to the 1940s and even beyond, successive governments, a high proportion of whose members entered politics through the Gaelic League, worked to institutionalize rural Gaelic and Catholic values in the nation through changes in education, government recruitment, marriage laws and economic policies. Their success was not unqualified, and the Gaelic-Catholic settlement, long rigidified, is now crumbling. But the historical sequence here outlined does suggest that cultural nationalism is a recurring and, at times, a formative force, capable of channelling the energies of aspiring social groups 'blocked' by established statist patterns into new political directions. Indeed, the different visions of the Gaelic heritage presented by the three revivals indicate that it may remain a potential matrix of identity, should there be a revulsion against the currents of Europeanization now washing over Ireland.

The Contemporary Religious Revival

A Challenge to the Nation-state?

Since the 1970s many societies seem to have been swept by a religious revival. Islam is at war with secularist materialism on several continents. In Iran, Shi'ite clerics overthrew the Pahlavi dynasty in 1979 and established a state whose laws, education, morality, economy and foreign policy are purportedly determined by Islamic principles. This is only the spearhead of a wider movement that has shaken or transformed states in the Middle East, Africa, and Asia. In 1981 Islamic extremists in Egypt assassinated President Anwar Sadat for his Western tilt, and here, as in neighbouring Sudan, the organization known as the Muslim Brotherhood, dedicated to returning Egypt to Islamic principles, has become politically influential. In response, Sadat's successor, President Mubarak, has increasingly employed Islamic symbols, funded Islamic publications, imposed stricter censorship on television and, in foreign policy, sought closer ties with the Arab-Islamic world.[1] In the secular socialist state of Algeria Islamic parties won the 1991 elections; in Pakistan the regime of General Zia ul-Haq between 1977 and 1988 abolished the relatively secular constitution in favour of one based on Muslim religious principles. There has been a similar growth of religious influence in the politics of Libya, Tunisia, Lebanon, Afghanistan and Malaysia.[2]

In Latin America and the Philippines the Catholic Church has been active in resistance to authoritarian regimes, and Catholic priests became leading figures in the Sandinista Revolution in Nicaragua. The Catholic Church in former Soviet bloc countries such as Poland and Lithuania has played an important part in the downfall of Communism, and in contemporary Russia the

Orthodox Church is undergoing a major revival.[3] In India the secular state is threatened by Sikh nationalism in the Punjab and the rise of assertive Hindu-based movements.

The religious revival is not confined to the less developed world. In the USA since the 1970s Republicans have allied with resurgent conservative Protestant evangelical leaders, determined to reassert Christian values in family life, public institutions and foreign policy. The emergence of Pat Buchanan as a credible Presidential candidate throws into question the separation between state and church prescribed in the American Constitution. In the supposedly Westernized democracy of Israel, religious parties and movements since the late 1970s such as the Gush Emunim (the League of the Faithful) have become a significant force, influencing public policy and promoting the resettlement of the Biblical lands of Israel and an infusion of religious values into the state. Even in a heavily secularized contemporary Europe some intellectuals suggest that Christian traditions might bind together a faltering European Community that is concerned about prospects of large-scale immigration from Muslim North Africa.[4]

In these and other cases, religion is not simply a surrogate politics, an umbrella for opposition that has no outlet within an authoritarian society. Common to these movements is a moral critique of the anomie of secular modernity, which has resulted in rising levels of divorce, crime, alcoholism, drug abuse, nervous disorders, social conflict and levels of inequality, and a demand for a revival of essential religious principles as a basis of individual morality and social organization. Accordingly, they have often formulated wide-ranging proposals to change the constitutions, legal codes and economic systems of their societies to subordinate the modernization process to religious principles. After the Iranian Revolution, supreme political authority was invested in the institution of the rulership of the Islamic jurist, designed to guarantee the power of the *ulama*, the judicial system was modified to accommodate the *shari'at*, observance of Islamic rules on dress, entertainment and culture was made mandatory, and religious issues gained more prominence in the educational curriculum.[5]

Although many commentators regard such revivals as fundamentalist, by which they mean an attempt to impose a medieval
or pre-medieval theology on the modern world, such characteriza-
tions are simplistic. These movements vary in their goals and
strategy. Some (often called *reformist*) have sought to reconcile
religion and modern science on equal terms and have promoted
evolutionary modes of social and political change; whereas others
(often referred to as *neo-traditionalist*) are aggressively hostile to
secular modernity, and have sought to use modern political technologies in order to restore religious authority over public and
private life.[6] But whatever the differences between reformists and
neo-traditionalists (which is often one of degree), they are marked
off from religious revivals in the premodern period by virtue of
their political and activist character. What is also notable is that
the leadership of these movements is drawn not from traditional
but rather from modern social groups – doctors, lawyers, scientists, and engineers, who promote, as part of the revival, communal self-help and solutions to the problems of underdevelopment.
Hence, the Muslim Brotherhood in Egypt have organized programmes in health and adult literacy among the poor at the
municipal level.

The contemporary religious revival poses severe problems for
those modernization theorists who assume with secularization
(defined by them as scientific and technological advances and
associated social changes such as large-scale education, urbanization, industrialization, and cultural and political pluralism) that
political ideologies, including nationalism, imbued with new conceptions of human autonomy, would replace religion as the basis
of legitimation, social regulation and collective action. As they
did so, the state would determine the public arena (e.g. law,
education, culture) which was previously the domain of religion.
Religion would survive, but only as a private allegiance, for as
an otherworldly belief system it lacked the capacity to interpret
and shape social change.[7]

However, not only are the world religions failing to fade away,
they even claim an alternative vision of 'modernity' to that of
secular liberals, socialists, and nationalists. Indeed, they

powerfully challenge the nation-state, either seeking to redefine it in religious terms or, indeed, challenging its legitimacy. In Poland, religious groups struggle with secular Westernizers as they seek to purify a society of the materialist corruptions of atheistic communism by returning to a Catholic conception of the nation. Even Turkey, which under Atatürk was torn from its Islamic heritage and reconstructed as a nation-state on the Western model – with a secular constitution, a Latin alphabet, and European styles of dress – has felt the impact of the Islamic revival since the 1970s, manifested by an increase in mosque-building, a return to headcovers by women, and the rise of an Islamic party to become the third strongest in the country.[8] Many Islamic groups, indeed, seek not merely to reform but to abolish the nation-state and the conventional international (state) order as a secular Western conspiracy against Muslims. They regard the Iranian Revolution as proposing a superior version of modernity and a launching pad for a unification of the Muslim *umma* in one huge community. Gush Emunim in Israel, although employing modern technology, considers issues in Biblical categories. Thus the will of God, not international law or even the law of the state of Israel, is the sole basis of legitimacy.[9]

The current religious revival then forces us to reassess many of our assumptions about the relationships between religion, nationalism and the modernization process. The first section of this chapter will explore how the relationship between nationality and religion (defining the latter in terms of the great traditions of Buddhism, Hinduism, Judaism, Christianity, and Islam) has been conceived by interpreters of nationalism. The second part will then investigate the causes of the current religious resurgence and assess how far it presents a threat to the nation-state. Finally, we'll consider in the light of this what general lessons we can draw about the relationship between nationalism and modernization.

Nationalism and Religion

Although many societies remain heavily inflected by religious values, it is undeniable that since the eighteenth century nationalism over much of the globe has succeeded the great religions as the primary legitimation of the social order. Does this mean that we should regard nationalism and religion as essentially competitive and antithetical systems?

Pace Machiavelli, most scholars would argue that the two are conceptually opposed. For the great religions are universalistic and transethnic in their appeal and their organization; they have as their concern success not in this world but in a higher spiritual realm; and their written languages have historically been those of 'dead' tongues, generally those of the sacred texts in which the divine revelation has been inscribed. By contrast, nationalism is limited, directing loyalty to a particularist territorial and historico-cultural unit; it is this-worldly, promoting the welfare of an activist political community; and although historians and artists are given special importance as interpreters of the national essence, it is the living community – its way of life, language, customs, and so forth – that endows them with their creative power.

For these reasons analysts such as Elie Kedourie have argued that religion and nationalism are incompatible.[10] Many nationalists, of course, assert an intimate kinship between their community and one of the great religions. The modern Israeli sense of identity is charged with their biblical definition as God's chosen people. Arabs are proud of their status as the people of Mohammed and of the Book (the Koran) which is written in Arabic. Indians claim a distinctiveness amongst the world's peoples by virtue of their ancient Hindu civilization. Russian nationality has been shaped by assumptions that Russia was the home of the true (Orthodox) Christian faith and that after the heresy of the Church in the West and the fall of Constantinople, Moscow represented the 'third Rome'.

Kedourie, however, argues that this appropriation of the ancient religions for nationalist purposes is anachronistic, for nationalism is a novel outgrowth of the Enlightenment, and the nations to which it refers are modern fictions. It presents a mythical historicist view of humanity as composed of distinctive and competitive territorial communities forever seeking self-actualization. So, far from being allied to the cause of religion which preaches a distrust of this world in favour of salvation in the next, it is a species of secular millenarianism which promises the possibility of human perfection through the achievement of national freedom. If it has religious affiliations, it is with heretical millenarian movements that have periodically erupted at times of social despair, when the established political and religious authority has broken down, to proclaim the final days and the prospects of terrestrial utopia.

Nationalism is a modern-day equivalent, in this case caused by the impact of modernization on traditional communities, first in early nineteenth-century Europe, then in the rest of the world. It answers a need to belong, felt particularly by the young and those disoriented by disruptive social change, by providing a utopian vision of a unique integrated prosperous self-actualizing community which is supposedly rooted in nature and history. In fact this primordial national community is an invention, and nationalism can offer no resolution of the dilemmas of modernity. But in the urge to (re)create the nation, nationalists are driven to seek any cultural marks which can differentiate their population from others and give it lustre. As a result, many nationalists have turned to the religious heritages of their societies, transforming them from universalistic belief-systems into emblems of national creativity. As they do so, the meaning of the religions is secularized and particularized. Indian nationalists transformed the Upanishads, whose theme was spiritual struggle, into a temporal call to arms; Islam became an exemplification of Arab genius and a justification of Arab nationalist goals. By this means nationalists have been able to able to channel the traditionally minded masses, both rural and urban, into nationalist campaigns.

Kedourie's analysis has much to recommend it. Medieval Latin Christianity was a transnational culture that stood over and above the different cultures of Western Europe, united by adherence to an international institution, the Papacy, and to a common Latin language, which on occasion could mobilize the kingdoms of Europe on a religious crusade to recover the sacred places of the Holy Land. Moreover, the universalist claims of the Papacy came into conflict with the burgeoning national assertiveness of European states not only in the medieval period but also in the nineteenth century. One of the most spectacular clashes occurred in 1870 when the Pope refused to recognize the legitimacy of the Italian state after the Italian government seized the Papal territories for the nation and made Rome its capital. In similar fashion, the Greek Orthodox hierarchy resisted the struggles of the Greeks and other Orthodox populations against the Ottoman Empire for national independence, fearing – correctly – that this would lead to the break-up of the Orthodox community into national autocephalous churches. Yet again, claims of nation and faith clashed in the new Turkish nation-state of Atatürk, who, believing that Islam was a barrier to modern progress, identified with the secular West, dissolved the Caliphate that for centuries under the Ottoman Empire had been regarded as providing religious leadership and protection for Muslims world-wide, and made Turkey a secular state.

None the less, Kedourie oversimplifies the relationship between modern nationalism in at least three ways. Firstly, he neglects the close relationship between religion and premodern ethnic identities in many areas of the world. Secondly, he overlooks the religious as well as the secular roots of modern nationalism. Thirdly, he fails to do justice to the varieties of the world religions and their differential ability to accommodate or resist secular modernization.

Historically, ethnic and religious identities have been closely intertwined, with the latter providing the former with origin myths, sacred symbols and rites, languages, literatures, diets and dress, heroes and heroines, and territorial sites of historical significance.[11] Of course, the most obvious case is that of the Jews, whose holy books singled them out as chosen and whose religious institutions preserved a sense of Jewish identity for nearly two thousand years after their dispersal from Palestine.

It might be argued that few groups had their own religions, but universal religions everywhere acquired local ethnic characteristics merging in the countryside with earlier 'folk' practices, and displayed tendencies to develop distinctive saints and rites and even to fall into schism. Neighbouring Catholic states such as England and France fought mutual wars under the banner of their national saints, St George and St Denis, and indeed, wars on the frontiers of faiths helped fuse ethnic and religious loyalties. A Catholic Spanish identity was forged in the struggle to oust Muslims from the Hispanic peninsula in the late fifteenth century. Military campaigns of the Russian Tsar in the sixteenth century against Catholic Poles and Protestant Swedes contributed to the crystallization of a Russian Orthodox identity. The wars of Shi'a and Sunni sects in the early sixteenth century, resulting from the imperial expansion of Shah Ismael Safavi, contributed to the identification of Persian ethnicity with Shi'ism.[12]

Kedourie is of course correct to argue that modern nationalism operates from premises radically subversive of the cosmologies of the world religions. In the eyes of the former, power and value derive from the historic community rather than from a supramundane deity who, if acknowledged by nationalists, speaks through the nation rather than through religious figures or institutions. In this sense, modern nationalism is a rival to traditional religious systems and its triumph is predicated on the erosion of religious authority as previously conceived.

But it is an oversimplification to regard nationalism as an outgrowth of Enlightenment rationalism and as necessarily hostile to the concerns of religion. Many nationalist movements have arisen out of religious reform movements which, in order to reconcile traditional belief systems with ideas of secular progress and popular sovereignty and to make their faiths a living reality amongst the people, have linked the purification of religious values to the revival of ancient vernacular languages and cultures. The Bernacacina movement of Catholic clergy in the late eighteenth century promoted collective self-help and education and pride in a historic Slovak culture credited with converting the dominant Magyar community to Christianity. Another example is the Arya Samaj movement of the late nineteenth century which celebrated India as the Aryan founding civilization of the world and, in advocating a return to its ethos, rejected the caste system and current obscurantism of Hindu society as unauthentic.[13]

Militantly conservative or, as they are usually labelled, neo-traditionalist religious movements which aggressively combat the advance of secular modernization – exemplified in scientific rationalism, urbanization, secular education, and individualistic credos – have also allied with nationalism and used modern techniques and institutions such as the press, modern party structures, and vernacular languages, to 'restore' a stable social order regulated by a theocracy or by traditional-authoritarian rulers. In nineteenth-century Japan Shintoism was fused with xenophobic sentiments by the Meiji Emperors who sought to achieve a conservative modernization from above; in early twentieth-century Ireland, lower Catholic clergy established literacy and temperance campaigns that evoked an idealized image of Gaelic Ireland as a spiritual Catholic rural society protected by a fatherly clergy which was now threatened by English-inspired urbanization and its concomitants, an immoral popular culture of hedonistic licence.[14]

Observing this, Anthony Smith has argued that modern nationalism arises out of a crisis of dual legitimation generated by the impact of secular modernization as mediated by the modern bureaucratic state on societies regulated by traditional religiously derived norms.[15] The social authority of religion in the past relied on its apparent ability to answer the problem of arbitrary suffering and evil in the world by positing a mysterious supramundane plan and promising benefits in the afterlife as a consequence of adhering to religious ethics. But this solution loses force as science and rational modes of inquiry and organization offer the possibility of overcoming the evils of poverty and deprivation in this world. The authority of science and its executive institution the modernizing state begins to challenge that of religion over increasing dimensions of social life (for example, education, welfare and family law). At the same time the continuously self-reflexive character of rationalism threatens to disenchant the world of all stable meaning, overturning those beliefs (religious and otherwise) which provided individuals and collectivities with identity and purpose.

Hence the dual legitimation crisis as educated individuals face a dilemma of choice. Some (modernists) plump for the secular solution, rejecting religion and tradition; others (neo-traditionalists) seek to combat secular modernism and restore the authority of tradition using its own weapons against it; still others (the reformists) seek an accommodation or synthesis between the two worlds, 'modernizing' religion so that it becomes a continuously evolving phenomenon adapting itself in each era to the march of progress and seeking to address the secular as well as the spiritual ills of society.

According to Smith, all three solutions can generate a nationalism, for each is driven to appeal to or revive ethnic myths and memories to sustain its project. The secular modernists, although their goals are in principle universal and cosmopolitan, in practice discover that there are profound cultural gaps between populations, that their own formulation of these universal goals is culturally inflected, and the attempt to realize them engenders resentments and a sense of humiliation on the part of 'backward' populations. Disillusioned, modernists turn back to their own cultural and territorial population to realize their visions of enlightened progress in a more limited setting by establishing an independent nation-state.

The neo-traditionalists, although in principle suspicious of concepts of popular authority and particularism, are forced to appeal to group memories and myths in order to mobilize people in powerful political campaigns against the modernizing state.

Finally, the reformists, in seeking to purify their religion of dogmas and integrate it with modern progress, are in danger of making it too abstract to answer the needs of a living community. They are compelled to search the past for a concrete illustration of how religion stimulated both spiritual and temporal progress in order to provide a model for the future. In the course of their historical excavations, religious beliefs become nationalized: gradually the emphasis changes from celebrating the people of a religion to evoking the religion of a people and how it contributes to communal distinctiveness and achievement. The nation increasingly replaces religion as the guide and stimulus to collective purpose.

There are, then, three different secular and religious projects, which elicit the kind of politicized ethnicity we call nationalism, each with its own objectives. The secular modernists have as their aim the establishment of a dynamic state which will promote the mobility of the people as a whole; reformists seek the integration of religion and the secular, tradition and modernity; and the neo-traditionalists promote the defence of a hierarchical, religiously ordained order. They construct quite different conceptions of the nation, based on very different myths of origins and golden ages.

The Greeks have divided, with the middle classes opting for a 'Western' democratic version which evokes as its golden age Hellas, the cradle of Western civilization, while the Orthodox clergy and peasantry idealize the Byzantine Empire and Greece's leadership of Eastern Christianity. In like fashion, in nineteenth-century France there was a deep schism between liberals and socialists who invoked the French Revolution as the heroic period of national history, and conservatives and clericals who idealized the Catholic Middle Ages of Joan of Arc.[16]

There may be intense conflicts within nationalist movements, but this does not stop these projects combining. Indeed, one of the strengths of nationalism is its ability to mobilize a range of interests and social strata (from urban secular middle classes to traditionalist peasantries), and indeed, various intellectuals may shift between modernist, reformist and neo-traditionalist positions, either out of conviction or calculation. In the short-term, the character of any particular nationalism, Smith argues, is heavily shaped by the strength of particular groups in the leadership positions of the movements.

If religion plays a much more active role in shaping nationalism than Kedourie would allow, it can also be argued that a much more differentiated discussion is required of the abilities of the great religions to counter secularization. This analysis needs to take account of the fact that a politically induced secularization can take different forms, and that the great religions vary considerably in their idea-systems and types of organization and hence in the resources they can mobilise against the state.

D. E. Smith has identified five analytically separate forms of state intervention that may come under the label of secularism.[17] The first is where the state makes a separation between the religious and the political and thereby ceases to perform traditional functions of defending and promoting the faith. In the second, the state expands into areas formerly the domain of religious regulation; in the third, secular legitimations of the political community replace those of religion; in the fourth, the political process is secularized so that religious leaders, interest groups, and parties wane in power; and in the fifth, radical secularist regimes recognize no area of religious autonomy.

Religions, he argues, also vary along two continua. First, their cosmologies may be *historical* (Christianity, Islam, Judaism), where God intervenes in history, which has a meaning as the working out of the divine purpose; or they may be *ahistorical* (Buddhism, Hinduism), where time is endlessly cyclical and lacks a moral direction. Second, they may be *church* systems (as in Theravada Buddhism, Catholicism) and hence though within society also separate from it; or, alternatively, (as in Hinduism and Islam) they may be *organic* systems which tend to equate religion and society, focusing on such structures as caste or sacred law as the mechanisms by which the divine regulates societies.

Smith claims that historical religious cosmologies have advantages over their ahistoric counterparts in developing a religious ideology of social change and building bridges with secular ideologies. Because of their institutional autonomy, church rather than organic systems are more able to develop a coherent and well-organized response to problems of social change. Moreover, organic religions will be particularly threatened by different aspects of secularization. Organic systems will be more endangered by the expansion of the secular into law, education and so forth; church systems by the separation of state and religion.

None the less, in spite of these qualifications, Smith is pessimistic about the long-term capacities of the religions to withstand secularization. In a later study he observes that there have been many revivals in the modern period, notably the Buddhist revivals in Burma and Sri Lanka of the 1950s, and before that a Gandhi-inspired Hindu revival in the 1940s,[18] but he argues that these tended to be superficial and in most cases there are structural impediments to religious movements achieving or sustaining political power. In Burma, Buddhist monks, through the Union of Presiding Monks Association, played an important role in sweeping U Nu into power in 1959, and they played a comparable role in ensuring the victory in Sri Lanka in 1956 of Bandaranaike's Sri Lanka Freedom Party over the secular, Westernized, United National Party. Although Buddhism became the state religion in Burma, the achievements of the religious groups were, according to Smith, 'decorative' rather than substantial. By this he means religious practices were enforced (for example, on holy days the state broadcast religious programmes, closed government offices, and forbade the sale of liquor), but as a religion Buddhism was primarily concerned with the cycle of life and rebirth and had little interest in the regulation of the life of the laity apart from injunctions against stealing and killing, and the expression of a general rhetoric of equality, compassion and virtue. Hence, it was unable to shape social structures, and as a result of these limitations becoming apparent, the resurgence had faded by the 1970s. Similarly, he doubts the ability of Hinduism to offer a basis of mass politics because of the centrality of caste in its conception of the world.

Ernest Gellner, however, has recently maintained that Islam, alone of the world religions, may be capable of resisting secular modernization and the march of nationalism.[19] He argues that the central characteristics of high Islam – a severe monotheism, emphasis on rule-observance (of the sacred law) rather than ecstatic practices, on direct contact between God and the individual, and its puritanism and scripturalism – are strikingly compatible with modern industrialism which, according to Weber, is a rational, orderly, work-oriented and disciplined culture that rejects excessive display and patronage networks.

It is true that until recently this high Islam was generally confined to urban scholars recruited from the mercantile middle classes, and that a folk Islam emphasizing magic and ecstasy and centred round local (living) saint cults was dominant among the rural tribes, surviving repeated cycles of reformation in which the urban version has imposed itself. But with the challenge of modernization Muslim societies have turned to high Islam, which has functioned in ways comparable to nationalism in other contexts. As the impact of Western modernization revealed to Muslims the relative backwardness of their societies, they were able to escape the dilemma of having to choose between an alien but functionally superior high culture and a native but inferior folk culture, by rejecting folk Islam in favour of a 'fundamentalist' return to high Islam which was both indigenous and compatible with a modern economy and culture. Moreover, with the development of modern administrative, communication and military technologies, the balance of social power has now shifted from low or folk to high Islam. Hence, the appeal and momentum behind the Islamic revival which may be a permanent feature of the modern world.

Current Religious Revival: Causes and Prognoses

How far then do these historical and sociological discussions throw light on the causes, prognoses, and consequences of the current religious revival, which, as we have noted, sometimes runs in alliance and sometimes in antagonism with nationalist movements?

As we have observed, the revival is very widespread, ranging from the rise of the religious right in the USA to the current resurgence of Jewish religious nationalism in Israel, the revival of Islam in Africa, Asia and even Europe, the recent return to Orthodoxy in Russia and elsewhere, and to the drive of Sikhs in India to obtain their own independent state. A number of common factors have been adduced for this widespread revival such as the crisis of the family, a perception of elite corruption and distance from the people, defeat in war, and a growing disbelief in the secular state's abilities to deliver the benefits of modernization.[20]

A precondition for this resurgence was that religion was still powerfully embedded in the daily life of these societies, and hence available as a basis for social regeneration. Thus, it is plausible to argue that a nationalist evangelical revival in the USA – an industrial society unusual for its high indices of religious commitment – was inspired by the spectacles of social breakdown and the anomie of the major cities, disillusionment with the political system after Watergate, a sense of decline after the defeat in Vietnam, and the rise of Soviet military power.

As we shall see, such factors were important triggers, but it will be suggested that Smith's model provides a more comprehensive interpretation of the origins and trajectory of these movements. The following discussion, however, should be considered more as an illustration than as a rigorous testing of his model (which would require an extended and intensive empirical analysis), and the focus for the sake of simplicity will be on the aspects of the widespread Islamic revival and also the rise of Gush Emunim in Israel, both of which phenomena occurred in states which paid lip-service to popular religious sentiments but which in practice were aligned to secular nationalist values.

Breaking with the secular establishment, Gush Emunim and contemporary Islam have looked to divine guidance to reconstruct the community, but show heterodox traits in the leading role played by the educated laity in defining socio-religious goals, and also in their divergence from much earlier religious revivals. For in the case of the Iranian Revolution at least, the return to the past is not with the (traditional) aim of reapplying the *shari'at* to existing society, but rather to discover a political model in the first Muslim community by which to shape the modern world, an objective that in some cases has meant overriding the *shari'at*.[21]

THE ORIGINS OF REVIVAL

If we investigate the formation and expansion of Gush Emunim in the 1970s into a significant socio-political movement, we will find it did originate in the disillusionment following the 1974 war. But it was rooted in a dual repudiation both of the secular Zionist project, which had been embraced by most Jews and structured the state of Israel, and of traditional religious orthodoxy by important sections of younger educated groups who felt themselves 'blocked' by the political establishments. Instead they turned to alternative neo-traditionalist visions propounded in the early twentieth century by a leading religious figure, Rabbi Kook the Elder, in order to regenerate Israeli society. Its emergence reveals the unstable accommodation between secular and religious principles in the new Israeli nation-state, heavily shaped by a religious ethnic heritage. The origins of Gush Emunim can also be interpreted in terms of Smith's model as one of a series of responses to the dilemmas of legitimation generated in Jewish communities from the early nineteenth century by the impact of Enlightenment and its political incarnations (first liberalism, then socialism) on their traditional religious beliefs and structures, which had preserved their identity as a people over nearly two thousand years as a diaspora, dispersed throughout Europe and the Middle East.

The establishment of the state of Israel in 1948, based largely on the mass migration of the two-thousand-year-old Jewish Diaspora from Europe, had seemed to embody the triumph of the Zionist secular nationalist project of the nineteenth century.[22] This had emerged out of the failure of traditional religious structures and universalist ideologies to provide Jews with a sense of direction in the modern world. Whilst in the course of the nineteenth century modernizing European states abolished discrimination against Jews, many Jews rejected the religious ghettos to assimilate as citizens in a new progressive humanity only to find that, by the late nineteenth century, the assimilationist option was undermined by a growing exclusive nationalism, hostile to ethnic minorities, that resulted in pogroms in Eastern Europe and a revived anti-Semitism in Western Europe. In response, Zionists such as Herzl, while rejecting a return to religious orthodoxy, argued the only way that they could participate on equal terms in the modern world was to abandon the Diaspora and settle in a territory (preferably the Biblical lands of Palestine) to form a nation-state of their own.

To many Orthodox Jews the whole Zionist project was an act of blasphemy, for the return of Jews from exile to the Holy Land had to await the coming of the Messiah; for people to actively organize for this return was regarded as showing a lack of faith in God's purpose. But Zionism in the twentieth century, aided by the experience of the Holocaust, became the dominant political force. And secular nationalists, increasingly influenced by socialism, gained significant support from sections of Orthodoxy, led by Rabbi Isaac Kook, regarded by some as the most important Jewish religious thinker of the early twentieth century. Kook argued that although Zionist nationalism was a secular phenomenon, it was God's instrument to achieve the in-gathering and its emergence was a sign that the messianic age was at hand.

At the time of the founding of the Israeli state, the dominant political bloc of Zionism was socialist. With its base in the powerful trade union structures and the kibbutz movement, it derived a secular ideal of Israel from early Judaic traditions as an exemplary pioneering democratic and co-operative society. In the first general elections, religious parties gained only a small minority of seats. None the less, even for secular Jews religious traditions retained a deep emotional significance as symbols of distinctive identity, and secular Zionists recognized the importance of accommodating Orthodox concerns, particularly since some sections of Orthodoxy refused to recognize Israel as a Jewish state at a time when the state was engulfed by myriad Arab enemies. Hence, Hebrew, the liturgical language, was chosen to be the official language of Israel, and the first Labour prime minister, Ben Gurion, not only included the National Religious Party in the governing coalition but also legislated to ensure public observance of the sabbath and other religious holidays, the governance of marriage and divorce by Jewish law, and public finance of religious educational institutions.[23]

This did not prevent vigorous debates over the status of religious as opposed to secular law which were never fully resolved; indeed, disagreements prevented the formulation of a constitution for the 1948 state. None the less, facing the challenge of building a new state surrounded by hostile Arab neighbours, Labor governments seemed to achieve a pragmatic *modus vivendi* with organized religious groups that secured the Zionist vision. In return for being given their way on essential religious matters, including appointments to such ministries as education, organizations such as the National Religious Party have allowed the governments a free hand on the substantive matters of the economy, defence and foreign policy.

After independence Labor Zionism linked itself to the Histadrut (or Jewish Labor federation), which owned a wide variety of economic interests, and was able to become hegemonic, consolidating its authority and marginalizing the power bases of its opponents by constructing an extensive public economic sector so that by 1973 over 50 per cent of workers were employed in state enterprises or services.[24] None the less, by the 1970s there was large-scale disillusion with Labor, one of whose symptoms were the sudden emergence of a grass-roots movement, Gush Emunim, which in seeking to reorient Israelis to a higher religious mission was prepared to confront the existing state. The key triggers in the rise of Gush Emunim were military, the wars of 1967 and 1973. The almost miraculous conquest of the historic lands of Israel, including the holy city of Jerusalem, against overwhelming odds in the Six Day War was regarded as confirmation of the imminent coming of the messianic age, whereas the near defeat of Israel in the 1973 war was regarded as a sign of Divine disapproval of the failure of Jews to undertake the settlement of these lands. But the underlying cause was a sense that the secular Zionist experiment had failed, with rising inflation and economic inefficiency as a consequence of the bloated public sector, corruption in public life, and a sense of discrimination on the part of the growing numbers of Oriental Jews. Labor in continuous power seemed to have lost its original ideals of founding a distinctive pioneering co-operative society, having instead made Israel a materialistic society like any other.

This was the setting which encouraged the emergence of Gush Emunim, formed by young educated Jews from religious backgrounds, many schooled at the educational *yeshiva* of Rabbi Zvi Yehuda Kook (the son of Isaac). Alienated from the dominant Labor power structures and angered by the apparent complicity of the religious parties of their parents in Jewish decay in return for power and 'symbolic' concessions, they offered a renewal of the pioneering ideals of the kibbutz era by making the Israeli state the instrument of the Jewish religious mission through its reclaiming and settling of the sacred homelands as a preparation of the messianic age.

In support of their settlement activities they have employed many arguments: strategic (Israel's exposed geo-military position), political (the illusory nature of Arab peace initiatives), historical (Jews can rely only on themselves and the territories are integral to Jewish history), and Zionist (their settlement represents a return to the pioneer dream now lost because of excessive materialism). But their ultimate principles are religious: the state of Israel is a sacred instrument of God to usher in the messianic age. And this Divine law ultimately overrides any national democratic mandate the government may claim.[25]

This zealotry has seen Gush Emunim developed into a para-state network with a semi-autonomous character, with much of its support coming from Oriental and American Jews, attracted to Israel to escape the assimilative drift of their diaspora community into a materialist US culture. Its early apostles were active in settlements in the wake of the Six Day War, but it was not until 1974 that the group was formed as a faction of the National Religious Party when, in the wake of the 1973 war, demobilized soldiers and religious students united in their aim to resettle the promised land in its entirety. When some of the NRP's leaders (in coalition with Labor) showed a willingness to make territorial compromises with the Arabs in return for peace, Gush Emunim broke away to become an independent movement.[26]

Its initial attraction was notably strengthened by the election in 1977 of the secular right-wing nationalist Likud party, also committed to expansionist goals, which provided it with resources. Initially, Likud inspired great hopes of mass settlement of the conquered territories, but possibilities of the movement being co-opted were checked by Likud's confusing peace negotiation with Egypt which led to the return of the Sinai peninsula. Disillusioned, Gush Emunim founded Amana, an alliance of settlements which provided structures for joint action in support of common goals. Through this and other agencies it has formed something of a parallel state on the West Bank, with municipal administrations, an educational system, paramilitary organizations, and a religiously based alternative ideology to both Labor Zionism and the Orthodoxy of the Chief Rabbis.[27]

If we turn to the contemporary Islamic revival in the Middle East, we see a similar story. Again the trigger was defeat in war which in 1967 brought the catastrophic loss of the holy places of Jerusalem, but this was regarded as a Divine condemnation of the dominant Arab nationalism as a Western secular response to the problems of modernization and of the corruption of the Muslim *ulama*. Although Muslim clerics were active in this revival, the key figures were ambitious members of a young educated generation who, feeling excluded from power by corrupt elites, turned to Islam as an alternative matrix of modernity. Once again, we see the fragility of secular-religious accommodations in state elites (whether Nasserite, Ba'athist, or dynastic) nominally committed to Islam but in reality overlaying Western ideologies on deeply traditional populations, and how this is destabilized by the continuous dynamic of modernization. We can also witness the long-term and fluctuating engagement of religion with secular ideologies to provide a matrix for socio-political as well as personal identity.

The background to this recurring debate was the growing penetration of Western powers into the Muslim world from the sixteenth century, but the cultural conflict between Islam and the 'scientific modernity' of the West became manifest in the early nineteenth century, when Muslim *secular* intellectuals, aware of the power and dynamism of Western European states compared to the stagnation of their own societies wondered whether and how they could reconcile their religious faith to Western science and technology.[28] There were different responses to this question in the late nineteenth and early twentieth centuries, including the Islamic modernism of al-Aghani. Many Muslim intellectuals were attracted to the power of the West but it was generally agreed even by these that total assimilation was not possible and that there should be a selective borrowing from the West, preserving the best in their own societies with the result they could become equal partners with Europeans in world progress.

In the first half of the twentieth century, with most Middle Eastern societies under Western tutelage, a liberal anti-colonialist nationalism became dominant. Particularly influential was Ata-türk's adoption of the secular nation-state model in Turkey when he enforced a Westernization of the legal system, educational system, alphabet, and dress, and relegated Islam to a private allegiance. Westernization also earlier evoked a neo-traditionalist response in the formation of the Muslim Brotherhood, founded in Egypt in 1928 by Hasan al-Banna, which demanded the restor-ation of the authority of the *shari'at* over society. But although the Brotherhood quickly gained a hold in many Arab countries and on the Indian sub-continent, these religious concerns remained secondary in the mind of Arab activists to the anti-colonial struggle.

Following the Second World War – after which many Arab countries achieved independence – liberalism, increasingly identi-fied with corrupt old elites and Western colonialist powers, was overthrown by a younger generation of Muslim leaders, but in the name of alternative Western secular political traditions.[29] Dedicated to providing solutions to the problems of national underdevelopment and to raising the living standards of the masses, and influenced by the material progress of the Soviet Union, figures such as Nasser turned to socialist models which would liberate Arabs from dependency on the capitalist West. In Egypt Nasser's radical socialist nationalism and in Syria and Iraq the Ba'athist parties engaged in accelerated industrialization, large-scale nationalizations and Soviet-inspired planning. This was accompanied in the late 1950s and the 1960s by forthright secularization in the fields of education, the abolition of *shari'at* courts, attacks on orthodox Islam as an obstacle to progress, and the domestication of the leading *ulama* by the regimes. Organizations such as the Muslim Brotherhood were driven underground and their leaders imprisoned. For a time Nasser's seizure of the Suez Canal from Britain and France gave him immense prestige throughout the Arab world which he used to advance the cause of Pan-Arabism. But by the late 1960s, this Arab socialism was increasingly discredited, and there was a widespread shift to religious conceptions (both reformist and neo-traditionalist) which sought in Islam an indigenous model of political and social development, untainted by corrupt secular ideologies and, indeed, superior to the West.

The major catalyst of this shift was the comprehensive defeat in 1967 of the Arab armies at the hands of a bitter Jewish foe, regarded as a surrogate for the West. This, however, was perceived as confirmation of the final bankruptcy of the grandiose socialist nationalist experiment which had not only failed to liberate the Arabs from dependency on their historic Western enemies but had also resulted in the further alienation of ruling elites from the bulk of the population by increasing the opportunities for official corruption in the expanded public sector. The key recruits to an Islamic politics came from the aspiring lower middle classes, who were frustrated by their lack of prospects, and who in Egypt were sometimes downwardly mobile youths who had dropped out of university.[30] Contemptuously rejecting the traditional *ulama* as collaborators with infidel regimes, they turned to lay organizations such as the Muslim Brotherhood in Egypt and the Sudan which became important actors in their national politics. In Iran, where Shi'ism had traditionally remained at arm's length from the state, the *ulama* led by Khomeini were the spearhead of the campaign against the Westernized Pahlavi regime.

Islamic revivalists both reformist and neo-traditionalist looked to religious conceptions of law (the *shari'at*), education and finance (for example, repudiating the charging of interest) as superior bases for the broad-based development of the life of the masses. Neo-traditionalists were suspicious of the world order of nation-states as the construction of Western colonialist powers which, after the Second World War, carved the world's Muslim populations into forty-four new nation-states, thereby leaving one third of Muslims as minorities dominated by religiously and ethnically alien communities. This prompted a Pan-Islamic revival.[31]

Several developments in the 1970s lent force to this resurgence by supporting perceptions that Western secularism, broadly conceived, was in decay in its heartlands both at the moral and material level. In the early 1970s the West's dependence on Middle East oil was revealed. This emboldened Muslim intellectuals not simply because it appeared to supply a powerful weapon against the imperial powers. It also encouraged doubts about the long-term viability of Western expansionist capitalism.[32] This decade saw the USA, the leading superpower, in apparent long-term decline, demoralized by its defeat in Vietnam, the Watergate corruption scandal, and impotent to rescue its hostages in Iran. The Egyptian-led Arab successes against Israel in the 1973 war appeared to Muslim eyes a vindication of Sadat's shift away from Nasserism and his apparent accommodation with the Muslim Brotherhood. The overthrow of the Shah's Western-oriented regime by the Muslim masses despite its military might and the failures of the Soviet armies in Afghanistan were further indications of Divine approval of the revival.

The growing influence of a Pan-Islamic sentiment has been strengthened by the spread of transport, communications, mass literacy and literary publications, and media technologies which have diffused a heightened consciousness of common threat at the hands of the West and helped overcome the huge geographical diversity and distribution of peoples. The migration of Muslim workers of many different nationalities to the oil-rich Arab states and to Europe has been a contributory cause. When Egyptians, Palestinians and Jordanians find themselves discriminated against in Kuwait and Saudi Arabia, the result has been a rejection of Pan-Arabism and a common assertion of Islamic identity.[33] As a result the revival has spread throughout the Middle East and has gained a hold in many African states, including Nigeria and the Sudan, and Asia, notably Pakistan, Malaysia and Afghanistan.

As many commentators have indicated, it would be a mistake to depict this revival as a monolith. There are many varieties within it, and in local contexts it has often fed into existing national loyalties (in, for example, Egypt, Pakistan, and Malayasia). Neo-traditionalists define Islam in much more restrictive terms than reformists, and, whereas the former empha-size the importance of separation from the larger society and the establishment of their own godly society, the latter assert the social responsibility of Muslims to society and the politics of persuasion rather than terrorism. Nevertheless, there is strong agreement on many questions, including a belief that the period AD 600–661 represents the essence of Islam.[34] Moreover, they present a novel, political Islam that in its focus on the organiz-ation of the state rather than on the *shari'at* marks a heterodox challenge both to established secular regimes and to the tra-ditional *ulama*.

CONSEQUENCES OF RELIGIOUS REVIVAL

It is not clear that the previous analyses of the growth of such religio-political movements as competitors to secular nationalism unambiguously confirm Smith's dual legitimation thesis. Smith indicated that, although rival religious and secular projects would form in response to the impact of modernization, proposing quite different pathways to the future, each would generate a national consciousness. Certainly, Gush Emunim can be regarded as a religio-nationalist movement, but there are many Islamic revival-ists who explicitly reject nationalism.

The above analysis also raises two further questions about the effects of such movements. Firstly, how successful have they been in shaping social change? And, secondly, to what extent do they offer a permanent or deep-rooted challenge to the secular nation-state and the international system? In inquiring into the second question, we will help clear up the ambiguity about the extent to which religious movements can propose solutions to the dilemmas of modernity independent of nationalism.

In assessing the capacities of religion to effect social change, one must note that religious revival movements have generally been minority phenomena, particularly in the developed West. Because of this, or, in some cases (as in Buddhism, Catholicism), because of prohibitions on clergy entering the formal political process, they have tended to exercise influence only indirectly through alliance with secular leaders or governments. In the USA it was the decision of secular Republican conservatives to ally with the religious right to further their political chances against the Democrats that greatly boosted the political and social influence of Falwell and others by giving them access to legislators and a bigger platform in the media.[35] After the Pakistan-Bangladesh civil war, which raised fundamental questions about the Pakistani national identity, the secular socialist Ali Bhutto adopted Islam to obtain wider Arab support and to secure domestic legitimacy.[36] In Israel the strength of Gush Emunim was substantially boosted by the Likud government, which used it to promote further settlements and also to ward off foreign pressure by pointing to domestic opposition to territorial compromise. But the fact that secular politicians were so engaged is an indication not of the weakness of religious movements but rather their wider social legitimacy. By bringing Islam into the centre of public life, Bhutto strengthened the religious and political forces that were eventually to overthrow him.

Nor should the fact that these are minority phenomena lead to an underestimation of their political and social efficacy. This is especially so in populations where religion is closely linked to national or communal identity. As David Schnell has argued, in Israel Gush Emunim has forced a broadening of the religious question beyond a concern with prohibitions on particular activities on the sabbath to embrace the moral basis of fundamental national issues, in particular the legitimacy of Jewish claims to the occupied territories and the rights of non-Jews in Israel.

With its image as a people of land-based scholar-warriors projected through programmes that combine religious study with military service, Gush Emunim has succeeded in establishing communities drawn for different religious backgrounds. This religiously inspired idealism, combined with its determination to resettle the occupied territories at considerable risk, evokes a widespread admiration that cuts across all parties, even amongst those who reject their, at times, terrorist methods. Thus, even Labor sympathizers can find in this organization a return to the ascetic pioneer spirit of the early Zionists, which contrasts with the bureaucratic careerism of contemporary Labor politicians. By the late 1980s there were 60,000 Israelis in over a hundred settlements in Judea and Samaria. Gush Emunim has helped reshape many Israelis' perceptions of the conquered territories – which they refer to by their ancient names (Judea, Samaria and Jerusalem) – as Jewish rather than Arab. Because of this Gush Emunim exercises an influence on the political process and potentially on the peace processes (which they are determined to resist) out of all proportion to its numbers.[37]

In many Third World societies where there is still a strong public commitment to religious values, religious movements and parties have often attracted large-scale support. In Iran they spearheaded the revolution and Islamic figures now control the government; in Algeria, Islamic parties were on the verge of winning democratic elections in 1991; and in India, Hindu revivalist parties have won power at the state level. They can strongly shape political action even when, as in the case of the Muslim Brotherhood in Egypt and also in Sudan, they deliberately remain outside the party political process, preferring to advance Islamic goals through whichever political parties secure power.[38]

Both Sadat, after succeeding Nasser, and Mubarak, who became President after Sadat's assassination by Muslim zealots angered at his peace treaty with Israel, hastened to make concessions to the Brotherhood to cement their hold on power. Although it is clear that throughout the Middle East, Islam is increasingly permeating public life, because of the divisions within the revival it is difficult to make an easy assessment of its overall effect. The reimposition of the veil might be perceived to be part of a regression to a patriarchal society, but, as Cantori argues, its effects may be quite different in permitting lower middle-class women to move with confidence into modern office employment.[39] Moreover, although it has a terrorist wing, the mainstream revival may have been a force for stability in countries such as Egypt, where the Brotherhood has provided adult literacy, health and welfare services – fields in which the state has been ineffective.

If the impact of the contemporary religious revival is undeniable, the question remains whether or not it represents a significant and long-term threat to secular nationalism. As D. E. Smith has observed, it would be a mistake to see this as an unprecedented phenomenon: there have been many religious revivals in the twentieth century, including an Islamic resurgence in Saudi Arabia in the 1930s. As we have noted, he has argued that in many areas the changes effected are symbolic rather than structural, and there are deep-seated impediments to religions producing fundamental change. In the long term, he maintains, none of the great religions can resist secularization.

But does not Islam, as Gellner suggests, stand out as an exception to this? Does not the pan-Islamic movement, advocating a universal Islamic revival, offer an alternative vision of modernity to that of the nation-state? Some have argued that Islam is unique among the major religions in that it refuses to make a distinction between the religious and the political. The state must be guided by religious laws (*shari'at*) and scripture demands the unification of all Muslims in a single community or *umma*. There is no room, therefore, in Islamic doctrine for the nation-state as a unit of loyalty in so far as it would subordinate religion to the sovereignty of the people and divide the loyalties of believers: all peoples have equal status under Allah.[40]

This rejection of nationalism is exemplified above all in Iran, where power is invested in the hands of religious specialists led by an Imam. The constitution prescribes that all laws must be in accordance with the *shari'at*, which is regarded as above society, and the interpretation of the *shari'at* is in the hands of the *ulama* and the ayatollahs. Thus the various sectors of Iranian life are religiously regulated; Islamic dress codes are enforced, education is permeated with religious values, and Islamic prohibitions against the practices of usury operate in the banking system.

Moreover, the example of the Islamic revolution in Iran,

spread through modern communications, has inspired Muslims everywhere, even non-Shi'ites. This is especially true of younger intellectuals, among whom one can see the emergence of a 'global' Islamic perspective that explicitly rejects the West and its concepts. A radical section of the Iranian regime rejects international organizations as a tool of satanic great powers and renounces normal relations with other states in favour of exporting the revolution to peoples. Iran has been at the centre of a transnational movement of groups with Pan-Islamic goals, who offer mutual financial support, the exchange of information, and training.[41]

In spite of these arguments, there are grounds for doubting whether fundamentalist Islam, either in its reform or neo-traditionalist versions, can offer a sustainable alternative to nationalism and the international system. For in the first place, although Islam claims that the political realm must support Muslim values and practices, it does recognize that they represent different institutional spheres of life. Currently, the leadership of most Arab states remains heavily secularist while paying lip-service to Islam. Secondly, whatever its commitment to a unity of the *umma* and its division of the world into the *dar al-islam* (believing realm) and the *dar al-harb* (infidel realm), Islam from early in its history has been divided into rival Sunni and Shi'ite branches, and, partly because of such differences, recognized in theory and practice the realities of a world formed into competing states.[42] Ottoman and Crimean Sunni armies not only waged war periodically on the Safavid Shi'ite state of Iran, but the latter sought alliances with Christian powers against their foes.[43] The weaknesses of any Pan-Islam movement are revealed by the fate of twentieth-century Muslim Congresses established to unite and liberate the world-wide Muslim populations subjugated by the Western powers. These Congresses, bedevilled by rival claims (Egyptian, Saudi and other) to leadership of the Muslim world after the collapse of the Ottoman Caliphate and by the enormous diversities within Islam, failed even to establish a permanent organization or a single centre to pursue their goals.[44]

It might be argued that the Islamic revolution in Iran, which overthrew a state based on Persian nationalism, can provide a spearhead for a Pan-Islamic movement. For Khomeini, the world was divided into those who followed the path of righteousness and those who followed Satan and disbelief (i.e., the imperialist powers); and although Islam represented the former, only the Iranian Republic was properly based on Koranic principles. Its role was to unite one billion Muslims and overthrow imperialist hegemony.

Yet its universal slogans were belied by its practice for several reasons, which were reinforced by the war with Iraq. Firstly, Iran was the only state with a large Shi'ite majority. Secondly, in spite of attempts by the Islamic regime to eliminate all pre-Islamic influences which provided the cultural and historical basis of nationalism, these were rooted in popular consciousness. Thirdly, although the Iranian population was multi-ethnic, Persians composed over 50 per cent of the population and the government adopted Persian as the language of the revolution despite the anger of various minorities. What crystallized all these elements was the Iraq–Iran war in which most Arab states supported Iraq as a fellow Arab state against their ancient enemies the Persians. This evoked a reactive Persian nationalism which even Khomeini felt compelled to canalize to muster support for the war effort.[45]

The result was a hybrid religious nationalism. Moreover, on becoming aware of the dangers of isolation in 1984, Khomeini had curbed the radicals by recognizing the need for Iran to work through existing international organizations and to establish diplomatic relations with all but a few nations (with notable exceptions such as Israel, the USA and South Africa).[46] As Piscatori has pointed out, entrenched differences of interest have meant that there has been no unified response on the part of Muslim states and populations to Khomeini's revolution, or indeed to the Soviet invasion of Afghanistan.[47]

Although this undermines claims that the universalistic principles of Islam can provide an alternative social and world order to that of the nation-states, Voll has pointed out that where the concept of national identity has little to do with Islam, the presence of large Muslim populations makes problematic the viability of nation-states.[48] Where, on the other hand, there has been a long historical conjunction between say Egyptian and Muslim identity, the legitimacy of the nation-state is not in question. Furthermore, in countries where the nation-state is a colonialist construct which has created Muslim minorities, Islam has undermined its status. Hence in Nigeria, the large Muslim minority is potentially destabilizing, since Muslim thinkers cannot vow allegiance to an entity which enshrines the will of the (largely non-Muslim) people as the supreme basis of authority as opposed to the divine laws and revelations of Mohammed and his successors.

In spite of this, it is an undeniable fact that most Muslims are born, educated, work and die within a nation- or would-be nation-state. Although there is a minority tradition that is hostile to the nation-state system as such, much of this antipathy arises from a sense of frustration with the failures of Arab developmental strategies and the humiliation of the military failures against Israel. It is likely, Piscatori argues, that Muslims will in time seek the creation of Muslim nation-states which will be hybrids, purged of Westernization and devoted to Islamic conceptions of social justice which will guide their development programmes.[49]

Nationalism, Religion and Modernization

What conclusions can be drawn from this analysis about the relationship between nationalism and religion in the modern period? And what light does this throw on the modernization paradigm?

To begin with, the discussion of the Islamic revival would throw doubt on those who suggest that the world religions can provide autonomous solutions to the problems of modernization. As we have seen, in intervening to create a theocratic state capable of overcoming the problems of underdevelopment on Islamic lines, the Iranian political clerics have begun to embrace heterodox tendencies that, in leading them to disregard the *shari'at*, may in the long run secularize their faith. Instead of standing for unchanging spiritual values, the faith may now be judged by its success in resolving temporal problems. Already, to legitimate their state, they have had to shift positions and appeal increasingly to national sentiments. In this regard, Anthony Smith's dual-legitimation thesis, which predicts the nationalization of religion, is confirmed.

At the same time, although this might support D. E. Smith's prognosis that the world religions *qua* religions do not have the capacity to effect long-term social change in the modern world, it is also clear that where religious and national identities are historically linked in states such as Israel, religious values are still strongly institutionalized in the wider society and can provide the inspiration for alternatives to the established order. In Israel, even secular Jews have regarded it as essential to preserve the Judaic character of the state, have accommodated religious concerns in such spheres as education and laws regarding citizenship and marriage, and regard as (nationally) sacred such sites as the Wailing Wall in Jerusalem. It is from the products of this religious socialization – the *yeshiva*-educated middle class – that movements such as Gush Emunim have formed to offer an alternative mode of organizing communities when secular ideologies seem to have failed.

These remarks indicate the difficulty of treating modern nationalism and religion as discrete entities, since many nationalisms contain secular and religious components, which act sometimes as complements and sometimes as alternatives to each other. They also suggest the complexity of nationalism itself, which is never concerned simply with modernization but also with identity. Does this at times ambiguous relationship between secular and religious projects within nationalism undermine those modernization theorists who argued that, because of ever increasing social differentiation, supramundane religion will give way to nationalism as the ideology of modernity?[50]

Modernization theorists might counter that these findings only call for a modification of the secularization thesis to acknowledge that it is a more complex, non-unilineal process. For although the religions have proved their ability to mobilize to shape the modernization process, they have become politicized in the process, and this in the long run will lead to them being evaluated in secular terms – on their ability to provide answers to problems of underdevelopment – and to a transfer of peoples' loyalties from supramundane to secular ideologies.

As we have seen, there are indeed tendencies for religious revivals to become nationalized and secularized. But the problem with this position is that it does not perceive equivalent tendencies of secularists to revert to religious roots. In short, these arguments rest on an unproblematic (early Enlightenment) view of modernization as a process leading individuals and communities from darkness to ever greater autonomy: given freedom and the technological capabilities to overcome the problems of suffering and injustice that provided the wellsprings of religious adherence in the premodern world, human beings increasingly turn to more rational ideologies. Such theorists fail to sufficiently recognize the dislocating aspects of modernization which recurringly lead people back to the solace of religion. As Gellner has argued, the processes of modernization are inherently uneven, since the innovations on which it is based are inherently unpredictable. Modernization thus destabilizes power relationships between states, often engendering conflict and war; moreover, revolutions in transport, as well as providing benefits, allow the transmission of disastrous crop diseases (such as the potato blight that resulted in the Irish famine) and of plagues such as the current Aids epidemic. Improvements in basic nutrition and medicine have advanced the standard of living in advanced industrial societies but contributed to a vast population growth that threatens to shatter the ecology of many Third World societies. These unpredictable by-products of modernity – wars, plagues, economic failures – have frequently led, as we have seen, to a revulsion against secular ideologies and a return to the 'deeper' cosmic images of religion.

From this we can conclude with D. E. Smith that although it is likely that the current religious revival will fade, it is also likely that as long as the modernization process continues, religious resurgences will recur to feed into and at times confront nationalism.

As we have noted, the religions lack the ability to establish the basis of a lasting modern political community and a conception that can replace the current international order. None the less, the confrontations between nationalists and religious zealots can be bruising. Where religious traditions stand apart from those of the nation-state and have deeper roots, as in many of the 'invented' political units in Africa and Asia, they can severely compromise the functioning of the state. Even where religiously inspired movements are not in themselves hostile to the nation-state, they can pose major problems to its successful viability in a plural world, for where religion unites with nationality in a situation of conflict – as in the Middle East – it can add a fanaticism to international conflicts that may prevent their resolution.

Finally, we might observe that to conclude that religions will survive as significant actors but only within a world structured by the nation is to assume the continued vitality of the Enlightenment project of human emancipation. But should the modernization process falter through nuclear or ecological catastrophe, then it is likely that the nationalist project founded on ideas of collective autonomy would collapse, and it would not be surprising to see a return to the old gods. The great religions which have endured many vicissitudes and powerfully shaped our identities and civilizations over many thousands of years might well come back into their own.

The USSR, 1991

Fall of the Last Empire, Failure of Communist Modernization, or Warning for the West?

Few events in modern history have been more astonishing or dramatic than the sudden collapse of the Soviet Union and its Eastern European bloc into would-be nation-states. Marxism has been one of the great rival political principles to nationalism this century, proposing a supranationalist vision of a future humanity emancipated from religious, class and ethnic divisions. Since the Bolshevik Revolution of 1917, the citadel of world communism has been the USSR, established on the boundaries of the Tsarist Empire.

As a multi-ethnic state, the USSR was a formidable test case for the communist project, for although the Russian nationality at its inception composed over 70 per cent of the population, the state contained over a hundred ethno-linguistic groups.[1] From the beginning its leaders forecast the eventual merging of these ethnic populations into a single Soviet socialist people. Although this optimism was qualified under Andropov and Gorbachev, in 1986 the Congress of the Communist Party of the Soviet Union declared the national question as inherited from the past to be successfully solved.[2] Yet within five years, the USSR had disintegrated into would-be nation-states. Since then the break-up of the former communist states of Czechoslovakia and Yugoslavia into their constituent nations testifies to the apparent failure of communism to overcome nationalism.

The collapse of the USSR has produced a flood of valuable commentaries by Sovietologists who have brought to bear their expertise to explicate recent events.[3] I wish here to investigate the relationship between the stability of modern political systems and the presence of cohesive ethnic core populations and, in par-

ticular, to examine the way in which an avowedly supranationalist project sought to deal with the problem of
transforming a multi-ethnic and multinational population. As we
will see, Lenin's strategy was to create an ethnic federal system
which would effect the transition to a single Soviet socialist identity. One of the purposes of this chapter will be to discover how
this ethno-political system worked and why it broke down.

The discussion is organized in three parts. The first examines
how communists dealt with the multi-ethnic realities of the USSR
and sketches the framework and practice of Soviet nationality
policies from the Revolution to Gorbachev. The second part
analyses the causes of the collapse, identified as the interrelation
of geopolitical pressures, inter-ethnic competition, and Gorbachev's reform programmes. Finally, there is a review of the larger
implications of this demise for our understanding of the role of
ethnicity in political systems: did the collapse represent the fall
of the last (Russian) empire, or the failure of communism as a
modernizing project, or does it highlight the vulnerabilities of
multi- and supranationalist projects in the modern world?

The chapter, therefore, addresses three major questions:

1 How did an avowedly supranationalist state committed to the
   eventual transcendence of nationality deal with the national
   question?

2 What explains the breakdown of the USSR and the revival of
   nationality as the basis of political identity?

3 How do we understand this collapse? Was it the collapse of
   the last empire or does it highlight more the general problems
   of cohesion encountered by multinational states?

The Nationalities Question

LENINIST DOCTRINE AND THE NATIONALITIES

One of the inescapable facts about the Soviet Communist state
is that it was formed on the boundaries of the Tsarist Empire

based on the dominant Russian *ethnie*. Between the sixteenth century and early twentieth century Tsarist power had expanded from its Muscovite source to extend from Finland to the Far East, incorporating a huge number of ethnic groups differing greatly in their level of self-consciousness and of socio-economic development.

The processes by which this expansion occurred varied, ranging from Russian conquest, to elite co-option, to simple settlement. But it is important to note that the expansion of the empire preceded the crystallization of a modern Russian national consciousness. When this emerged in the nineteenth century it was characterized by a strong imperialism, an uncertainty about where the boundaries of Russia began and ended, and an insensitivity to the concerns of other ethnicities. The imperial state imposed haphazardly on all populations an institutional and political Russification which carried with it in addition strong connotations of cultural Russification. Although at first these state policies sprang from a drive for uniformity rather than a commitment to Russian nationalism, by the 1890s a Russian imperialist nationalism had gripped certain sections of the government. This generated among some of the more developed non-Russian *ethnie* a reactive nationalism at much the same time as revolutionary socialist movements were emerging in the urban centres of Russia in particular. Although in Russia the revolutionary outbreaks of 1905–6 had a strong class basis, in the rest of the empire they were as much a nationalist revolt against the imperialist policies of the regime.[4]

Thus from early on Lenin had to address the question of nationalism, and subsequent Soviet nationality policies were derived from his formulation of Marxist theories of history and revolutionary practice, first in his role as revolutionary conspirator and then as first leader of the USSR.

Like Marx himself, Lenin had little to say about the nature of nationalism as such: his stance in this regard was primarily tactical. Nationalism was regarded as a phenomenon principally of the bourgeois capitalist phase which would fade as socialism united all humanity in a global order: revolutionaries should assess it according to whether it supported or opposed the movement of history. When it was regarded as promoting a popular consciousness against feudal oppression it was progressive, but where it was used by bourgeois interests to thwart the formation of an internationalist proletarian solidarity it was reactionary.[5]

Accordingly, as a revolutionary leader in the Tsarist Empire, Lenin had rejected Russian nationalism as a tool of the feudal imperialist regime and, hoping to tap the anti-Russian nationalism of the non-Russian peoples, supported their claims to self-determination, arguing that the nationalism of peoples struggling against oppression was progressive.

When many of the non-Russians, including the Ukrainians, Azerbaijanis, and Georgians, took advantage of the chaos to declare independence after the 1917 Revolution, prominent Bolsheviks were prepared to accept an alliance between sovereign socialist states. Rights to secession, however, were subordinate in Lenin's eyes to the aim of advancing the socialist revolution. Thus, Bolshevik armies (largely Russian in composition) during the civil war (1918–22) enforced their integration into a Union of Soviet Socialist Republics, based on the boundaries of the former empire.[6]

Lenin, however, when establishing the new socialist state, rejected the idea preferred by Stalin of a unitary structure dominated by the Russians in favour of a federal system. For he feared that the communist project would be torn apart by the dangers of greater Russian nationalism, on the one hand, and a reactive separatist nationalism among the non-Russian populations on the other.

According to this federal 'compromise' the central government, organized through a Soviet communist party, would have powers over international relations, international boundaries, social and economic policy, education, and the union-wide budget. In addition national republics and (lesser) autonomous republics were established on ethno-territorial grounds. The former (some fifteen), were granted to the major nationalities (including the Russians, Ukrainians, Belorussians, Armenians, Georgians, Moldavians, and Azerbaijanis) after whom they were named.

These had their own communist party organizations (with the exception of the Russian republic), flags, legal codes, powers over light industry, official recognition of their languages and cultures, and a policy of *korinezatsiya* (meaning indigenization) was followed with respect to major positions of the republic.[7]

This arrangement was justified as a dialectical solution to the nationalities problem. There would be two modes of development: the long-term drive to socialism would be directed by the Soviet Communist Party and central organs of the state through its economic, educational and other policies, which would establish the infrastructure for communism and equalize conditions throughout the USSR. At the same time, the limited autonomy given the republics would allow for, in populations still at a backward stage of development, a flowering of national popular cultures in co-operation with the centre. As a socialist division of labour developed in each republic, equalizing economic and social conditions, there would be a coming together of the nations followed by a spontaneous merging of the national proletariats (*sliyanie*) in a common Soviet socialist identity and culture.[8]

This dialectical solution might seem to be naïve, merely building contradictions into the Soviet state. There would be, on the one hand, the activities of the centre (operating through the army, security apparatus, and the Party, whose networks extended down to the most local level and economic planning agencies) aggressively dedicated to a revolutionary overthrow of those traditions, strata and practices inimical to socialism. On the other hand, the policies of semi-autonomous political units would be governed to a large degree by ethnic principles. But in practice Lenin planned for the centre to keep control by planting its own personnel in key positions of the local republican administrations responsible for internal security and the appointment of staff.

In fact, through this structure the Bolsheviks used existing nationalities and deliberately engaged in nation-building in order to address three major obstacles to their goal of constructing a common and secure Soviet socialist homeland identity. Firstly, alliances with national elements allowed them to promote a common culture with the aim of overcoming the immense diversity of nationalities. Secondly, they accelerated the creation of a socialist division of labour in the many backward regions and hence the goal of equalizing conditions between populations that varied enormously in their level of socio-economic development between regions. Finally, they served to divide potentially solidaristic religious populations in strategic areas who might otherwise represent both an internal and external threat to the communist project.

THE USE AND ABUSE OF NATIONALISM

The first problem was how to create a common Soviet identity and culture out of such ethnically diverse populations. Lenin and his successors 'solved' this problem by building the core of the Soviet state on the majority Russian nationality (in 1922 c.70 per cent of the population). This was settled not only in European Russia but also disseminated as a result of Tsarist empire-building policies throughout the territory, exercising a powerful cultural force in the cities.[9]

Lenin sought to establish his supranationalist state by balancing ethnic groups. Russians dominated disproportionately the Soviet communist party, army, and security services. They tended to be the 'proconsuls' in the national republics, when, as Second Secretaries, they vetted key appointments and reported on security matters to the centre. Russian was the official international language of the state, and Russians were used as the major labour force outside their native republics to advance Soviet industrialization and, particularly in Stalin's time, to Sovietize non-Russian populations.[10] By 1979 nearly 24 million Russians had been relocated in the non-Russian republics.[11]

At the same time, care was taken to avoid the danger of the Russians swallowing the communist state. Alone of the major nationalities, the Russian republic was denied a separate communist party, a capital, and cultural organizations of its own. Russians could only have a political and cultural voice as Soviet citizens. Bolshevism over time achieved a symbiosis with traditional Russian (Orthodox-derived) messianism with its deep suspicion of the Latin West in forming a Soviet state that declared its world destiny to emancipate humanity from (Western) capitalism.

There were dangers in this policy which became apparent under Stalin, but the leaderships of major non-Russian nationalities were compensated for Russian dominance at the centre by being given their own republics in which they were allowed privileged status, a limited political autonomy, and resources to develop their own language and culture. Hence, although many of these republics contained significant ethnic minorities, the titular nationality (i.e. the group after whom the republic was named) were favoured in recruitment into the Party and state apparatus and their language was employed in all Party and state business.[12]

This accommodation with the political and socio-economic interests of the national intelligentsias of the major non-Russian populations enabled Bolsheviks to address their second problem: how to achieve a common socialist transformation throughout a vast territory with huge social and economic disparities, much of which lacked a proletariat. By allying with what was sometimes the only 'modern' social category, a small national intelligentsia, they located a group with a vested interest (because of the policy of indigenization) in forcing through the socialist modernizing programmes (ideological, social and economic) of the centre, using despotic controls of censorship and surveillance to quell potential opposition at the elite and mass levels.[13]

The motto for this policy was that republics were national in form but socialist in content. Centrifugal tendencies were checked by the republics' dependence on subsidies from the state reserves which in a majority of cases covered more than 60 per cent of their budgetary expenses. The poorer republics were particularly dependent on the centre to finance their expanding administrative, professional and cultural occupational structures and their provision of social infrastructure (housing, healthcare, pensions and the like).[14]

Support for the secular national intelligentsias served a third purpose of the Bolsheviks: to subvert religious solidarities which were regarded as hostile to the Soviet state. As total belief systems, they offered a fundamental challenge to an atheistic materialist ideology that demanded absolute allegiance to its tenets. These allegiances were of particular concern where they were connected to ethnic identities (as was later the case in Lithuanian), where they might orient communities to external centres of power (e.g. the Papacy), and where they might link Soviet populations to those of bordering states.[15] The Muslims of Central Asia, some 40 million strong and sharing borders with Muslim Turkey, Iran, and Afghanistan, although composed of many different ethnic groups, were regarded as a special danger.

In the early 1920s, during the struggle between religious leaders who wished to unify the Muslims in one powerful republic and the relatively weak Kazakh, Kirghiz, Turkmen and Uzbek nationalist intelligentsias, the Bolsheviks sided with the latter, who in turn looked to Moscow as the bearer of Western Enlightenment values by which they might modernize their societies. The Soviets thereby divided the Muslims into several republics, and by encouraging the creation of linguistically differentiated cultures helped to create embryonic nations with elites committed to secular socialism overlayered on a mass religious base.[16] In these ways Bolsheviks advanced the construction of national identities for socialist purposes while at the same time attempting to domesticate nationalism by giving it a secular linguistic cast, and detaching it from anti-system religious memories.

LENIN'S SUCCESSORS

This then was the framework established by Lenin, and continued at first by Stalin. Despite the intentions of their founders, by the late 1920s it produced a burgeoning of national consciousness among most of the major Soviet peoples. This was exemplified in flourishing national histories, (often novel) vernacular literatures, and the de-Russification of cities in the many republics. A new national communism was forming with many republics, including the powerful Ukraine, now lobbying for powers over economic development, inspired by fears that further industrialization would result in new waves of Russian in-migration.[17]

By the 1930s, however, Stalin (1926–53) had shifted the balance of power decisively to the centre, combining this with a

Russification of the regime. Regarding federalism as an obstacle to his plans both for the collectivization of agriculture and for his Promethean programme of heavy industrialization, he sought to reduce the legal autonomies of the republics. To expedite his goals he destroyed the old Bolshevik leadership, which had had a cosmopolitan flavour (containing many Jews, Poles, Latvians and Georgians), through purges and an extensive recruitment into the expanding state and industrial bureaucracies of plebeian youth drawn extensively from the Russian and Ukrainian peasantry.[18]

This centralization drive was accompanied by a programme of Sovietization tied to a xenophobic celebration of Russian culture. The Russian people were extolled as 'the Elder Brother' of the Soviet peoples who through their language, history and culture (vigorously promoted in schools throughout the Union), were elevated as leading the other nationalities to modern progress. During the 1930s the Tsarist Empire, previously criticized in Soviet histories as the Russian prison house of nations, was lauded as a progressive phase in history.[19]

As the most powerful non-Russian republic, the Ukraine bore the brunt of this assault: between 1930 and 1933 its leadership was murdered, the resistance of the peasantry was crushed by a terrible forced famine, the Ukrainian Autocephalous Orthodox Church was liquidated and a fierce programme of Russification of the Ukrainian language was inaugurated.[20] Many republics suffered in similar vein. The alphabets of most nationalities were Cyrillicized, detaching them from their ancient literatures. Some, like the Tartars, with a rich literary past, had to change twice, once from Arabic to Latin in 1927, then from Latin to Cyrillic in 1939.[21] Russian 'colonization' was expanded. Campaigns of persecution were intensified against members of churches too closely identified with national identity (the Uniates in the Ukraine, and, after the annexation of the Baltic states in 1939, the Catholics of Lithuania).

These Russifying tendencies and religio-national persecutions reached new heights during the Second World War, when sections of the Ukrainian, Baltic and Georgian peoples allied with the German invaders, and during the early post-war period when national resistance continued, particularly in the Baltic lands and those territories annexed in 1945: the Western parts of the Ukraine and of Belorussia, and Moldavia. Various ethnic minorities such as the Volga Germans, Crimean Tartars and Chechens were punished for their collaboration with the Germans by exile from their homelands into Central Asia.

After the Second World War, Stalin was at the height of his authority, having raised the USSR to the status of a superpower that controlled a security bloc in Eastern Europe and was leader of a socialist community of states. But, although able to truncate the political and cultural autonomy of the republics, he was never able to abolish them and they remained dominated by the titular nationalities. On Stalin's death the republics regained ground. As part of a general de-Stalinization in the 1950s, Khrushchev (1953–64) initiated a limited cultural liberalization which produced in all the major groups a national revival in history, literature, and the arts. Intellectuals in the 'old' nations (e.g. Georgia, Armenia, and Lithuania) asserted the independence of their historical traditions, whereas in Central Asia they sought to establish their populations as nations and to connect them with culturally progressive pre-Islamic traditions.[22] This was accompanied by a partial decentralization of the political and economic system that strengthened local elites in the republics.

The Brezhnev era (1964–82) saw a reversion to cultural repression and centralization. Russian and Slavic influence was strengthened in the central organs of Party and state.[23] Sovietization (heavily Russian-based) campaigns, begun under Khrushchev, were heavily promoted through the educational system, youth organizations and the army to combat cynicism within the system generated by the revelation of Stalin's crimes, and to engender a Soviet patriotism.[24] At the same time Brezhnev sweetened the pill by giving republican leaders security of tenure, allowing them to build up independent patronage networks which encouraged a rampant corruption and economic inefficiency. Under Andropov and Chernenko various anti-corruption measures were introduced to revitalize the system but this brief interlude before Gorbachev's succession did not materially affect this structure.

With what success then between Lenin and Gorbachev had Soviet communism addressed the nationalities problem? In terms of their major goals, Soviet nationality policies must be counted a failure. Instead of federalism effecting a spontaneous merging of the nationalities into a Soviet identity, it had strengthened and even helped create national identities by allocating regional political authority on ethnic principles. Through its redistribution of resources between republics the centre helped to ensure a considerable rise in the provision of education throughout the Union, but it failed to homogenize living conditions.[25] As perceptions of economic decline intensified under Brezhnev, there was anger among the more developed republics such as the Ukraine at the diversion of resources to Siberia, while Central Asian leaders demanded greater investment to improve the life of their underdeveloped and rapidly growing Muslim populations.[26] At the same time there was apprehension at the continuing relative demographic decline of the Russian population on which the core of the state rested from $c.70$ per cent of the total population in 1922 to 52 per cent in 1979.[27]

None the less, it would be foolish to deny the emergence of some degree of Soviet identification, even if it was the product of external threats and conflict rather than of the progress of socialist modernization. The sense of pioneering the first socialist society, memories of common suffering and triumph during the Great Patriotic War against the Germans, the Cold War and evocation of a nuclear threat from the West, and the world power status of the USSR undoubtedly generated a Soviet patriotism.

This identification with the state was strongest among the Russians, who accepted as natural their dominance, but the regime appeared also to find acceptance among the next leading nationality, the Ukrainians (particularly those in the eastern provinces closely linked by history, language and Orthodoxy to Russian culture) whom it was co-opting in significant numbers into the central institutions. Even in the 1980s, scholars assumed because of this apparent accommodation of the two major nationalities there was little prospect of Soviet disintegration.[28]

Why then did a mighty world power with such powerful instruments of control suddenly disintegrate in peacetime into separate would-be nation-states, after surviving over seventy years the challenges of civil war, the traumatic years of collectivization and the purges, German invasion and national revolts?

The Collapse of the USSR

Since this collapse occurred during an attempt by a new leader, Gorbachev, to democratize the Soviet system, it is plausible to suggest a Tocquevillian answer: that revolutions occur after a period of rising expectations suddenly checked, and 'the most perilous moment for a bad government is when it seeks to mend its ways'.[29]

There is much to be said for this interpretation, for, as we shall see, as General Secretary of the Soviet Communist Party, Gorbachev's advocacy of reform in domestic and foreign policy in effect admitted the failure of the regime. He thereby robbed it of the mystique that had previously legitimated it, and opened up, in a country where the state claimed guardianship over every aspect of social life, a Pandora's box of grievances amongst its population. But such an analysis would be incomplete without an explanation of why an authoritarian and conservative system decided to risk reform, and of why the attempt to reform led to an unravelling along ethno-territorial lines, with the deathblow being dealt by the effective secession of the nationality – the Russian – most identified with it.

For a full answer we have to look at the interaction of three processes. The first was a deteriorating geopolitical position developing from the 1950s that, having created a systemic military and economic crisis of the state by the early 1980s, compelled Gorbachev's radical initiatives and inspired intellectuals to seek alternative nationalist identifications. The second was an increasingly competitive struggle for resources from the 1960s onwards between federal and republican elites as a result of economic decline that led to richer republics campaigning for more autonomy. The third was, itself, the reform drive in foreign and domestic affairs which produced further political and economic chaos and intensified the expression and mobilization of national discontent against the centre to the point that the USSR fell apart.

GEOPOLITICAL PRESSURES AND A CRISIS OF THE STATE

During the post-war period there were recurring national 'revivals' among the intellectuals, rejecting the destructive moral and material impact on their societies of a tyrannical state-imposed socialist modernization and seeking alternatives in a pre-Bolshevik past.[30] The catalysts for an open expression of this (at first) largely cultural nationalism were, firstly, Khrushchev's brief and limited 'liberalization' during the 1950s, and then Gorbachev's reform drive.[31] Both these attempts at reform from above were inspired by a perception of a steadily worsening crisis of the Soviet state during the post-war period, pressed by geopolitical competition with the West and the need to demonstrate the superiority of its socio-economic system over its capitalist rivals.

The problem that the state faced was of geopolitical overreach, a result of the expansion of its power deep into Europe and Asia after the Second World War and its promotion of communist revolution world-wide. By this it had multiplied its adversaries (USA, the European NATO states, Japan and China) whose combined resources now exceeded its own, and it had also stumbled into an inferior strategic position in facing a ring of resolute enemies round its borders.[32] Increased military competition placed greater financial burdens on a polity with an inefficient command economy that was undergoing a dramatic decline in returns on industrial and agricultural investment and in rates of labour productivity since the 1950s. This in turn put severe pressure on living standards.[33]

As part of his attempt to eliminate the excesses and inefficiencies of Stalin's totalitarian command system, Khrushchev denounced Stalin's crimes (including his forced mass resettlements of peoples), promoted limited political and economic decentralization, and permitted a partial cultural liberalization. Although he enjoyed moderate success in raising living standards, he was ousted, and his (unintended) delegitimation of most of the communist period resulted in a profound disillusionment on the part of many Soviet intellectuals with Marxist-Leninist scientistic dogmas. Some of these intellectuals formed dissident circles to achieve civil and democratic rights within the Union, while others turned to alternative national communitarian and religious models as radical social and political alternatives to a corrupt present. In Lithuania nationalism allied to Catholic activism, and in the Western Ukraine to underground Uniate campaigns.

Although a clampdown occurred under Brezhnev, this was never complete. Indeed, during the 1960s there was a sustained revival of nationalism amongst educated youth in Russia itself, which spanned the political spectrum from liberal democracy to a militant imperialism.[34] Noticeable was a strong return to neo-Slavophile and Orthodox rural traditions, as articulated by the All-Russian Society for the Protection of Historical and Cultural Monuments (founded in 1965) which claimed several million members. Opposing Soviet Marxism as an alien cosmopolitan and scientific-utilitarian ideology imposed on the people to authentic 'organic' conceptions of the social order, these Russian populists highlighted as symptomatic of a deracinated mass society the declining birth rates, widespread public corruption, sprawling anonymous high-rise slums of the cities, and large-scale pollution. They called for a moral regeneration of a historic Russia of local communities, expressed in their concerns with ecology, the preservation and restoration of Russia's architectural, religious, and literary heritage, and their encouragement of student pilgrimages to ancient towns, monasteries and churches.[35]

The response of the state to this Russian nationalism was ambivalent, oscillating between co-option and repression. During the 1970s the sense of moral and politico-economic crisis deepened within the regime, heightened by projections of demographic stagnation – the net increase in the Soviet workforce would decline from 24 million in the 1970s to 6 million in the 1980s – which would tighten further the competition between the economy and the huge armed services. Worse still, decline was forecast for the Russian population, the major source of skilled personnel for industry and the military, and, on the other hand, the major area of increase was to be in the Muslim population, largely rural, less educated and perceived to be 'less loyal'.[36] The failed intervention in Afghanistan highlighted the overextended nature of Soviet commitments and increased domestic discontent.

By the late Brezhnev years a large underground Russian nationalism had formed, penetrating much of the Russian intelligentsia and Party, some wings of which were imperialist and neo-Stalinist whereas others, presenting the Russians as victims, rejected the costs of empire.[37] Meanwhile, in the early 1980s the pressures on the state intensified to breaking point as a result of the application of computerization by the USA and its allies to nuclear defence (Star Wars systems) and conventional weaponry, which raised the arms race to a new technological plane.

The result was a growing perception in the communist and the military leadership that the system could not fulfil the contradictory demands placed on it. The military lobbied for better technology, but technological modernization required the diversion of resources from a military budget that was estimated to vary from 14 to 17 per cent of GDP. At the same time, to pacify popular discontent there had to be a boost in consumer living standards.[38]

These pressures explain the initial support given by broad sections of the leadership for Gorbachev's attempt to break out of this bind, by simultaneously scaling down the cold war and introducing *perestroika* at home.

ECONOMIC DECLINE, BLOCKED ELITE MOBILITY AND NATIONAL AUTONOMIST MOVEMENTS

Important though it was in signalling a potential legitimation crisis, a growing attraction of intellectuals to nationalism throughout much of the USSR would not in itself have threatened the system. None the less, it became increasingly salient when the economic decline of the state in combination with a loosening of Stalinist controls began to undermine the stability of the ethno-

federal system by disrupting the expectations of social mobility
held by educated youth. A classic situation of 'blocked mobility'
threatened to develop, thereby creating a broad social constituency for nationalism among those aspiring but failing to achieve
administrative, managerial, scientific and cultural positions, and
who could transform the projects of the intellectuals into a political threat to both the republican elites and the centre.

As we saw, the stability of the Soviet Union was maintained
by an ethnic balancing act that based the central institutions
disproportionately on the dominant Russian nationality, which
identified most strongly with the state and its superpower status,
and that provided the major non-Russian nationalities with their
own republics. In return for doing the centre's business and
exercising despotic controls over dissident groups and the population at large, the educated stratum of the non-Russian titular
nationalities was given privileged access over official positions of
its own territory, and it could work to extract resources from the
centre to expand such things as educational provision. The Baltic
and Transcaucasian republics (Georgia, Armenia and Azerbaijan) were particularly successful at fashioning affirmative action
policies and creating an indigenous elite.[39]

From the 1960s, however, this system of ethnic balancing was
beginning to unravel for two reasons. Firstly, Khrushchev's weakening of Stalin's terror apparatus and then Brezhnev's policy
of respect for cadres, allowed the republican officials a growing
autonomy so that they were able to establish their own patronage
networks and to lobby the centre.

Secondly, as republican cadres gained new freedom, they faced
increasing internal demands, for as the Soviet Union modernized
after Stalin's death, it generated a four-fold rise between 1959–
60 and 1980–81 in the number of non-Russians gaining a college
or vocational training.[40] As the educated stratum expanded, the
republics were pressed to find appropriate elite positions and to
finance a swelling of republican administrative and professional
superstructures.[41] Since the period showed an overall trend to an
equalization between the nationalities in educational opportunities and the employment of specialists with higher education, this

meant a redistribution by the centre of resources from the richer to the poorer republics (notably in Central Asia). From the 1960s, as it became more difficult for the republican elites to meet the expectations of ever rising numbers of their co-nationals for administrative and professional positions in the republic, this led to bitter political struggles between the republics and the centre for resources, and caused inter-ethnic conflict. These pressures became more and more severe in the 1970s in a climate of economic decline.[42]

In particular, the elites of richer republics (Latvia, the Ukraine, Azerbaijan, and, from the 1970s, Armenia and Georgia) resented the redistributive aspects of the system, and two strategies were developed to overcome the squeeze on employment of their co-nationals, both of which were bound to generate increased nationalist friction in the USSR. The first was to agitate publicly for more economic autonomy for the republic. The second strategy was to discriminate still further against minority nationalities (including Russians) within their republic; for example, by stipulations on the use of the titular language in places of employment. In a country where some 55 million people lived outside their titular republics, this was bound to create inter-ethnic tensions.[43]

Both strategies were employed in the powerful Ukrainian republic during the period of Shelest's tenure as Party chief (1963–72) which has been described as one of 'revival of controlled Ukrainian autonomism'. Under Shelest, the Party encouraged public criticism of the centre's subordination of Ukraine's economic interests to Siberian development and complained of the republic's high level of contributions to the All-Union budget. In 1963, as part of a thoroughgoing Ukrainization (and de-Russification) of the republic, the Party leadership expressed demands that all institutions of higher learning, authorities, factories and trades should do their business in Ukrainian.[44]

Such was the danger posed by this Ukrainian autonomism and the resentment aroused in the Russian minority that Shelest's regime was subject to a wholesale purge between 1971 to 1973 and nationalist intellectuals were attacked in other republics. Nevertheless, in similar vein the republics of Armenia, Georgia and Azerbaijan in 1978 declared the titular language to be the language of state. This provoked in Georgia protests that same year from Abkhazians who petitioned to join the Russian federated republic.[45] Claims of a programme of ethnocide heightened tensions in the Baltic, where, as a result of heavy immigration in the 1970s, the Russians had reached 27.9 per cent and 32.8 per cent of the respective populations in Estonia and Latvia by 1979.[46]

REFORM AND THE COLLAPSE OF THE CENTRE

Before Gorbachev took power in 1985, the centrifugal forces of nationalism were kept in check by the revolutionary mystique and aura of power of the USSR, the extent of its coercive apparatus, and the interest of local communist elites in not destabilizing a system which accorded them their political monopoly. But it is now clear that a long-term geopolitical and economic crisis had the effect of generating a nationalist unrest against the centre and between populations. Especially sensitive were relations between titular nationals and sizeable Russian minorities scattered throughout the USSR.

Gorbachev, however, as a loyal Soviet *Russian* communist was blind to this looming problem in his first few years. His preoccupation was with achieving a politico-economic transformation of a decaying command system by his policies of *perestroika* (which entailed economic decentralization and greater political participation), *glasnost* (openness), and normalization of relations with the West. Not until 1988 did he seriously begin to address the nationalities problem while still in the midst of an unsuccessful struggle to 'marketize' the Soviet economy. By then it was too late, and, ironically, it was his policies of reform that led to the rapid disintegration of the Soviet Union by dismantling the ideological and organizational foundations of its ethno-federal system.

Hence *glasnost* was intended to establish a critical Soviet civil society underpinning socialist reform against the entrenched *nomenklatura*. Instead, in weakening the police state and permitting open debate, it allowed the exploration and expression of long suppressed national grievances (for example, religious and political persecution, ecological damage, cultural Russification) against the Soviet system, the re-emergence of nationalist intellectuals who could make contact with nascent opinion, and the formation of nationalist popular fronts in the republics. As a consequence, counter-elites – often earlier dissident leaders of the 1960–80 period, such as Petrosyan in Armenia, Gamsakhurdia in Georgia, and Drach in the Ukraine – emerged to challenge office holders for the leadership of their communities.[47]

If *glasnost* squeezed local communists from below, *perestroika* could threaten them from above. As part of his plan to create a more efficient and accountable Soviet polity and economy, Gorbachev foreshadowed central intervention to replace the republics' corrupt and inefficient patronage networks based on ethnic favouritism by more meritocratic structures. Moreover, in 1988 by pushing through multi-candidate national elections to the Congress of People's Deputies he effectively broke the Communist Party's monopoly on political power.[48] The response of local communist regimes to this situation varied, but Party elites, now feeling threatened from the centre and challenged in their territories by ethno-political movements which regarded them as corrupt collaborators, were tempted or forced to ride the tiger of national autonomism, with mixed success.

In this combustible environment Gorbachev's foreign policy initiatives, designed to normalize the USSR in the world order, instead further weakened its integrity in two ways. Firstly, he thereby removed the sense of imminent threat from the West which had been used so relentlessly in the past by the regime's propaganda to hold a highly militarized society together. Secondly, when he conceded the illegitimacy of a post-war settlement in Eastern Europe, based on conquest, and acquiesced in 1989 in the popular overthrow of communist regimes, it became impossible to avoid flow-on effects within a union established by force. In a situation of gathering Soviet economic and political breakdown, this encouraged Baltic nationalists who had never accepted their annexation in the 1940s to switch from autonomist to outright separatist demands. Appealing to the international community for justice, these republics spearheaded a drive for full independence, which was followed by Moldavia, also annexed in the 1940s, and Armenia, Georgia and the Ukraine, which had memories of forcible incorporation into the USSR during the civil war.[49]

The impact of Gorbachev's reforms was uneven, with some republican leaderships long resisting them, and there were great variations in the development of nationalist movements. In Central Asia the Communist parties managed to suppress relatively weak oppositions, and the conservative leadership in the Ukraine, until its overthrow in 1989, kept a lid on nationalist activity. But by 1988 intellectuals and activists had formed national popular fronts in the Baltic republics, Armenia, and Georgia. They were fuelled by popular disillusion with Gorbachev's economic policies which had resulted in a deterioration in the supply of consumer goods and agricultural produce and in soaring inflation.[50] In the Ukraine and Armenia the disasters of Chernobyl in 1986 and the great earthquake of 1988 strengthened nationalist criticisms of the corruption and ineffectiveness of the Soviet system. In 1988 inter-national conflicts also broke out between Armenians and Azerbaijanis over the disputed area of Nagorno-Karabakh.

Gorbachev's inability to deal with these problems except on an *ad hoc* basis, together with his tolerance of demonstrations and the introduction of competitive local and national elections encouraged a mass nationalism to take off in 1988 and 1989. In November 1988 Estonia declared itself a sovereign republic, and most other republics were concerned to gain recognition of the titular language as the official language of state. This in turn excited a mobilization of national minorities in the republics, some of whom demanded their own autonomous republics, while others, like the Abkhazians, revived their demands for secession from Georgia and union with Russia.

Although military force was used spasmodically (for example, against the Georgians in 1989 and Lithuanians in 1990), Gorbachev's democratic credentials made it impossible to solve the problem in the traditional way. In 1989 he proposed a 'genuine' federation on the Leninist model, but without clarifying how this would bridge the widening gap between the centre and the republics, or protect the rights of minorities. By the end of 1990 all the

Union republics and most of the autonomous republics had been inspired by the revolutions in Eastern Europe to declare themselves sovereign, and several (the Baltic, Moldavian, Georgian, and Armenian) opted for full independence. This coincided with worsening economic disorganization (including a collapse in the distribution system) and accelerating inflation as a result of which many republics began to withhold goods from the centre.[51]

Although a serious problem, the nationalism of the non-Russians need not have been fatal to the integrity of the state. The Central Asian republics (net beneficiaries of the Union in budgetary terms) remained loyal. Moreover, the centre had many potential allies in the national minorities within the republics who sought protection against discrimination from the titular group, and it could exploit such traditional antagonisms between neighbouring nationalities as that flaring between Armenians and Azerbaijanis. What was more dangerous for the Soviet Union was the impact of this ferment and descent to political and economic chaos on the core Russian population which had identified most with the great power status and revolutionary mission of the state.

As we have seen, before Gorbachev, there was evidence from the 1960s of significant Russian disillusionment with the Marxist state because of its destructive impact on Russian society and culture, their lack of an independent cultural and political voice, and the burden of sustaining the 'lesser' peoples. But at least at this stage Russians could enjoy the prestige of running a state which challenged the USA in military and scientific prestige. Under Gorbachev, however, as Russians came to believe themselves victims of a failed system, devoid of revolutionary mystique, declining in world prestige and economically incompetent, they came to feel increasingly resentful of the grievances of other nationalities which were expressed not just in anti-Soviet but anti-Russian terms.

The Russian reaction took different forms, one of which was to assert an imperialist Russian nationalism that, in the name of defending the 25 million Russians outside the Russian Federation, demanded the imposition of order on the recalcitrant republics.

The major voice of Russian frustration, however, was Boris Yeltsin, who, tapping Russian populist and democratic themes, won election in 1990 to the chair of the Supreme Soviet of the Russian Republic and declared its sovereignty. Although Gorbachev moved to propitiate the Russians, shortages of food in the cities eroded support for the centre. In 1990 Yeltsin argued that the reform process, now paralysed at the centre, had moved to the republics. In 1991, as Gorbachev floundered, manoeuvring to right and left in an attempt to keep the Soviet Union together, Yeltsin grew in strength, winning an overwhelming victory for the Presidency of the Russian republic. His threat to withhold taxes from the Union forced Gorbachev to agree to a treaty that would transform the Union into a loose federation of largely autonomous republics.

This in fact sounded the death knell of a system based on the willingness of the dominant nationality to operate its central institutions – the Party, state administration, security services and the military. When within days of the signing of the treaty in August, orthodox communists mounted their coup against Gorbachev to reverse the disintegration of the centre, they discovered core elements in the Soviet army, security services, and the administration had already switched their support from the USSR to Russia. The coup failed, and the Soviet Union was at an end.

The Last (Russian) Empire, Failure of Communist Modernization, or Warning for the West?

What then are the implications of this disintegration of the USSR for an understanding of the relationship between ethnicity and the state in the modern world? No doubt there are many lessons to be drawn, but one can find three perspectives of particular interest. These are not necessarily mutually exclusive, and indeed, one can find many authors in the course of their subtle and illuminating analyses combining them.[52] But it is useful for the sake of clarity to separate their different assumptions.

From one perspective, these events represent the collapse of the last empire, implying that Soviet goals, operations and contradictions, were strongly shaped by the patterns of expansive conquest, colonization, and techniques of ethnic management established over the centuries by the Tsarist Russian state. A second option, focusing on the USSR rather as a distinctive, novel kind of modernizing state, is to regard the collapse as a demonstration of the failure of a universalistic communism to provide an alternative to nationalism as a basis of collective identity and organization in the twentieth century. A third viewpoint is to regard these events as exemplifying the vulnerabilities of all multinational states in the modern world.

DECLINE OF THE LAST (RUSSIAN) EMPIRE?

The continuity thesis comes in a number of versions, but the most interesting is the 'imperial overreach' interpretation of the sociologist Randall Collins, who in 1986 forecast on geopolitical grounds 'the future decline of the Russian empire'.[53] Multi-ethnic states, he argues, cohere or decay in so far as they secure a kind of 'national' legitimacy by virtue of their status *vis-à-vis* other great powers in the international arena. Successful states enjoy positional (i.e. they are marchland rather than interior states which are ringed with enemies) and resource advantages over their rivals.

Applying this to the USSR, he argued that the growing military and economic problems of the USSR in the 1980s were the product of a long-term geopolitical overreach that had developed out of the expansion of the Tsarist Empire. As a marchland state for many centuries, Russia had enjoyed a favourable geopolitical position over its rivals and its huge population was an important military advantage. But since the end of the nineteenth century and, more particularly, the Second World War, this situation had now changed for the reasons given above. Now military and economically overextended because of a ring of enemies and its inferior economic and demographic capacities, the USSR found itself in decline. Should several potential crises on its frontiers (e.g. in Eastern Europe and Afghanistan) coincide, it was likely they would present an insuperable challenge to the centre. At this point the state, now losing its legitimacy, would disintegrate round its 'ethnic fault lines'.

Although Collins is unique in giving a theoretical basis to the continuity thesis, it is widely assumed in Soviet scholarship that despite the supranationalist pretensions of the Soviet communist state, it was heir to the (Russian) Tsarist Empire both in its foreign and domestic policies. Such writers are not blind to the distinctive character of the communist state, but they argue that just as under Tsarism a Russian imperialism came to give the state cohesion while at the same time threatening it with disintegration, since it provoked the long embedded grievances amongst non-Russian nationalities. These regarded the USSR like its precursor as a prison house of nations.

As Robert Conquest has pointed out, the Bolshevik Revolution was largely Russian-based, and it was primarily Russian armies that regained much of the territory of the Tsarist Empire by overcoming the resistance of bourgeois nationalists who had attempted to secede after 1917.[54] Although the old Bolshevik party leadership had an 'international' character, under Stalin and his successors the communist state, in spite of its egalitarian doctrines, reverted to much the same ethnic hierarchies, with Russians and Orthodox Slavs dominating the core institutions and with Muslims at the bottom of the status ladder.[55] It pursued the same assimilationist and divide-and-rule strategies, seeking to co-opt sections of the Ukrainians and Georgian elites, and playing 'protector' to minorities. As in the Tsarist period, Russian migrants were used to cement state power in the peripheries and to advance a hegemonic Russian culture.[56]

Although during the early years efforts were made to control 'Great Russian chauvinism', as attention under Stalin switched from world revolution to achieving 'socialism in one country', a celebration of the historic civilizing mission of the Russian people infiltrated the state. The new state implicitly rooted itself in the earlier empire, by re-evaluating the centuries of Tsarist expansion as progressive because they brought 'backward' peoples under the sway of a more advanced socio-cultural (Russian) people.

Just as under Tsarism, these Russification strategies had some success, particularly among the Slavic populations of Belorussia and the Ukraine, which were culturally close to Russia. But in spite of the use of schools and the military (recruited by universal male conscription) the success of assimilation campaigns, measured by indices such as marriage patterns, linguistic usage, and propensity to migrate, was limited in Transcaucasia and the more culturally distant Islamic populations of Central Asia.[57] This empire of culturally differentiated peoples was held together ultimately by despotism.

As was the case under Tsarism, the nationalism of the non-Russian peoples was likely to be the Achilles' heel of the USSR, for this despotism rested on a weakening Russian hegemony. Demographic trends indicated a relative decline in the Russian population from $c.$70 per cent in the 1920s to under 50 per cent in the early decades of the new century and a rapid increase in the Muslim population, regarded as the least educated and reliable group in the Union.[58]

Collins' and these allied interpretations are useful in suggesting the geopolitical determinants of state legitimacy, and they illuminate a recurring facet of modern revolutionary regimes: how, after a universalistic messianic phase, they are compelled to ground their project in the history and culture of the dominant *ethnie*. They also highlight the in-built tensions of a multi-ethnic state with a long heritage of oppression.

But as it stands the analysis is too one-dimensional and can be criticized on three grounds. One problem is that the term 'empire' tends to be used somewhat polemically rather than analytically, as in Conquest's title *The Last Empire*. This seems to suggest without rigorous comparative analysis that the USSR was a unique anachronism (the Romanov Empire on a life-support system) doomed to collapse because it violated principles of national determination. There is some basis for arguing for the distinctive characteristics of the state based on the imperial pattern of Russian national formation mentioned earlier, but this draws an oversharp distinction between the USSR and other *modern* states, most of which (including avowedly nation-states) are multinational in composition and are based on ethnic hierarchies.[59] It also underplays the huge discontinuities between the institutions and practices of a traditionalist Tsarist state and those of a Soviet order dedicated to a messianic transformation that shaped the experience of its peoples.

A second criticism is that by tending to depict the federalist character of the socialist state as merely a façade for Russian dominance, it fails to give sufficient weight to a dynamic factor not present in Tsarism. Some have argued that Soviet federalism in practice resembled the system of indirect rule favoured by the dynastic empires, including Tsarism. But a commitment on socialist grounds to an equality between nations could only undermine the legitimacy of a regime based on a Russian core by highlighting the contradictions between principle and practice. Federalism also institutionalized national identities to the point where they could challenge in peacetime the continued existence of a superpower. It is true that, for much of the period, there was something of a symbiosis between Russian neo-Slavophilism and Soviet communism, but it is hard to explain why the majority of Russians themselves came to regard communism as an exploitative system if the USSR was simply a Russian empire. If the USSR was an empire, it was a communist one which subordinated Russians as well as other nationalities to its goals by denying them a political voice of their own.[60]

Thirdly, it also tends to present a primordialist view of nationalist resistance as driven by a strong sense of cultural (sometimes religiously based) difference, reinforced by oppression, which can be measured by such practices as linguistic usage, endogamy, and so forth. But this does not do justice to the extent to which the Soviet Union helped construct nations, often in alliance with secular elites who regarded Moscow communists as modernizing allies in their battle against theocracy. Neither (as was argued in chapter 1) do 'objective' indicators in themselves measure the existence of national consciousness, nor does the experience of oppression necessarily result in political mobilization. In Central Asia, where cultural distance was greatest, separatist nationalism was at its weakest. We have to look to a more sophisticated explanation that accounts for the fact that a radical nationalism was strongest, not in the most culturally different and backward regions, but in the richer and more modernized European regions of the USSR, those more exposed to Russification, where it was led by an educated generation with expectations of power, wealth and status.

These criticisms apply even to Collins' model (valuable though it is in other respects) which with its terminology of fault lines (particularly jagged in the frontier areas of the Baltic and Central Asia) makes ethnic resurgence an automatic process rather than a problem to be analysed. As I argued earlier, what is required is to show how an externally generated systemic crisis brought about the rise of alternative nationalist ideologies and impinged on the federal political structures of the communist state so as to create problems of blocked mobility in particular republics.

FAILURE OF COMMUNISM AS A MODERNIZING IDEOLOGY?

This perhaps suggests an alternative interpretation of the collapse, one that explains it not in terms of an antiquated imperialism but of the failure of communism as a modernizing project. Communists claimed that they had scientific insight into the laws of history and could catapult a country at a backward stage of social development over the heads of the leading capitalist powers. But their despotic command system was unable to compete with democratic capitalist states which were better able to tap the energies of civil society. Communism collapsed because of its inability to generate the resources necessary to meet growing aspirations of its own creation, and because of the resentments engendered by its dictatorial practices. As the command system fell into crisis *at the centre*, it lacked some of the positive incentives at the level of common interest that could be found in capitalist states to restrain the centrifugal momentum developing in the national republics. For these were economically integrated through the centre rather as in a market system, by mutual trade and comparative specialization. Hence, when the central economy collapsed, there were few horizontal ties to hold republics together.[61]

As an interpretation this would go some way towards accounting for the collapse of the Soviet state, but not for the growing momentum of nationalism. To explain this, Hobsbawm delves into social-psychology, suggesting that as the planned economy (and its social security system) disintegrated, it produced insecurity and disorientation, and people retreated to the simple certainties of belonging to a common language and culture.[62] Hobsbawm essentially accounts for the triumph of nationalism in hydraulic terms by the failure of communism, when he observes:

> ... as we can now see in melancholy retrospect, it was the great achievement of the communist regimes in multinational states to limit the disastrous effects of nationalism within them.[63]

But this is wrong in two respects. Firstly, it implies an antinomy between, on the one hand, the Soviet communist state and, on the other, the ethnic loyalties of the population, whereas, as Besançon argues, the communist system operated through its balancing of ethnic identities which acted both as energizers and inhibitors within a federal system.[64] Secondly, it explains in primordialist fashion current ethnic discontents as products of earlier precommunist conflicts, whereas they were to a large degree an effect of the communist mode of modernization.

To elaborate, Lenin, as was noted earlier, in establishing the federal system had the expectation that, as socialist modernization took hold, a Soviet identity would gradually replace a sense of nationality, and he was not afraid to co-opt national loyalties (even to the extent of helping to create them) to advance this long-term project. But an effect of creating quasi-autonomous territorial entities based on ethnic criteria was to institutionalize nationalities. By and large, ethnic ties were the key to social and political mobility for individuals seeking entry to the burgeoning administrative, scientific-technical and cultural apparatus. As a differentiated modern society emerged in the republics, it took national forms.

Although an internationalist Soviet proletarian identity was from the beginning vigorously promoted by the state through the education system, youth organizations, the armed services, and (later) festivals, its roots were thin. Stalin, requiring a massive centralization of power to push through his programme and aware of the centrifugal pressures in Lenin's system, realized he had to base his power solidly on the Russian core. Consequently, official Soviet culture was heavily Russified,[65] notably so at times of crisis (during the war with Germany, and in the wake of Khrushchev's demoralizing demolition of the Stalin cult). But although giving Russians 'Elder Brother' status might enable Stalin and his successors to mobilize Russian national sentiment behind the regime, it could only highlight the in-built contradiction with the Soviet doctrine of equalization between the nations. Sovietization to the non-Russian nationalities entailed their subordination. Although sections of the national elites in certain regions (e.g. the Ukraine) were co-opted, in setting up an ethnofederal system in this way the communist state had created irresolvable tensions.[66]

The increasing national anatagonisms then evident in the Gorbachev years cannot just be attributed, as Hobsbawm seems to suggest, to the reawakening of ancient feuds (though historical memories did play a part). Rather they were the result of a despotic command mode of modernization that had to operate within a formally decentralized system. To ensure the success of his agrarian and industrialization schemes, Stalin had to break the power of the republics and all other autonomous organizations by purges, forced famines, divide-and-rule policies, persecutions of traditional religious heritages, and the siting of substantial Russian populations in their territories both to advance economic development and to undermine local cultures. After Stalin there was some relaxation, but the practices of ethnic manipulation had to go on.

As we saw, what was increasingly damaging to the system was its failure to deliver the goods in spite of all the tragic human sacrifices and ecological ruin. By the 1970s, a drive for national autonomism was developing, but not everywhere. Indeed, it was the richer republics that mobilized against the centre. This would appear to lend support to those such as Roeder who reject, as too undifferentiated, primordialist interpretations that account for national resurgence in terms of a drive for identity and freedom, in favour of applying a (political) resource competition model to the communist state which is able to explain which populations mobilized against the state and why.[67]

This model interprets the rise of nationalist movements as the response of political entrepreneurs who, as part of a drive for power, use symbols of cultural difference and social grievance to mobilize populations experiencing disrupted prospects of socio-economic mobility. Roeder demonstrates how economic stagnation, together with the centre's policies of resource redistribution between republics affected the ability of richer republics to service the demands of an ever larger educated youth. It was the autonomist campaigns of these republics that fatally destabilized an ethno-federal system already under stress, but their underlying objectives until late in the day were to retain more resources (through economic autonomy), or to restrict competition by policies of cultural exclusion rather than to tear free from the system.

Roeder's analysis is powerful. It suggests that although the contradiction between nominal goals of equality among nationalities and the reality of ethnic stratification made the legitimacy of the system problematic, it did not of itself inspire serious political dissent. (After all, it exists in most modern societies.) The threat came from the sense of resentment felt by relatively privileged groups against the centre's redistributive policies. For nations as exclusive cultural groups are not so concerned with achieving equality with others as obtaining what they *perceive* to be their due (which may be superiority and privilege). They (here particularly the beneficiaries of redistribution) are also restrained by a consideration of what they will lose from quitting a political system. It is also correct to say that without a substantial aggrieved social base the cultural concerns of the intellectuals themselves will never disturb an existing political system.

None the less, this political conception of ethnicity is too narrow in two respects. Firstly, it reduces the revivals to the function of producing symbols for political agents engaged in the purposes of collective differentiation and mobilization, trivializing their central part in creating alternative identities and meaningful systems that had a *directive* effect on subsequent political action.[68] Secondly, in examining the dynamics of the political system, it fails to give sufficient attention to its dependence on the (Russian) ethnic core.

One of the major shortcomings of the prevalent political interpretations is the failure to address the profound *moral* dimension of the crisis generated by communism's destructive assault on the religious and cultural heritage of the Soviet peoples. It was in this context that the emerging national revivals, which long preceded Gorbachev, crystallized to offer fresh but 'authentic' social models and become dynamic agents of political change. In a situation of some fluidity they shaped events by throwing up charismatic leaders, energizing popular communities, intensifying identities by cultural conflicts with other groups, assembling broad alliances in opposition to the system, and elaborating options for political leaders as the system slipped into chaos.

As we saw, notable national intellectuals – Petrosyan in Armenia, Gamsakhurdia in Georgia, Drach in the Ukraine and (later) Lansbergis in Lithuania – as longstanding symbols of opposition in many republics were elevated by peoples wishing a break with the past to become authentic leaders of their nation's future. The national revivals they presided over offered positive alternatives to a decaying social system and distinctive cultural forms by which to express them, thus liberating energies drained by anomie and confusion. In the Baltic republics the mass choir festivals and the great commemorative rituals (above all, the human chain of more than a million people stretching from Vilnius to Tallinn in 1989 to recall the fiftieth anniversary of their annexation under the Nazi-Soviet Pact) raised popular emotions to a high intensity in pursuit of the campaign for independence.[69]

As the revivals developed, so did conflicts between rival nationalities in mixed areas over such matters as ownership of the past, cultural icons and shared territories. In the Ukraine the 1988 celebration of the millennium of the Christianization of Kievan

Rus antagonized Ukrainians because of the Russian Orthodox insistence on treating it as an (imperial) Russian event to be celebrated in Moscow.[70] In Transcaucasia a bitter dispute reawakened over the constitutional status of Nagorno-Karabakh which led to an unofficial war between the Armenians and Azerbaijanis. Such disputes both hardened boundaries between populations and intensified and elaborated a sense of distinctiveness within them, adding a new and unpredictable element to an uncertain situation.

This intensification and filling out of a sense of distinctiveness *vis-à-vis* others contributed to the mobilization of diverse interests (religious and secular) in umbrella popular front organizations in the Baltic and Transcaucasia. As society seemed to be differentiating into countless voluntary groups, only national ideals provided a point of integration. Although the very diversity of these political movements inevitably generated internal debates, such arguments, framed by a consciousness of a common enemy, served to create a sense of national political community and to define the possibilities and constraints for the new national leadership. In this way nationalism can be said to have had a directive function in articulating the shifting options available to political leaders as they sought to command a continuously changing situation.

Charting the dynamic development of nationalism in this way among certain of the non-Russian populations has its interest. But the decisive effect of this ferment was to cause a crucial retreat on the part of large segments of the Russian population on whom the system depended from a generalized identification with the Soviet territory as a whole to an ethno-territorial nationalism. As we observed, Soviet communism had reinforced the imperial character of Russian nationalism that had developed under Tsarism, by granting the Russians dominance in core Soviet institutions, while denying them at the same time any political and cultural autonomy as *Russians*. Consequently, the Russian elites – the military, police, state and Party bureaucracies – as well as substantial sections of the people (and in particular Russian migrants) tended to identify with the Soviet territory.[71]

Yet it is arguable that because of their closeness to the centre the Russians as a people were exposed more than other nationalities to the destructive aspects of the regime.[72] From the 1960s a communitarian nationalism formed, advocating a rejection of empire, reidentification with the historic land of Russia, and support for Russian freedom. The context was a growing fear among millions of educated Russians that the absorption of Russians into the running of a Communist imperial state had resulted in their decline. Concerns were expressed about demographic trends which were transforming them into a minority in the Union and, as the economy stagnated, about the diversion of capital investment from their republic to others.[73] This was only one nationalist response: neo-imperialists, by contrast, pleaded Russia's historic destiny and demanded a reassertion of central controls over ungrateful republics. But the popular focus on Russian territories by those disillusioned with the Soviet state was significant, and contestations between Russian nationalists began to problematize the historic relationship of Russians with the territorial state and its populations.

With this background in mind, we can see how the Gorbachev era intensified the alienation of the Russian core, already sensitive about status decline, from the Soviet state. The sapping of the USSR's great power prestige with the loss of the external empire, and *perestroika* demoralized the Russian military and civilian elites. But perhaps more shocking to a people used to deference and aggrieved at its own unique lack of political autonomy was the proliferation of nationalisms, which, in demanding autonomy, expressed their resentments of the Soviet state in Russophobic terms. This evidence of widespread unpopularity (for the first time highly visible under *glasnost*), to a group perceiving itself in decline, encouraged many Russians to redefine the Soviet territory as alien and to identify the Russian territory as their homeland.

Again, as in the 1960s, many varieties of nationalism flourished in Russia, but Yeltsin's election as President of an autonomous Russian republic indicated a popular support for a Russian territorial nationalism.[74] This was the deadly blow to an imperial system that depended on the suppression of an independent Russian identity. When Yeltsin as President of Russia selected Moscow (the capital of the Union) as the republic's capital, he effectively established a position of dual authority in the USSR, paralysing Union government and speeding disintegration. He countered Gorbachev's repression of the Baltic Republics by announcing Russian support for their independence. By the end the Russian President had become the leading political figure, and the Soviet state under Gorbachev had declined to an empty shell.

WARNING FOR OTHER MULTINATIONAL POLITIES?

The above interpretation would certainly indicate that the processes of communist modernization not only failed to uproot national identities, but even created or reinforced them. The subsequent disintegration of Yugoslavia and Czechoslovakia suggests the failure was generic rather than particular to the USSR.

It is possible to maintain that this set of events has a still more general application in the modern world to what are close parallels in contemporary Europe. For, as Laitin points out, in spite of their self-designations as nation-states, most European states are in reality multinational, dominated by a single nationality and regulated by historically embedded ethnic status hierarchies.[75] Moreover, one can make useful comparisons between the imperial decline of the USSR and that of Western Europe in the post-war period when five states – Britain, France, Holland, Belgium and Portugal – were compelled to surrender their colonies, a process that peaked in the 1960s. As in the Soviet case, a widespread perception of the decline of the European great powers has been accompanied by a resurgence of minority national movements in Britain, France, Spain and Italy, which gained further momentum from the sudden economic downturn in the 1970s.

During this period aggrieved national minorities in the West, experiencing unexpected breaks on their expectations, have contrasted the universalistic claims of liberal democratic states with their perception of systematic discrimination in favour of the core nationality. Does this not indicate a vulnerability of all *multi-national* states to the unpredictable shocks of modernity – sudden military involvements, economic recessions, and so forth – which impact unevenly on their constituent populations?

Probably not, for two reasons. Firstly, the core nationality in Western nation-states has a greater commitment to maintain the integrity of the state. The French or Spanish could regard the state as *their* state because it was suffused with their name, myths, history, and culture. In contrast, although the USSR, like Western nation-states, was run through a dominant ethnic core, because of its formal supranationalism, the Russians had less stake in the unity of the state. As Conquest asserts, the Soviet political community was unique in the world in having no ethnic or territorial reference in its name.[76] Although sections of the Russian core did and still do identify with the Soviet territories, the animosity of non-Russians sharpened in others an ambivalence that made them prepared in the end to desert the USSR in order to build a better future in their homelands. Divisions paralysed the state, paving the way for full collapse.

Of course, there are other multinational states where the core nationality exercises power through a civic rather than an ethnic identification. The English dominate their state as Britons even though they unconsciously conflate Britain with England, much to the irritation of the Scots, Welsh and Irish. But here as elsewhere in Western Europe, the core nationality is much more dominant than were the Russians in the USSR (who had declined to barely 50 per cent of the total population) and there are many fewer minority nationalities to control.

Another important difference between the two cases is the democratic character of the western European states. But democratic norms and institutions, although they may serve to moderate conflict in a state, will not in themselves resolve nationalist disputes – as the persistence of terrorist campaigns of the IRA in Britain, ETA in (post-Franco) Spain and Corsican extremists in France attests. None the less, it can be asked if the unity of Soviet territories might have been preserved had a more farsighted Gorbachev moved early to dismantle the communist despotism in favour of a looser democratic capitalist federation, perhaps on the US model. Such a state would have had to make key decisions which would affect the life chances of its peoples: about the official language of state, the balance of authority between centre and republics, and the degree and direction of resource allocations between regions.

The portability, however, of the US model is limited since it was born out of a successful popular war of liberation which provided the new state with a foundation myth and a sense of unique community, and, in any case, its ethnic population was distributed throughout the state rather than settled on historic territories. By contrast, Soviet reformers could tap few positive transnational sentiments or sets of interests that would bind populations to obey the regulatory and redistributive decisions of a central state. Indeed, any new multi-ethnic state based on the territorial structures of Tsarism and communism would carry the burden of memories of Russian domination of the central institutions, political tyranny, persecution of national and religious minorities, and economic and social failure.

Given this unpromising heritage, prospects of maintaining the integrity of the territorial state would have been bleak. In any federation the problem would have been that the Russians as a bare majority would be insufficient to rule decisively while being sufficiently powerful as to arouse the fears of the other nationalities. The break-up of the state was on the cards, whatever options were tried.

Although this analysis does stress the distinctiveness of the Soviet Union *vis-à-vis* other states, the discussion suggests that its collapse has wider implications. Certainly, it demonstrates the importance of geopolitical competition and patterns of state modernization as important causal factors in the rise of nationalism. But it also highlights the necessity to analyse the moral as well as the political dimension of systemic crisis, that is too often overlooked by political scientists, but out of which nationalism so often forms. In this regard, the continued salience of cultural nationalism as a dynamic agent of change in the late twentieth century is confirmed in spite of being repeatedly buried by commentators.

Finally, although it is evident that the triumph of nationalism was dependent on the collapse of state controls, this discussion demonstrates that even universalistic ideologies such as communism, possessing all the machinery of a modern technological state to achieve its aims, have ultimately to operate through ethnic core populations. It confirms the seminal importance of Anthony Smith's recent work on ethnic cores.[77] Further and detailed comparative investigation would be required to corroborate the next conclusion. But the analysis of this chapter may lead one to propose that for a state to achieve stability (particularly one undergoing democratization), these cores must be demographically dominant and strongly identified with the state and its territories. Without these conditions multinational states are likely to be regularly destabilized by the unpredictability of modernization processes which upset the existing ethnic status order.

The End of the European Nation-state?

With the dissolution of the USSR and its security bloc, the new states in Eastern Europe have hurried to establish their own armies, create distinctive currencies and economic policies, revive national symbols and cultures, and in many cases 'cleanse' 'their' territories of foreigners. In short, with the collapse of communism, they appear to be adopting as their political model the classical norms of the nation-state as it has formed in Western Europe. This model as we saw earlier has several constitutive elements:

1 The nation-state is the sovereign actor in world politics, its power only qualified by its relationships with other such political units in a competitive interstate 'society'.
2 It is sovereign within its territory, subordinating all intermediate authorities – regional, religious, class – to its law-making and law-enforcement powers over security and the economy.
3 It is culturally unique, exemplified in its distinctive history, values and institutions.
4 It is based on a homogeneous citizenry who have equal rights in the nation.

How ironic then that this shift to nation-statism in the East should be occurring at a time when it has recently been argued that the assumptions on which this model is based are no longer valid, and that even in its own European heartland the nation-state is increasingly anachronistic as a result of the processes of internationalization.[1]

Such critics argue that with the advance of an interdependent international economy, success in war for industrial societies now requires their pooling sovereignty through military and economic co-operation with allies, as testified by the experiences of the two world wars and the post-1945 organization of the industrial world into rival military blocs such as the Warsaw Pact and NATO. In the economic sphere the growth of multinational organizations and the development of global financial markets severely limits the economic autonomy of the nation-state and this has led to the formation of supranational organizations like the EC and the development of regional trading blocs. The growth of global satellite communications systems is creating a world Anglophone hegemony which even the most powerful national cultures, such as the French, find impossible to resist. Finally, extensive post-war immigration particularly from Third World countries into many Western European states in order to sustain economic growth during a period of demographic decline in the West, has transformed these states into multi-ethnic and multicultural societies with awkward implications for national identity.

Such processes, it is argued, lie behind three different but increasingly interrelated challenges to the European nation-states in the post-war period.

The first comes from supranational organizations such as the European Community. The EC is not the only significant organization of this character: in the military field, NATO places restrictions on the autonomy of most Western nation-states. But the Community, building on the European Coal and Steel Community (formed in 1952) and then the European Common Market (established by the Treaty of Rome in 1957), represents potentially the most systematic challenge to the autonomy of the nation-state. For it provides institutional form to a movement embraced by ever expanding numbers of nation-states towards European economic and political union that has resulted in ever deeper economic integration, the growth of political and legal powers by Community institutions, and hopes for a Community foreign and defence policy.[2]

The second threat comes at the local or regional level from largely ethnic-based movements which have emerged since the late 1960s and have rejected the bureaucratic (nation-)state in favour of cultural or political autonomy. Some, like John Breuilly, have discounted this ethnic and regional revival as a transient protest phenomenon.[3] Indeed, many of these movements – the Occitanians and the Cornish, for example – have appeared to express only the romantic fads of a few intellectuals; none (even those with a significant social base, as in the Basque lands and Northern Ireland) has come close to seceding from the state; and the support for nationalism fluctuates markedly over time.

Nevertheless, the eruption of grievances by ethnic and regional populations across the continent since the 1960s reveals the fictive claims of the European nation-state. Moreover, in the 1980s many activists supported the movement towards European political union as enabling a Europe of the nations or the regions to replace the Europe of nation-states.[4]

A third challenge derives from the increasing polyethnic character of the European states since 1945 that makes problematic the correlation between nationality, democracy and citizenship rights.[5] Declining birth rates and the increase in large-scale immigration into Western Europe from the Mediterranean region and later from Third World countries have led to the development of large permanent alien communities who are denied many of the rights reserved for citizens. Since this means the exclusion of a significant section of the working classes from the franchise, it has led to a growing tension between the principles of democracy and nationality and to a drive to change the national definition of the state by a recognition of the multicultural character of key institutions. Current European Community agreements, which give residents of member states mobility and employment across borders, and the possibility of new waves of migration into Western Europe from the impoverished post-communist states of the East, presage an intensification of such tensions.

In the light of this analysis, I will investigate in this chapter the following questions:

1. Is the future of Europe supranational?
2. Is the Europe of nation-states likely to break up into a federation of nations?

3. Is polyethnicity likely to result in post-national political co
    munities?

As we shall see, an important underlying issue is the relationship
between the (European) nation-state model and modernity. Must
societies transform themselves into unicultural and ethnic polities
if they are to be viable in the long run? Or is the nation-state
only a contingent political formulation? If the nation-state is
weakening in its European heartlands, this may have considerable implications for all world societies.

Towards a Supranational Europe?

To a generous observer the vision of European unity shared by
a few statesmen in the immediate post-war period, oppressed by
the devastation of their continent twice this century by national
rivalries, has been impressively vindicated in the rise of the European Community. Although the first organization, the European
Coal and Steel Community (ECSC), founded in 1952, was economic and its membership confined to Belgium, France, Holland,
Italy, Luxembourg, and West Germany, its initiators envisaged
it as the first step to a European Political Union. In 1958 the
ECSC was succeeded by the European Economic Community
(EEC) which went well beyond the economic to embrace the
legal, cultural and political (and increasingly the field of security),
and as this has happened the membership has also increased to
encompass 90 per cent of the population of Western Europe, and
it could by the end of the century expand to take in much of the
rest of Europe.[6]

Thus the EEC, as well as creating a common market between
these countries, established a supranational policy-initiating
bureaucracy, the European Commission, subject to a Council of
Ministers and scrutinized by a European Parliament, and whose
directives are ultimately enforced on national governments by a
European Court. From the 1960s the following were put in place:
a common agriculture policy, a regional development policy, co-
operation in high technological industries (e.g. aerospace), and

137

ary system (1979). Moreover, a system of Euro-
operation, designed to co-ordinate foreign poli-
hed and the membership expanded from six to
accession of Britain, Denmark, and Ireland in
1981, and Portugal and Spain in 1986. This
expansion has been accompanied by a strengthening of the authority of Community institutions, notably through the rulings of
the European Court; direct elections to the European Parliament
were introduced in 1979, and a European Council of Heads of
State and government was instituted in 1974.

In 1987 there was a further deepening of European institutions
with the Single European Act, which aimed to establish by 1992
a single European market, monetary union, a social charter, and
the abolition of customs and separate immigration controls. The
EC has now assumed the character of a political system, with
(small) independent powers of taxation; common agricultural
and (limited) industrial and cultural policies; authority to negoti-
ate trade policies for the twelve member states; policies of
resource redistribution between states for Community goals; and
there are proposals to develop common internal and external
security policies. There is now an EC flag, and anthem, and a
set of cultural and educational policies, designed to promote a
European identity.

European analysts point to a marked increase in patterns of
social and economic interaction across Western European
borders (e.g. financial flows, trade, tourism, labour migration,
educational interchange) since the 1960s which indicates the EC
is undergoing a transformation from a set of national economies
to an integrated region. By the 1980s, the proportion of EC
members' trade resulting from exchange with their partners
varied from 55 per cent to 80 per cent.[7] Increasingly then, the
EC in the eyes of some of its supporters will take on 'in some
form most of the responsibilities of a nation-state with responsibilities of external security and stability being among the most
important'.[8]

Proponents acknowledge the unevenness of integration, notably in the area of defence policy, but such is the gathering

momentum of the Community that most other European countries in Central, Northern and Eastern Europe have or are in the process of negotiating for membership. Confident predictions are made that by the early twenty-first century, the European Community will provide a federal political framework for the whole of Europe and a model for the world at large.[9] Although those committed to the European project speak in more chastened tones post-Maastricht, they are confident that the difficulties of the early 1990s are but temporary interruptions to the achievement of their goal.

What then is the meaning of this impressive story of European progress? Is a new (supranational) political organization emerging that will replace the nation-state?

SPILLOVER THEORIES

The answer is yes, according to one influential set of theorists, referred to as neo-functionalists, who argue that the evolution of the European Community from economic to more enveloping political, legal and cultural forms of co-operation exemplifies the unfolding of an internal dynamic of interdependence.[10]

This arises from a recognition by Europeans that economic development in the contemporary world necessitates agreement on a common framework of rules that goes beyond what can be provided by individual states. An agreement to establish supranational authority in one sphere to resolve disagreements between different national interests 'spills over' to other sectors as protagonists encounter resistance or an absence of rules in these sectors that might negate the original decision. For example, once there was agreement to establish a single market to accelerate the economic growth of the Community, even steadfast defenders of national sovereignty such as Britain supported the principle of majority voting as opposed to unanimity with respect to the Single European Act in order to achieve agreements necessary to harmonize specific markets. These included the development of European policies on environmental standards. As increasing numbers of groups experience the benefits of such co-operation, the result is a gradual process by which the supranational institutions extend their authority to supercede the sovereignty of nation-states, and as this occurs interest groups will come to switch their loyalty to the supranational authority.

This interpretation has been extremely influential, even to the extent that in the 1950s and 1960s it became part of the official ideology of Community officials.[11] Full of historicist assumptions (in the Popperian sense) that European unity is inevitable, it presents European identity as an endogenous outgrowth of still-to-be completed processes of integration and as futuristic. These tenets are still present in Community rhetoric. Hence, the European project is a train which people must catch and the goal is presented in terms of a moving image (ever closer union) rather than of a specific station to be reached.[12]

Although the spillover hypothesis does identify mechanisms of change, its immanentist logic can and has been criticized on several grounds, including its conception of spillover as an automatic process and its assumptions that collective identities will form out of a set of stable and mutually beneficial interactions based on common interest.[13] For spillover can be blocked or even reversed, as de Gaulle demonstrated in the 1960s when he curbed the creeping supranationalist powers of the Commission by institutionalizing the capacity of states to veto its proposals where they intruded on vital national interests. Moreover, although the increasingly dense patterns of economic and social exchange within the Community has produced strong interest groups – political, business, public service, academic – networking throughout the EC which give powerful support in all member states to the cause of integration, the indifferent turn-out at elections to the European Parliament suggests a much greater identification at the popular level with national institutions.[14]

It is more plausible, others would argue, to attribute progress towards European political union to two major factors: concerted purposive action by European elites deriving from a sense of shared commitment to a common federalist goal, and visible external regional security and economic threats which has encouraged even defenders of the nation-state to seek their goals within a larger framework.[15] In this interpretation, the origins of European federalism in the early post-war years can be traced to the recognition on the part of leading French, Italian, and German statesmen and intellectuals of the need to overcome the national rivalries that had resulted in the devastation of the continent twice this century, and to co-operate in order to sustain restored democratic systems endangered by serious economic hardship. This sense of vulnerability was reinforced by the external military threat to Western democracies from the Soviet bloc. From this came the initial drive for the development of the ECSC and EC. The European identity that emerged was constructed from above and in the image of the Cold War as a community of democratic states.

Critics of spillover point out that this momentum came to a halt during the 1960s as a result of obstruction from de Gaulle in defence of national sovereignty. Although membership expanded in the 1970s, this decade is generally labelled a period of 'Euro-stagnation', and the low popular turn-out in direct elections to the European Parliament in 1979 and 1984 revealed a failure to generate a European identity despite initiatives by the Commission and the increasing role of the European Court in overriding national legislatures.

Nevertheless, there followed a renewed drive to union in the 1980s. This was exemplified by the adoption of a Community flag, anthem, emblems, stamps and common border signs, by the introduction of cultural policies in education and the media to advance a European identity, by attempts to create a common foreign policy and, above all, by the creation of a single market.[16]

This growing activism by European leaders at the symbolic level was a recognition of the necessity to create a visible Community identity to overcome the problem of legitimacy posed by popular apathy. At much the same time a growing awareness of a European geopolitical interest distinct from that of the USA and the USSR in foreign policy developed out of a realization of European (as opposed to a US) dependence on Middle East energy sources in the 1970s and the popular reaction against both the superpowers as they fought out a frightening nuclear arms race largely on European terrain in the 1980s. Finally, the impetus to the SEA came from an awareness of Europe's vulnerability to oligopolistic competition from technologically based multinational companies in the USA and the rising economies of Japan and East Asia in the 1980s.

As yet the results of these initiatives are necessarily inconclusive, and the effective collapse of the Exchange Rate Mechanism in 1993 amidst popular disillusionment with the Maastricht Treaty makes the euphoric hopes of yesteryear appear naïve. But adopting a long-term perspective, we can ask whether a combination of European initiatives from above, together with a process of differentiation against significant others in the field of foreign and trade policy, is likely to gradually create a European supranational identity capable of overriding national sovereignties.

Some have argued this is possible.[17] Admittedly, at present such a European identity is still vestigial and 'artificial' with not much of a European dimension taught in the educational curricula of the nation-states, and little cohesion is as yet seen in European foreign policy. Moreover, it is unclear where the boundaries of Europe are: do we mean the Latin (as opposed to Orthodox) civilization of the West or Christian Europe (excluding Turkey) or, again, societies shaped by Enlightenment values?

In reply, the proponents of European unity maintain that the nation-state was an artificial and novel construct with changing boundaries in the nineteenth and twentieth centuries. It was born out of a combination of formal structures created from above by state-building elites, involving linguistic standardization, conscription, discrimination against aliens, and of informal economic and social networks generated by industrialization. Today the similar formation of a European political community from a mixture of deliberate institution building and the 'spontaneous' emergence of a European regional economy cannot be ruled out, particularly in a world evolving into competing regional or continental economic blocs. The problem of boundaries may be solved in the next decade with the accession of most of the European democracies into the Community.[18]

The problem with this argument is the dubious analogy

between the formation of nation-states and that of the European Community. For, as we observed in chapter 1, what has given dynamism to the modern nation-building enterprises of European political elites has been their capacity to use historic ethnic identities based on myths and memories, possession of unique cultural attributes, and popular identification with a concrete territory that has crystallized over centuries of warfare with neighbours.

By contrast, Community leaders have tended to focus on a deliberately nebulous future, for there is little of a common past by which to unite Europeans (unless it is the history of the Crusades!). A focus on the European past is more likely to ignite memories of religious and national conflicts. It is true, of course, that on the other side of the Atlantic the formation of the USA in the nineteenth century was inspired by a future-oriented ideology of a Redeemer nation, destined to exemplify a new society transcending Old World ethnic differences through its dedication to liberty and opportunity. But this great experiment could succeed because it was a territory formed of immigrants who had in effect rejected their ethnic attachments for a new American identity, whereas the European enterprise has to co-exist with the strong national identities of peoples settled in 'historic' territories.

Cultural attempts to rechannel allegiances away from the nation have as yet had little success. In spite of formal attempts to create a European culture – through media policies, educational networks, and so forth – the informal patterns of cultural interaction extend well outside European boundaries. Britain is enmeshed in the larger English-language world culture of the USA and the Commonwealth; Spain and Portugal in the larger Hispanic cultures that include much of Latin America; France has its own extensive Francophone 'Empire'.[19] The question of which will be the normal international language of the Community is a vexed one. Nor have attempts to co-ordinate the states in a common foreign or defence policy achieved much success. Attempts to create the European Defence Community foundered in 1954 on French opposition to the renunciation of national sovereignty, a resistance that continues to this day.[20] The efforts of the EC to co-ordinate a common policy addressed to the economic problems of Eastern Europe and to the war in the former Yugoslav territories has only exposed major national differences.

This lends support to the thesis that the fundamental driving force behind the development of the EC has not been federalist idealism or external imperatives but national interest among its major parties, and that where the interests of the major states diverge, blockage occurs.[21] In other words, what the chequered story of European development exemplifies is not a subsumption of national identities into a larger European identity so much as a set of calculated and conditional decisions to pool sovereignties in order to achieve national goals of security and prosperity.

From this perspective the EC was essentially founded on the common interest of France and West Germany in co-operation as a means of avoiding a repetition of the disasters of the past. France sought a means of tethering permanently to Western Europe a German Federal Republic that was temporarily weakened through division and defeat, but which history demonstrated was potentially the dominant military and economic power in Europe. West German politicians wished for a way of permanently identifying their country with the Western democratic traditions in order to regain, after the crimes of the past, a legitimacy for their country, without which there would be little hope of national reunification.

The structure established was the EC, in which final authority rested with an intergovernmental rather than a supranational forum, or to be specific, with the Council of Ministers rather than with the European Commission or the European Parliament. The result was that, in return for its acceptance of French political leadership of Europe and a policy that protected the French agricultural sector, West Germany was able to rebuild its industries within a large European market to achieve national prestige as the world's third economic power. The French have for their part regarded the Community as a bulwark against an Anglo-Saxon world cultural hegemony.

It would be simplistic, however, to consider the EC in purely intergovernmental terms. As Keohane observes, as an organization it has evolved quite unique supranational features that do infringe on matters of national sovereignty in several respects.[22] The EC possesses a coherent executive body (the Commission) capable of initiating measures; its laws override those of the member states; it has considerable financial resources; and it negotiates common trade policies with the rest of the world which bind its members. Hence Keohane argues that the EC is something between a state and an intergovernmental organization: a network or international regime, whose supranationality rests not so much on its powers as on a style of decision-making that works for compromise between member states.

Some hope that eventually it will succeed in evolving into a federal state; others regard it as simply a new type of political organization, more appropriate in its overlapping sovereignties as a description of how power actually operates in an increasingly interdependent world than the mythical claims to sovereignty of the nation-state.

Be this as it may, it is doubtful that one can perceive a European identity emerging out of the previously discordant nation-states of the continent. True, there seems to be a commitment to Europe in smaller countries such as the Netherlands, Belgium, and Luxembourg, whose sovereignty was trampled under foot in the two world wars. But it is evident there is a widening gap between the peoples and political and economic leaders who use the EC as a means of regaining a role for their continent on the world stage that had been lost this century with the rise of the USA and the USSR and the collapse of the European overseas empires.

It is also the case that the major nation-states are still unwilling to surrender powers over what are regarded as areas central to sovereignty. The French state has insisted on retaining its independent defence policy, notably its nuclear strike force, while the German state has ignored the worries of its allies in opting for a speedy national unification.[23] Essentially, the major states have used the EC as one among other international organizations to achieve as much power as they can over areas perceived to be central to the national interest. European integration has ultimately been based on the *contingent* convergence of nation-state interests. In the 1980s, the crusade for a single market developed in an atmosphere of deregulation and privatization in the major states after the discrediting of the command economies in Eastern Europe and of state interventionist Keynesian policies in the West. A common perception of external economic threat provided a further incentive to economic integration.[24]

This emphasis on the contingency of European agreements raises doubts about how much momentum there is for political union and whether the process could unravel. For there are already several points of dispute about such issues as whether the priority should be the widening or the deepening of the Community, in other words whether the Community should become a free-trade umbrella to protect the fragile and storm-tossed emerging democracies of Eastern Europe or whether it should concentrate on becoming more of an integrated political reality based largely on its present West European membership. Whereas the British, suspicious of European federalism, would prefer the former option, the French, fearful that a looser framework would release Germany from its Western moorings to further its traditional geopolitical stance of dominating *Mitteleuropa*, have argued for the latter.[25]

The most pressing issue, however, is how German unification in the context of a power vacuum in Eastern Europe will affect the balance of power in the Community. Unification and the new uncertainties resulting from the disintegration of the communist bloc threaten to undermine the calculations on which the Community was built. These events appear set to make Germany the economic hegemon of Europe, to release it from its dependence on Western allies to secure cherished national goals and to open up opportunities for it to resume its dominance over a dependent Eastern Europe. France, previously leader of the Community, can no longer assume deference from an increasingly assertive Germany whose economic power means its decisions effectively shape the policy parameters for its partners, thereby arousing old fears and resentments of dominance.

At the same time the (perhaps temporary) disappearance of a frightening enemy removes one of the bonds of cohesion between the Western democracies which, in finding it difficult to agree on a common policy to deal with complex issues such as aid to Eastern Europe and the war in the Balkans, tend to make decisions which follow their own geopolitical interests.

These considerations suggest that there is no necessary or indeed strongly visible trend towards the formation of a supra-national European identity or polity focused on the European Community, and that national identity is still the potent driving force behind major decisions. At the same time, they do not suggest the disintegration of the EC, whose survival and, indeed, development over the past forty years indicate that its members have found that it has provided and will probably continue to provide in a world organizing into regional blocs a useful frame-work for decision-making on a variety of issues, economic, environmental, and humanitarian. But this raises another possi-bility: could it be that the EC, by showing its capacity to offer many of the facilities of the nation-state to the population of Europe, will undermine the existing nation-states to create eventually a Community of nations?

A Europe of Nations?

National loyalties have proved to be an awkward opponent not just to supranationalist projects but also to the European nation-states themselves. Most of these polities until recently have pre-tended in their policies to be undivided nation-states whose members are integrated through equal citizenship rights. But as Krejci and Velimsky found, sixteen out of the twenty-nine Euro-pean states in existence in 1980 contained significant ethnic minorities settled on compact territories who might aspire to independence.[26] Most European states are, in reality, multi-national in composition, generally the product of conquest, and still dominated by a single nationality whose history, language, religion, sports, customs and leadership determines – often in a coercive fashion – the character of the institutions of state.

Since the 1960s we have seen within most of the major nation-states the rise among these minorities of nationalist movements, some constitutional, others insurrectionary, seeking political autonomy. Britain has seen the revival of a largely constitutional nationalism among the Scots and Welsh, and of a constitutional and physical force nationalism among the Catholic Irish of Northern Ireland; in Spain there have been constitutional and revolutionary movements among the Basques and Catalans; in France rumblings from the Bretons and the 'Occitanians' as well as the Corsicans; in Belgium violent agitations between Walloons and Flemish; in Italy, there have been autonomist movements in the South Tyrol and Sicily. Although such movements went into electoral decline in the 1980s, in the 1990s there has been another upsurge, in part inspired by growing EC integration, which in the eyes of many activists offers the prospect of dismantling existing nation-states in favour of a Europe of nations and regions.[27]

What then is the basis of this nationalist resurgence against the nation-state? To what extent is the EC likely to encourage a dissolution of the existing state structures? I shall explore these interrelated questions in turn.

NATIONALISM AGAINST THE NATION-STATE

The eruption of nationalism against the nation-state in the postwar period is only the most recent of a series of recurring reactions over the past two centuries on the part of European minorities against the integrationist policies of the major nation-states. In the early twentieth century, *fin-de-siècle* romantic nationalists such as W. B. Yeats, in rejecting the imperialist character of the great European states, prophesied in apocalyptic terms that their power drive would lead to a catastrophic war out of which would emerge a new small-scale Europe of the national peoples. During the two world wars many minority nationalists exploited the collapse of established states to achieve with varying success national autonomy. The First World War resulted in the formation of many new 'nation-states' out of the former Habsburg, Ottoman and Tsarist Empires, and even in the West the secession of much of Ireland from Britain. In the Second World War many nationalists in Western and Eastern Europe (Bretons, Croatians, Slovaks,

Ukrainians) sought freedom from their existing states by an ill-fated collaboration with Nazi invaders.

None the less, the reappearance in the 1960s of ethnicity as a matrix of political mobilization within and against the nation-states took most observers by surprise. Many of the minority nationalist movements, although expressing romantic themes of authenticity, were modernist in outlook, attracting – in addition to the standard constituency of lawyers, teachers and journalists – support from a new technical intelligentsia of economists, administrators and social specialists.[28] Their left-wing communitarian ideology evoked links with contemporary Third World national liberationist movements against the imperialist capitalist states and in some cases inspired campaigns of revolutionary violence. Such rhetoric has faded in the 1980s and 1990s, but rejections of the overcentralized bureaucratic state, support for local economies and cultures, ecological issues, access of minorities to media and communications have been some of the continuing themes, and the movements have become institutionalized in modern European politics.

The recognition of ethnicity as a deep-seated problem has encouraged some analysts to explain the contemporary nationalist resurgence in terms of a longer range pattern. One of the most influential has been the 'internal colonialist' approach of Hechter, who claimed that the persistence of ethnic cleavages within the modern state was explained by the fact that the Western states were essentially formed through the imperial conquest by one ethnic group of others.[29] A hierarchical cultural division of labour was established which shaped the subsequent processes of industrialization in so far as elite positions were reserved for adherents of the dominant culture, and the economy of the peripheral groups was subordinated to the interests of the centre. The emergence of minority nationalisms citing economic and cultural grievances against the European states is thus explained by reference to institutionalized patterns of discrimination in resource allocation.

This long-range perspective is a valuable one, for the nation-state has systematically discriminated against minority nationalities, a legacy that has continued into modern times. In passing the Education Act of 1870, the British government outlawed the Welsh language until 1889, and as recently as 1925 the French government banned the teaching of the Breton language.[30] But any theory of ethnic revolt based on explanations of the economic exploitation of peripheries or of relative deprivation will not hold, because movements for autonomy in Western (just as in Eastern) Europe can begin amongst relatively wealthy populations such as the Basques and Catalans.[31] In contemporary Italy, the greatest threat to the integrity of the state comes from the Leagues of the prosperous North (notably the Lombardy League), who complain bitterly at their domination by a corrupt and economically decaying South.[32]

Others have identified the major factor as a crisis of the European states in the 1960s which had both external and internal dimensions that loosened the allegiance of minority nationalities.[33] The external aspect was the loss of world power and status by the European polities as a result of the loss of their empires, and this has to be set in the general context of a general decline of Europe since 1945 *vis-à-vis* the superpowers, the USA and the USSR.

With the loss of military-imperial power, competition for status between the European states was increasingly displaced to the field of economic growth, and with governments newly confident as a result of Keynesian theories of their ability to manage the economy, governments all over Europe engaged increasingly in technocratic dirigiste policies in the fields of education, industry and social welfare to boost their position in economic growth leagues. As a new pragmatic welfare capitalism emerged, so class lost its centrality as a mode of identity and organization.

In tending, however, to focus responsibility for the economy on governments, the Keynesian consensus politicized disparities between regions and led further to regional development policies from the centre which would utilize underdeployed labour and iron out embarrassing inequalities. The results were on the whole unimpressive, and one effect was the rise of ethno-nationalist movements articulated by a new aspiring professional, technical and administrative middle class which had formed from the expanded educational and public sectors but many of whom felt underemployed.

Two major themes which varied according to region were prominent. The first was cultural: the need to defend a way of life – focused on such things as language in the case of the Welsh and Basques – that was threatened by the social 'distortions' of an ineffectual interventionist technocratic state imposing 'alien' norms and values on the regions. The second was more political: the demand for a real decentralization of decision-making powers to the communities in the regions.

These movements have differed greatly in their measure of support, the degree of autonomy sought, and in the methods employed. Most movements have pursued goals of limited auton-omy through constitutional means (e.g. those in Scotland, Wales and Brittany). But although attracting only minority support, revolutionary organizations (e.g. Northern Irish Catholic, Basque and Corsican) have sustained violent campaigns for over twenty years.

So far the nation-states have responded to such movements by various devices. Military measures have been applied against revolutionary groups such as the IRA and ETA, but, in addition, limited measures of autonomy to the regions have been offered in many contexts which have reduced support for the more militant demands. In Spain in 1977 the post-Franco democratic govern-ment granted regional governments to the Basques and Catalans with powers over finance, economic planning, energy resources and justice; in 1981 the French Socialist government, as part of a general scheme of regional devolution, set up elected assemblies for the Bretons and Corsicans and permitted the teaching of Corsican in schools; in 1975 the British Labour government arranged referenda on proposals to establish elected assemblies for Scotland and Wales which failed to achieve sufficient support.[34]

The result of these concessions was the opening up of divisions within nationalist ranks over how much further to go. Govern-ments were able to exploit the problems of nationalists in periphcral regions whose grievances about the inadequacy of resource transfers by the centre to their populations would be worsened by more autonomy.[35] Since the 1970s autonomist campaigns have slackened, but they have not been eliminated. Indeed, in recent years there has been something of a revival throughout most of Europe (with Italian regional demands achieving a new prominence and taking on something of an ethnic colouration), and some have linked this to prospects of closer European union as undermining the necessity of the nation-state.[36]

It is indeed, relevant to ask how far the potential development of the EC as a Pan-European unit with budgetary powers and increasing redistributive abilities could undermine the existing nation-states and enhance autonomistic trends by reducing the costs of secession. But to pose the question in this way is to assume that the cohesion of the European nation-states is based merely on coercion or the fear of going it alone in a world dominated by large-scale economic and military units, and that there is little sense on the part of minority nationalities of identification with their states. It is also to assume that individuals and groups do not maintain a system of dual loyalty. This may be the case for some, but there are considerable variations in attitude to the nation-states on the part of minorities, depending on the extent to which leaders of given groups have been readily included on favourable or equal terms into the dominant culture and institutions at the time of the political incorporation of the group or whether they have been excluded altogether. Whereas substantial sections of Northern Irish Catholics, excluded early on as Catholics, certainly feel estranged from the British state, a large proportion of Scots and Welsh find no incongruity in participating vigorously in British public life and institutions while remaining self-consciously national. In Spain, whereas in the 1980s some 40 per cent of Basques claimed to be just Basques, only 15 per cent of the population of Catalonia described themselves as solely Catalan.[37]

None the less, if one assumes there is always a potentiality for minority nationalities to estrange themselves, the question remains, to what extent is an EC committed to a Pan-European political system of some kind likely to engender centrifugal pressures on the nation-states?

Obviously, the answer to this is dependent on whether and how successfully the EC develops in its budgetary competence, security reach, powers over immigration and so forth. But it should be pointed out that Pan-continental identities and structures are not necessarily inimical to the nation-state, but have been used by state elites to argue against fragmenting existing political structures on ethnic lines which it is claimed would make the continent vulnerable to powerful external foes.

In Africa, Pan-Africanism was envisaged in the early twentieth century as a means of creating a strong independent United States of Africa out of peoples arbitrarily divided by European powers without respect to ethnic affiliations into separate jurisdictions. But once the African nationalists obtained independence for their individual territories, Pan-Africanism was used by the new state elites to justify co-operation in preserving the existing political structures against common dangers of ethnic secessionism and irredentism which they claimed would lead to the Balkanization of Africa.[38]

Although there is not such a radical disjunction between ethnic and political maps in Europe as in Africa, there is a common interest of several members in checking any EC attempts to deal with national groupings over the heads of nation-states. It is said that Spain has expressed a reluctance to accept any future Scottish application for independent membership of the EC for fear of its effects on the Basques or Catalans.

From the point of view of the EC, it is unclear that a dismantling of the nation-states would enhance its operations, for it would mean a multiplication of actors which would complicate and slow down the decision-making process to such an extent that there would have to be a move to majority voting and a relinquishing of the veto wielded by nation-states on questions of vital national interest. Even were the nation-states likely to surrender this power (which is doubtful), the expansion of Community authority would probably exacerbate national conflict, for the interventions of the EC have generated opposition from the regions of Europe as much as from the metropolitan states. The *länder* of Germany have regarded the assumptions of powers by the EC in the areas of education and the environment as a direct challenge to their jurisdictions, granted under the federal constitution of Germany. Indeed, the upper house of the German parliament (representing the *länder*) delayed approval of the Maastricht Treaty until the concerns of the German regions were met.[39]

Although, at present, some minority nationalities might consider the EC as a lever by which to free themselves from the domination of their nation-state, there is no guarantee that the growth of a powerful EC redistributing resources from richer to poorer regions of the Europe and making controversial decisions (for example, on immigration) would be acceptable to the losers. Were the EC to be seen as making itself available as a lever, it would be likely to excite the same centrifugal forces on the continent that helped tear apart the Soviet Union.

Polyethnicity and the Nation-state

If the analysis so far suggests that it would be premature to write the obituary of the nation-state, it does indicate that the multi-ethnic character of such states is becoming increasingly institutionalized through the public recognition in schools of minority languages, provision of special television and media services, and grants of regional autonomy. When one adds to the recognition of minority nationalities within the European states the economic dependence of these states since the Second World War on large-scale international migration from the European peripheries (Southern Italy, Greece, and Turkey), from North Africa and other parts of the Third World, it becomes possible to ask whether the myth of the ethnic nation-state has had its day, and whether Europeans should look to civic and polyethnic conceptions as the basis of a cohesive collective identity.

One of the most wide-ranging and long-term perspectives on this question is provided by W. H. McNeill, who argues that the nation-state is an aberration in world history whose brief hour has passed. According to McNeill, until recently ethnic politics have usually been associated with peripheral and backward regions; the major centres of civilization from the Roman Empire in the West to the Chinese Empire in the East have been polyethnic. He gives many reasons for this, including the practices of war and long distance trade, but he highlights demographic factors. Until the nineteenth century the cities – which were the centres of civilization – were never self-sufficient demographically because of the high mortality from diseases which forced them to import labour. When, as was frequently the case, spontaneous immigration from the surrounding countryside was lacking, populations further afield were enslaved to meet economic and military needs. The result was large-scale ethnic mixing in the major centres of government.[40]

In accounting for the rise of the nation-state as the dominant political model between 1750 and 1920, McNeill identifies several long-term factors. These include, from the late medieval period, the growing influence of ideas of civic humanism in the expanding Western European cities, and the centralization of political and administrative authority; and from the seventeenth century, the development of standard vernacular languages, and the military revolution which, in requiring a loyal and highly drilled infantry, encouraged reflection on models of classical antiquity which linked military training with the duties of citizenship.

However, he argues that what made possible the rise of political systems based on a concept of ethnic homogeneity in Western Europe was an extraordinary and unexplained rise in population in the eighteenth century. The cities still needed to replenish their population from the countryside but they could now draw on the surrounding areas and this resulted in a more homogeneous population. In the Western European states the subsequent definition of citizenship rights and of democracy itself took place within a national context.[41]

McNeill notes that, of course, even in Western Europe the idea of the ethnically homogeneous nation-state was a myth in the nineteenth century. But although it proved then to be sufficiently plausible to act as a powerful mobilizing device, he argues that in the twentieth century it has become untenable as a model of political community. He gives a number of reasons for this, including the increasing military and economic interdependence of countries. He also observes the difficulties the model has imposed on the ethnically mixed populations of Africa and Asia, who adopted it as a result of European conquest or out of a desire by native rulers to emulate the West.

The major factor he cites, however, is demographic: since 1945 there has been a dramatic slump in birth rates in all Western industrial societies which to sustain their growth have had to recruit substantial numbers of foreign workers. This fact will compel a reacceptance of polyethnicity on the part of Europeans and others as the price to be paid for continued social and economic progress and political harmony. A commitment to the nation-state idea, he implies, will once again relegate societies to the backward peripheries of world civilization.[42]

Some of these issues have been addressed in a recent important study by the Swedish social scientist, Tomas Hammar, who observes that in several states foreign residents (workers and their families) whom he calls denizens compose between 10 per cent to 25 per cent of the labour force.[43] The presence of such a high 'foreign' population compels a fundamental rethink of the dual commitment of modern European states to both nationality and democracy. Hammar argues that it will be impossible in the long term for states committed officially to democratic values and ideals of equality of opportunity to exclude this 'foreign' presence from citizenship, and the exclusion itself poses dangers to social stability.

How have the European states responded to this problem? In general, they have tended until recently to shut their eyes to what they considered a temporary issue, although it is interesting that states vary considerably in their policies regarding the acquisition of citizenship, and an important determinant is the extent to which they adhere to an ethnic rather than a civic-territorial definition of national identity.

Germany, committed to an ethnic conception of membership of the nation-state, has discouraged naturalization by demanding ten years residence together with a knowledge of the German language and culture, and high naturalization fees. In the wishful hope that the economic necessity was short-term and that the 'guest' workers would return to their homelands, Germany, like many other states, refused to grant easy access to citizenship, allowing them the protection of the law and some rights to welfare. France, holding to a more civic and territorial conception of national membership that goes back to the Revolution, has been relatively liberal, granting citizenship automatically to second generation migrants at their majority.[44] Nevertheless, even in countries with a civic conception, the post-war period has seen the growth of substantial communities (many now third generation) largely excluded from the political process but who pay taxes and participate in labour markets.

The difficulty for the European states is more deep-seated than it appears and cannot be resolved simply by liberalizing their naturalization procedures for two reasons. The first is that foreign residents are now more likely to retain their identities as a result of labour market discrimination, easier and cheaper travel, and new technologies of the telephone and the mass media through which such groups can keep in touch with their homelands.[45] Many would be unwilling to acquire the citizenship of their host country at the expense of citizenship in their country of origin, because of feelings of loyalty or of the difficulties that would be imposed by their homeland, which could entail the loss of property or restrictions on their re-entry to visit relatives.[46] The consequence is the formation of extensive ethnic diaspora communities who are having a growing impact in international as well as national politics.[47]

Some, focusing on the political dimension of this problem, have argued for the introduction by states of dual-citizenship arrangements whereby denizens could participate in most of the rights of the native citizenry, in particular in local elections.[48] This has traditionally been anathema to the nationalist idea of the nation as unitary by indicating a dilution of allegiance at best and conflicts of loyalty at the worst. Hammar has acknowledged the difficulties with dual citizenship, notably where there are obligations to perform compulsory military service, but he finds that they are not insuperable.

Indeed, against such 'nationalist' critics, Hammar has argued that it is anachronistic to expect identities to be singular in a world marked by a steady internationalization in the fields of trade, migration and communications. Multiple loyalties are becoming the norm. Such proponents of change draw comfort from the impetus given by another instance of the increasing internationalization of society, namely the expanding field of international law which since 1945 has resulted in a series of declarations at the level of the United Nations and the Council of Europe, protecting such human rights as the right of the citizen to participate in the public affairs of his or her country.[49]

None the less, Hammar acknowledges that such trends to liberalize voting rights have been checked since the late 1970s by growing popular anti-immigrant sentiment fuelled by outbreaks of international terrorism and recurring economic recessions. Even in France, home of the Revolution, according to an opinion poll on the eve of the national vote on the Maastricht Treaty, 51 per cent were opposed to those Treaty provisions that entitled EC nationals to vote and stand for municipal election in countries other than their own.[50] Were such formal rights granted, it is doubtful that this would change underlying assumptions, for in countries such as Britain the automatic grant of full political rights to Black immigrants from the British Commonwealth has not saved them from economic and social discrimination by virtue of their race and culture.

This highlights the second and more fundamental obstacle to resolving the problem of ethnic pluralism, namely the deep ethnocentric attitudes pervading even civic nations such as France: although equality is offered, the tacit assumption is that the minority will assimilate as individuals into the French culture. For this reason others have urged the necessity of a shift at the cultural level to promote, through multicultural policies in key institutions such as schools, a recognition of the value of other cultures and of the human enrichment that comes from membership of an ethnically plural society.[51]

However, such demands in Europe for a broader multicultural conception of the state have been engulfed in the 1980s by the

Salman Rushdie affair and fears about the threat posed to a national way of life by an influx of impoverished Muslim peoples from North Africa and also from potential mass migrations from Eastern Europe.[52] Governments in Britain have responded to such multicultural challenges by attempting to define a core educational curriculum in which British history would be integral. In Germany the revocation of liberal asylum laws has been accompanied by the disturbing resurgence of neo-Nazi violence against foreigners. Even in 'civic' France the persistently strong showing of Le Pen's National Front in elections and proposals to make citizenship less automatic to denizens indicate the increasing trend to exclusive ethnic values across the political spectrum. A few years ago the French left was outraged by a Muslim girl's breaching the secular republican traditions of the nation by wearing religious dress in school, which has been regarded as one of the principle agents of assimilation. In all the EC countries there is strong public support for tight restrictions on further immigration.

All this suggests that the growing presence and visibility of ethnic minorities in contemporary Europe is no guarantee of an 'advance' to a multicultural conception of community. It is clear that there is often a tension between the economic policies of nation-states and their cultural concerns. Yet nationalists are quite capable of wanting to have their cake and eat it, in the sense that they may continue to refuse to extend civic rights to ethnic minorities even though they benefit from their services. Moreover, as the internecine violence in the former Yugoslavia demonstrates, populations once inflamed by ethnic hatreds will ignore rational economic and social calculations. Although one might reasonably hope that the commitment of increasing numbers of European states to liberal democratic values since 1945 will moderate the excesses of a xenophobic nationalism, the atrocious treatment of minorities on the European continent this century should make the proponents of the inevitability of poly-ethnicity pause for reflection. The existence of such 'alien' communities may indeed heighten nationalist sentiments.

...... are the lessons we can draw from the preceding analysis? We should begin by recognizing that trends towards internationalization in the late twentieth century are more than just rhetoric. The dangers of nuclear armaments and their proliferation; the greenhouse effect and the world-wide destruction of our planet's ecology; the spread of global technologies; mass international labour migrations and the need to protect the human rights of these peoples have all spurred the development of international organizations and fora, and require that limitations be placed on the sovereignties of the nation-states.

None the less, there is no evidence that the European model of the nation-state is obsolescent. As we noted, the states within the EC have agreed to enhance their power by pooling their sovereignties in selected fields rather than subsume their identities within an all-embracing supranationalist organization. It is also unlikely that the dream of some European federalists for a trans-ethnic United States of Europe will ever be achieved, for it is unclear where the sense of identity necessary for the cohesion of such a polity could be formed.

Different approaches have been mooted or attempted to strengthen the EC, but they have had only limited success and serve rather to highlight the strength of the national model and the importance of founding it on ethnic sentiments. We have noted the failure of functionalist spillover strategies to generate a sense of emotional loyalty alongside a recognition of an interdependence of material interests. In recognition of this, the EC during the 1970s and 1980s tried a more activist identity-building model, but this – with its introduction of an EC flag, anthems, and advocacy of common foreign and defence policies that would unite Europeans against significant 'others' – was 'borrowed' from the nation-states. Nationalism was to be transcended by creating a European nation-state!

The lack of progress achieved also makes clear how many of the vital ingredients are missing to make the recipe work. States such as Britain and Switzerland have succeeded in forging both a sense of territorial and ethnic loyalty in their multinational/ethnic populations because of their shared experience in war and in building distinctive institutions, and their clear sense of territory by virtue of Britain's island status and Switzerland geostrategic position between the great powers. But there is insufficient sense of a common European past or even of what Europe means in a territorial sense for the EC to build on. The European Community is most likely to be successful if, held together by Pan-European sentiments, it settles on a framework that decentralizes power to the nation-states.

Indeed, theorists such as John Hall have argued that the emergence of an interstate system which permitted diverse and competing national states was one of the conditions of the dynamism of Europe in world history.[53] This historical point should in turn remind us of two things: firstly, that the European nation-states are much more various in their forms than the ideal type presumes; and secondly, that we should not regard the relationship between nation-states and internationalization, as is implied by some scholars, in zero sum terms but should rather view it, as I argued in chapter 2, as a creative interaction.

After all, the European nation-state was established as the hegemonic norm in the nineteenth century, during the greatest period of international trade in human history, and the example of Japan attests that it continues as a viable model of political economy in the contemporary world.[54] It is the unpredictable impact of (internationalist) modernization on traditional status orders that inspires a return to national pasts to discover alternative social models, and the construction of diverse and competing *national* modernities is one factor in generating further innovation. Indeed, one could go further to state (as I argued in chapter 1) that there is no modernity, only national modernities.

But this is not to say that the classic conceptions of the European nation-states as ethnically homogeneous and unitary political structures remain unchallenged. The experience of the past twenty years has highlighted the fact that these states are much less integrated than has seemed to be the case, and now have to accommodate the nationalism of minority groups which reject them as ossified and oppressive. Drawing a contrast between the states' public commitment to a liberal and 'democratic' ideology and alleged historically based patterns of discrimination practised by ethnic core populations on minorities, these groups have in many cases compelled states to restructure their institutions to reflect their cultural and linguistic diversities and to weaken their unitary basis in favour of regionalist devolution.

In some cases, however, notably former Yugoslavia, this clash between statist and ethnic principles has had tragic consequences. Rather than perform a postmodernist celebration of the multiplicity of identity, populations have opted for an absolutism to be achieved by 'ethnic cleansing' – a euphemism for murder and terror.

It is implausible that we will see a repetition of this disaster in Western Europe where liberal democratic institutions tend to moderate conflicts, and even where there are irreconcilable enmities between dominant and minority groups in Europe, a collapse of or secession from the nation-state is unlikely. For, unlike the cases of the Russians in the Soviet Union or the Serbs of Yugoslavia, the core nationalities of the Western polities strongly identify with the integrity of the state which is suffused with their ethnic name, symbols, history and culture, and are in demographic terms more dominant.

In contemporary Europe there now seems to be an in-built interplay between supranationalist or Pan-European pressures, nation-statism and minority nationalism. Managing these pressures so as to achieve a secure existence for the peoples of the continent will not be easy. Under these circumstances, an optimistic prognosis is for the continued co-operation under different international umbrellas of the European nation-states, whose liberal democratic principles will lead to an emphasis on territorial and civic rather than ethnic forms of identity and thus ensure a respect for the rights of minorities through policies of multiculturalism. But a more exclusive ethnic nationalism could ensue if Western Europe continues to face pressures of potential mass migrations from Eastern Europe and North Africa.

What then are the implications of this discussion for the rest of the world, to whom the European nation-state was once held up as a model? As we noted, the arbitrary imposition on multi-ethnic populations in Africa and Asia of European ideal types has been disruptive, creating endemic problems for many post-colonial states. But we might conclude that an analysis of the contemporary experience of actual European nation-states does have lessons for other countries. One lesson is that the nation-state is not dead: a strong ethnic core seems to allow for political stability, but at the same time in a world committed to human rights and democratic values we must also allow for the expression of minority groups. To the problem of reconciling ethnic loyalties with civic and territorial principles in multi-ethnic populations, there appears to be no easy answer.

Pioneers of Post-nationalism or Insecure Parvenus?

The Cultural Politics of New World Societies

I have argued that, for the foreseeable future, Europe, both Western and Eastern, is a lost cause for those who wish to see the 'backward-looking' nation-state, as traditionally conceived, replaced by future-oriented societies dedicated to tolerant poly-ethnic principles. But a case can and has been made that these ideals flourish in the New World societies of Australia, Canada and the United States. These are countries, designated by Anthony Smith as 'immigrant nations', which were originally founded by colonists from a predominantly English (and, in the case of Canada, also French) ethnic core who, dispossessing the indigenous inhabitants, established an independent state and later admitted waves of migrants from many ethnic backgrounds, seeking to absorb them through equal citizenship rights. In the course of this an ethnic community was transformed into a multi-cultural territorial political community.[1] There are important differences between these societies, in their size, political power, cultural status and economic might, but they have shared a self-image of themselves as distinct from and superior to the 'Old World' from which they came, as pioneers of multicultural policies and practices which have resolved the problems of ethnic hatreds that still bedevil their 'parental' societies. Indeed, many of their intellectuals have proclaimed these countries to be post-national models for an increasingly internationalized humanity.[2]

In this chapter I propose to test such claims by examining the commemorative festivals of their origins staged by these countries in the contemporary period for what they tell us about the society's self-image and cultural politics. Each focused on a different kind of moment: in 1967 Canada celebrated the centenary of its establishment as a federal state uniting French and English settlers; in 1976 the USA had its Bicentenary of the Declaration of Independence; and 1988 was for Australia the Bicentenary of its settlement by Europeans.

None the less, they shared important features that make a comparative analysis feasible. Although there had been earlier commemorations of the national founding in both Australia and the USA, they were the first officially organized territory-wide commemorations to be staged by these countries. As we shall see, they represented ambitious and self-conscious experiments in nation-building, extending over a year and involving a considerable public investment, both in terms of planning time over several years and money.[3] In each case the festival planners constructed roughly similar formats and themes which generated similar sets of controversies extending over several years from their initial planning stage to the commemorative year itself.

A second reason for studying these events is that such festivals have been employed since the French Revolution to construct at times of contestation a hegemonic identity of the political community that will mobilize support for a ruling regime. Hobsbawm amongst others has discussed how national identities were constructed from 'above' during the late nineteenth century in the second French republic and Wilhelmine Germany.[4] In this case, however, we will be investigating the origins, characteristics and effects of official festivals in liberal democratic federal societies in which governments, although concerned to use the occasion to give a directive stamp to their societies, were explicitly committed to a communitarian format of celebration.

In this chapter, after examining their common features, origins, controversies and effects, I shall argue that the study of such festivals reveals three things. First, governments in such societies possess only limited capacities to engage in explicit programmes of nation-building. Second, even in 'immigrant nations', supposedly more tolerant of multicultural diversity, ethnicity underpins foundation myths and the distribution of power, and can pose major problems for social cohesion. Third, such nations, as New

World societies, are marked by distinctive 'status anxieties', formulated in a language of maturation, that require them to assess periodically their progress through time and to construct landmarks as galvanizers of future action.

Common Aspects of the Three Festivals

COMMUNITARIAN STRUCTURE

Despite their status as state events, the festivals had a similar communitarian ethos and structure that derived from the liberal-democratic and federal characteristics of their societies. This was exemplified in several ways.

First, the drive to have celebrations came from outside the federal government. In Canada, businessmen influenced the decision of the government in 1959 to stage official celebrations. In 1956 (long before the US government's 1966 commitment), Philadelphian municipal representatives developed plans for an International Exposition, and President Kennedy was lobbied as early as 1963; Bicentenary commissions were established in Massachusetts (1964) and Virginia (1966) – two of the original thirteen colonies. In Australia, the government's announcement in 1978 was preceded by the agenda of social visionaries such as Donald Horne.[5]

Second, the planning agencies themselves – the Canadian Centenary Commission, the American Revolution Bicentennial Commission, and the Australian Bicentennial Authority (to be referred to henceforth as the CCC, ARBC and ABA, respectively) – were established by the governments in a bi-partisan spirit, given quasi-autonomous status (although appointments were made by the President or Prime Minister), and organized on a federal basis. These agencies each emphasized that the occasion was not 'a party put on by the government' but a celebration of the people, and they articulated their role as catalysts rather than definers of the event. In order to achieve maximum participation at the community level, they presented a 'horizontal' view of group status: all had equal rights in the celebrations.

Third, in keeping with this communitarian ethos, the agencies confined their role as project initiators to a few central events, especially those based on the nation's 'birthday'. They relied heavily on state or provincial and municipal energies and also on private initiatives; for example, co-ordination with voluntary organizations, notably in Canada with the Canadian Centenary Council, a body of business and professional people. Similarly, there was an emphasis on obtaining sponsorship from the business community, as is evident from the key appointments to the agencies and their funding. John Fisher, Chief Commissioner of the CCC, had been Executive-Director of the Canadian Tourist Association; Daniel J. Mahoney, Chairman of the ARBC (1970–74), had been Chief Executive Officer of Norton Simon Inc.; John Reid, Chair of the ABA (1979–85), had been Chairman of James Hardie industries.

Fourth, although the agencies sponsored 'high culture' initiatives of a permanent and temporary character including national archives, cultural centres, historical and science museums, there was a special effort to ensure popular interest in the commemorative year by the inclusion of mass sporting events (e.g. in Canada, the Winter Olympics and the first Pan-American games), the provision of leisure and sporting facilities, popular concerts and spectacles.

COMMON THEMES: NEW WORLD EXPERIMENT, ETHNIC DIVERSITY, CONQUEST OF DISTANCE

Although the content of founding myths of the countries varied, each festival celebrated three major themes: the nation as a unique New World experiment as yet unfinished and oriented to the future; as exemplary multi-ethnic collaboration; as representing the triumph of human will (through politics and technology) over continental nature.

Political symbols and ceremonies celebrating the 'success' of the liberal-democratic federation were central. In the USA, the Declaration of Independence, the Constitution, and the Liberty Bell were highlighted; in Canada, the historic voyage of the Fathers of Confederation from Quebec to Charlottetown of 1864 was re-enacted; and in Australia a new Parliament House was opened by the Queen.

But perhaps the major theme of the commemorative year was that of the nation as a heroic journey undertaken by different waves of pioneers. In particular, the role of technology and communications in creating a nation, uniting territories and peoples was central: the tall-ship parades in both the USA and Australian Bicentenaries, celebrating multi-ethnic origins; the Canadian Confederation Train Exhibition, travelling on the Canadian Pacific Railway, whose completion in 1871, linking western and eastern provinces, helped make federation practical; the Conestoga wagons and prairie schooners re-enacting in reverse the conquest of the western frontier in a two-year journey across all forty-eight states of continental USA; the Australian Travelling Exhibition, which portrayed the theme of Australia as the product of three migrations.

These exhibitions by their mobility embodied the theme of the nation as a continuing voyage of discovery and triumph over distance. President Ford's address on 4 July 1976, to the Conestoga wagons at Valley Forge linked futurist and trans-ethnic themes to those of the frontier when he referred to his country as:

> . . . at the beginning of a continuing adventure . . . [the] US remains today the most successful realization of humanity's universal hope. The world may or may not follow, but we lead because our whole history says we must.[6]

CONTROVERSIES AND RECEPTIONS

A third distinctive feature is that from their early planning stage, in spite of their communitarian-participatory format, the celebrations generated a series of prolonged controversies over several years that went far beyond a discussion of the commemorative moment to engage in prolonged critical reflections on the entire past, present, and future of the national community. These debates were at first intermittent, confined to the elite (opinion-forming) level, and usually obscured by the 'foreground' of 'normal' politics; but they grew in resonance as public interest rose with the approaching anniversary and largely shaped the final definition of the occasion and its reception.

Although different views of the occasion were canvassed even before the official launch, controversy began only after the planning agencies began to formulate themes. This provoked four sets of overlapping controversies about: the financial and technical competences of the agencies; the respective weight given the states or provinces; the ideological agenda promoted; and the national vision presented, including the place given within it to non-dominant ethnic and indigenous peoples.

In all three countries there were recurring anxieties expressed by governments and the public about the pace of planning and its financial management. This led in the USA to the replacement in 1974 of the ARBC and its members by a streamlined American Revolution Bicentennial Authority (ARBA), and in Australia to the resignations of its two chief officers in 1985.

A second issue was the degree to which the festival should have a central focus and the weight given to particular regions in it. In Canada there were resentments expressed at the dominance of the 'central' provinces of Ontario and Quebec (notably the large sums given to the latter for the Montreal International Expo). In the USA controversies erupted first about the choice in 1970 of Philadelphia as the site of an International Exposition against the claims of other cities and states, and then because of its abandonment in 1972, which elicited claims that the Bicentennial had lost a unifying focus. In Australia several states protested that the national festival was, in terms of attention and prestigious events, a New South Wales affair.

A third argument centred round perceived political biases of the agencies. In the USA there were protests at President Nixon's rejection of the original liberal objectives to extending the democratic vision of the revolution by a federally funded renovation of the urban environment in favour of a celebratory populist ethos, dubbed the 'Buycentennial' by the left because of its emphasis on business sponsorship and consumerism. In Australia the ABA was criticized by conservative British monarchists for undermining core Australian values in promoting alien Labour republican (and multicultural) ideals pandering to anti-capitalist minorities.

Finally, the agencies provoked a storm of ethnic grievances. In Canada these were largely fought out within the CCC by Anglophone and Francophone factions or at inter-provincial level where the latter, resentful of English hegemony, insisted on the commemoration being renamed as one of confederation rather than of Canadian nationality (whose existence they denied).[7] In the USA, the ARBC was rocked by attacks on its alleged WASP character as reflected in a lack of attention to ethnic minorities, including Blacks and indigenous peoples. In Australia, 'British' Australian critics denounced the ABA's multiculturalist biases in favour of the 'new European' post-war migrants, whereas many Aborigines rejected the idea of commemorating the European invasion of their country.

The year (and a half in the USA) itself was marked by mass attendance (in the millions) at the central events (Op Sail in New York harbour on 4 July 1976; the arrival of the tall ships and the First Fleet Re-enactment in Sydney Harbour on Australia Day; the Canadian Centennial Train and Caravan exhibitions) as well as by vigorous participation at grass-roots level.[8] Nevertheless, participation was patchy: some groups and states showed little enthusiasm, and in some cases hostility to the whole occasion. In Canada, the absence of an official celebration on 1 January in Quebec province 'sounded a chilling note', and demonstrations in support of Quebec separatism dogged the year, climaxing with the visit of President de Gaulle.[9] In the USA, Blacks and many Indians were apathetic, and New Left groups and Puerto Rican and other activists staged noisy demonstrations. In Australia, the Aboriginal Northern Land Council declared 'a national year of mourning' and Aborigines organized vigorous protest meetings and marches on Australia Day and thereafter.

This brief overview of the festivals raises four questions to be explored in the rest of this chapter. First, why did societies imbued with an anti-centralist ethos decide to institute such elaborate official festivals for the first time? Second, why should festivals organized according to a 'horizontal' and communitarian format stir intense controversies? Third, what, if any, were the effects of such festivals? Fourth, what can they tell us about the problems of building cohesion in immigrant nations?

Why were the Festivals Staged?

Since these festivals were the first of their kind, there was no inevitability about their staging. Why then did these countries decide to commemorate their founding as a state occasion and in such an elaborate and extended fashion?

There are several reasons: the rise of the federal state as the embodiment of the nation; the need for cohesion; economics; the status anxieties of 'new' nations. It is probable that the first two reasons were dominant, but what weight these factors had, and at what times, in determining the unfolding design of the festival can only be answered by further detailed research. The first ensured that it would be an official occasion, given the financial and administrative backing of government, and be promoted internationally; the second that it would have a special intensity and moral character; the third that it would contain 'spectacular' events; the fourth that it would be highly elaborate, encouraging not only an extensive reflection of the national experience, but also a preoccupation with creating permanent memorials in order to mark the progress of the nation in space and time.

THE FEDERAL STATE AND THE NATION

The fact that these festivals were staged as official events with the expected participation of the citizenry reflects, in the perception of political elites themselves, the growing identification with the federal state in communities initially imbued with a strong anti-centralist ethos. In the early stages of planning, it is true, there was little likelihood of the governments presiding over the ceremonies, and they showed only a casual interest in the event. But as the year approached, it became perceived as a means of making an important statement about the international status of the political community among the nation-states of the world. The year itself was marked by a procession of heads of state to these countries.

We can observe these patterns most obviously with respect to the USA, where there was a shift in importance over its history from communitarian to statist symbols, focusing on the figure of the President and the Constitution.[10] Giving impetus to these trends had been the New Deal of the 1930s, two world wars, the moon landing and, above all, the cold war which had given the US a world role as the leader of the Western democracies against Soviet Communism. The Bicentennial became a form of international cultural politics, reinforcing American credentials to Western leadership by celebrating, in the words of the ARBA, the '200th anniversary of the oldest continuously surviving democratic republic in the world'. One quarter of the Bicentennial was predicted to take place internationally.[11]

By comparison, the federal state of Canada was much weaker, beset by mounting challenges from the provinces, especially Quebec, and with its economy increasingly penetrated by American capital. Nevertheless, by the late 1950s and the 1960s there was a growing Canadian anti-American nationalism, as expressed in Canada's independent stand on the Vietnam War and its sympathetic stance to the developing world. Thus in October 1963, Prime Minister Lester Pearson, in seeking to cement this international identity, announced as a central component of the Centennial, the International Development Programme to promote development in the Third World and give a dynamic outward and international dimension to the celebrations.[12]

In Australia, although the states still enjoyed considerable power, the federal government was growing in authority with the increasing economic integration of the country. Australian governments from Fraser to Hawke deliberately defined a foreign policy independent of a Britain oriented increasingly to the EEC, that made Australia a leading supporter in the Commonwealth of Black Africa's campaign against South Africa and linked it to its Asian neighbours. One of the five major goals of the Bicentennial was 'to achieve international participation and to strengthen relationships with neighbouring countries'.[13]

NATIONAL COHESION

A second important motive in all three countries was the need for national cohesion. Each festival was long preceded by a historical and cultural search for roots and authenticity. In the USA this was indicated by a marked rise in 'pilgrimages' to historic sites and parks from the early 1960s, one of whose peak years was 1976; in Australia, by the revival of interest in vernacular styles in building and landscapes and in the restoration of historic 'gold rush' towns; in Canada, by the return of artists from abroad to make their careers in Canada.[14]

A recurring theme was that the occasion be used to formulate adequate symbols of national identity and construct a new set of agendas for societies beset by deep-seated differences about the meaning of the national experience for the conduct of foreign policy, the operation of key constitutional and political institutions, and the power and status of ethnic and other groups. This theme was stressed more heavily as the year approached.

Canada's Centennial was sponsored at a time of rising tensions between French and English Canadians over Quebec's claims that the original federal compact between the two 'founding peoples' had been betrayed by federal governments. John Fisher, for many years before, appealed to Canadians in his radio broadcasts to seize the opportunity of the year to strengthen Canadian unity. In 1963 he stated:

> I know something is wrong somewhere. One of our prime jobs during the centennial will be to promote Canadian unity ... If we were not having a centennial, we would have to invent one.[15]

The quest for national cohesion intensified during the 1960s as Quebec-Canada tensions worsened over the issue of bilingualism, and as English Canada was convulsed by the divisive flag debate which saw the replacement of the Union Jack by the maple leaf on the national flag. Not surprisingly, this drive was reflected in the bi-cultural structure of the festival and in the orientation to youth, the 'coming generation'. One of the major projects was to promote interprovincial visits of young Canadians across

Canada, which the planners claimed was 'extremely important at a time in which the country is in need of inter-group and inter-regional understanding'.[16] Other projects included the formation of ethnic councils and events to give recognition to the multicultural dimension of Canada.

In the USA the establishment of the Bicentennnial was preceded by the assassination of President Kennedy, disorders engendered by Black demands for civil rights and demonstrations against the Vietnam War, and was accompanied by conflicts between largely Democratic supporters of federal activism in social affairs and largely Republican defenders of states' rights and the market.

Many of the initiators of the Bicentennial, such as Senator Matthias, advocated that the occasion be used to promote new federal programmes, that recasting the democratic and egalitarian vision of the Revolution would integrate embittered disadvantaged minorities such as the Blacks into American society by, for example, the reconstruction of the inner cities. This desire for unity strengthened as the year approached, and was reinforced by continuing Vietnam demonstrations and the humiliations and divisions of Watergate.[17]

The initiation of the Australian Bicentennial had been preceded by the bitter constitutional battles between Liberal and Labour parties after the dismissal by the Governor-General of the Whitlam government in 1975. In discussing the establishment of official machinery for planning the event in 1978, both the Prime Minister (Malcolm Fraser) and the Leader of the Opposition emphasized the unifying and positive aspects of the occasion. They were not alone: various pressure groups suggested from 1977 onwards that the event be used to end the embarrassing alienation of Aborigines from Australian society by making it the setting for the promulgation of a Treaty to redress Aboriginal grievances over such burning issues as land rights.[18]

As the year approached the theme of unity became more insistent, even as conflicts accelerated between Aboriginal and White Australia over land rights and between 'Anglo-Celtic' and 'European' Australians over multiculturalism and immigration. Thus John Reid claimed in 1985, 'the people have made it known that they are sick of divisions'.[19]

ECONOMIC MOTIVES

Economic motives, too, were a factor in the planning of the festivals, two of which had Expositions attached, and business representatives played a very prominent role in the planning. In part this was to ensure the financial viability of the projects; corporate sponsorship, to varying degrees (notably in the USA where the private sector funded well over half the activities), was regarded as an important funding source.[20] But, in addition, all three countries viewed the events as a means of boosting tourism and the leisure industries, increasingly important in post-war societies.

Thus in Canada, the Commissioner of the Centenary Commission, John Fisher, was prominent in the promotion of tourism. It was hoped to attract a record influx of visitors, particularly from the United States and from new areas, which would result in a tourist expenditure of $1 billion. Similarly, James Kirk, head of the ABA, looked to use the occasion to reinforce Australia's rising visibility as a tourist destination and gain new tourist markets, which would boost also the building and communication industries. One of the three major themes of the US Bicentenary was Festival USA, designed to encourage foreign visitors and, indeed, Americans to travel extensively to experience the ethnic and cultural diversity of the USA.[21]

This rationale was reflected in the design of the festivals: major international sporting events, military spectacles, and, of course, international expositions. Heritage projects such as the Australian Longreach Hall of Fame were financed to provide alternative industries in tourism for otherwise depressed areas. Furthermore, in the USA and Australia as the approach to the year coincided with a depression of economic activity, the festival was regarded as a counter-recessionary instrument.

A MATURATION RITE

Once the state had decided to mark the occasion, the festivals were likely to take on a reflective character, induced by the status anxieties of the intellectuals of New World countries who lacked the depth of an extensive past as a basis of their worth. Claiming instead a unique but (necessarily) unfulfilled future identity, they felt compelled periodically to reassess the entire experience of the collectivity to determine how far they had come in their cultural voyage.

Central to this anxiety was a deep-seated cultural ambivalence *vis-à-vis* the metropolitan culture from which they came and from which they had, to varying degrees, broken away. Thus on the one hand, they differentiated their societies, as dynamic youthful nations, from an exhausted Old World borne down by its past. On the other, they felt an inferiority complex before the cultural 'maturity' and depth of the 'parental' culture from which so many of their social institutions and modes of consciousness derived. The marking of the first or second centenary by an extended festival of self-assessment was in the eyes of some of its prominent advocates – notably the planners – to function as an important rite of passage – of *maturation* – creating some formative experience that would resolve these tensions and inspire the nation for the challenges to come.

This theme of maturation could be conceptualized in different ways. In Canada, it was framed as the process of nation-building itself: the Canadian planners sought to propel Canadians into a distinctive self-consciousness, claiming that, 'without fully realizing it', Canadians were participants in a unique human experience that had resulted in colonies achieving 'the status of a modern industrial power' which was 'recognized for its contribution to human welfare and the cause of peace in the world'.[22] In concrete terms, Canadians built permanent landmarks in the form of cultural centres: the brash former colony was to show its maturity by its entry into the world of 'high' culture. Expo '67 was also to demonstrate Canada as a sophisticated modern industrial society.

In Australia, David Armstrong, inspired by the Canadian 'coming of age' in 1967, promoted the Bicentennial as 'a unique, once-in-a lifetime opportunity . . . the focus for nothing less than a massive national programme of social and community development, a chance to complete unfinished business'.[23] Similarly, ABA chairman Reid suggested, in a striking phrase, that people wanted the occasion to leave 'monuments to the future', but ideas about this varied.[24] Many saw the Bicentennial as a historic opportunity to seize national autonomy from Britain by announcing a republic (thereby ending constitutional dependence represented by such institutions as the governor-generalship), and a new national anthem and flag. Thus John Warhurst argued that the Australia-British relationship was 'not a mature one . . . it was the relationship of a child to its mother'.[25] Others, in addition, enjoined their fellow citizens to show their maturity as a nation by their willingness to engage in critical reflection as well as celebration, and to acknowledge the need to give decisive redress for the evils done to the Aborigines during colonization through a constitutional treaty enshrining land rights.

Even in the USA, which had achieved auto-emancipation from Britain in the War of Independence, influential figures such as James Michener, who wrote the final report of the first ARBC, explicitly defined the occasion as 'a rite of passage' and 'as a coming of age'.[26] Here, too, conceptions varied with conservatives and radicals stressing either the need to face up to world responsibilities or to tackle poverty and historic wrongs (to Black Americans) at home.

Controversies and Cleavages in Immigrant Nations

The festivals were organized by non-governmental agencies, with a mandate to unify the nation and they offered, supposedly, equal participation to all. Why then were they almost immediately embroiled in controversies which continued largely to the end, some of which evoked fundamental questions about the legitimacy of the nation-state? There were several reasons.

First, with regard to criticisms of the managerial performance of the agencies, the problem was that, although in theory non-partisan bodies, the agencies were open to considerable pressure from the federal governments, which controlled appointments and finance, and which were heavily influenced by the electoral cycle. At first the agencies were paralysed by the inertia of governments unlikely to preside over the occasion; then changes of government led to changes of theme and personnel; and, as the year approached, there was further disruptive interference by governments concerned about their image in the eyes of the international community and of their own population. These problems were multiplied by the need to work through state (or provincial) governments.

A second problem for the agencies was that, because these were novel events, they had no precedents, as they repeatedly complained, for devising such an elaborate year of events. Planners had no obvious guidelines to follow or bank of expertise on which to draw at a national level, and this was the more onerous because the organizers had to combine several different and potentially antipathetic purposes. For similar reasons, there were inchoate expectations of the event, leading to complaints, particularly in the USA and Australia, of the failure of the planners to create appropriate national rituals or forms of celebration for the occasion.

A third reason for the intense controversies was that mounting a successful *national* festival was always going to be difficult in countries with only a comparatively recent history from which to construct a rich and inspiring occasion. This was compounded by the fact that much of this history was attached to states or provinces, many of which had preceded the formation of the federal state and remained powerful units of political and economic power, jealous not only of the centre but also of each other. There were attendant 'siting' problems: whereas in old centralized states such as Britain or France the capital cities, as historical, political, cultural and financial centres, were 'natural' sites of national ceremonies, Washington, Canberra, and Ottawa, built as 'compromise' capitals, were regarded by the citizenry as artificial politico-administrative constructs detached from the 'real' life of the country.

The agencies tried to get round this problem by mounting or sponsoring travelling exhibitions. Embodying the idea of the nation as the conquest of space, these sought to link the central experiences and symbols of the nation to locality by providing room within the exhibitions for the distinctive celebrations of the many small towns in which they stopped. Nevertheless, many of the founding events had specific territorial linkages which were jealously guarded, and so had the potential to be divisive as much as unifying.

These problems were most visible in the cases of the newer states of Canada and Australia which lacked a war of national liberation to serve as a founding myth. As the Canadian Centenary Commission admitted, Confederation did not generate the dynamism of a revolution, and there were 'few events to fire the imagination of Canadians everywhere in the country'.[27] In Australia, neither 1788 nor 26 January (the national day) had great national resonance: throughout the preparations for the festival, there had been arguments between the advocates of 26 January, Federation Day and Anzac Day as the most appropriate national day. Both countries had to borrow rituals and significance from Britain by having the Queen and the royal family preside over some of the major ceremonies.

A problem for Canada was that only four of the ten provinces (Ontario, Quebec, New Brunswick, and Nova Scotia) had federated in 1867. There were worries about the level of participation in some of the later arrivals, despite the decentralized format which guaranteed each provincial capital a major cultural centre.[28] In fact, the festival had an Ontario and Quebec thrust, though, as we shall see, English and French Canadians had different perceptions of the event.

The planners in Australia had another difficulty: how to transform an official (New South Wales) state occasion into a national event. Of course, '1788' – the landing of the First Fleet at Botany Bay, Sydney – had been commemorated Australia-wide in 1888 and 1938, and 26 January (the day of the landing) had long been the national day, but because the state of New South Wales had also appropriated the moment as the founding of the 'premier' state of Australia, this had excited interstate jealousies, especially between Victoria and New South Wales.

In trying to nationalize a festival associated with a particular state, the ABA was handicapped by the weakness of Canberra as a centre (although important ceremonies such as the opening by the Queen of the new Parliament House were held there); indeed, it felt compelled to set up its headquarters in Sydney, which reinforced complaints in the rest of Australia about the privileging of New South Wales. The ABA sought initially to detach the occasion from its Sydney moorings by downplaying the events of the year 1788, notably the landing of the First Fleet, but it could never fully succeed because of the activism of the New South Wales government which, with its own priority claims to make, alone of the states gave generously to its State Bicentennial Council (Aus$70m compared with Fraser's Aus$166m for the entire Bicentennial). The resulting proliferation of New South Wales projects reinforced the sense of exclusion felt by the other states, three of which – Western Australia (1979), Victoria (1985), and South Australia (1986) – were distracted in this period by the prospect of commemorating their sesquicentenaries.[29]

By contrast the USA had a powerful myth of auto-emancipation based on a large common store of symbols, legendary events and heroes of the revolutionary period which united the people, and most of its states had entered the union under the tutelage of the federal government. Moreover, the capital, Washington, had acquired, since the Second World War, more of a national status as the stage on which the USA strutted as leader of the Western world. Many of the major ceremonies were based there, including the 4 July weekend celebration of the sacred document of the USA, the Constitution. Regional groupings of states formed to co-operate in the design of Bicentennial projects. Nevertheless, the commemoration of the birth of the nation-state inevitably focused attention on the historically significant sites in the original thirteen states, between which there were strong rivalries.

The first ARBC (1967–9), which had a strong Virginian membership, was perceived to have an eastern bias when it adopted plans to base major activities in Boston, Washington, Philadelphia, and Miami. Although Nixon, in replacing its members in 1969, declared that the celebrations 'belong not only to the thirteen original states, but equally to the newest', in 1970 he selected Philadelphia as the site for an International Exposition to serve as a national focus (as in 1876).[30] This was criticized by other cities and states, and the ARBC had eventually to abandon these ideas for an *ad hoc* decentralized format that pushed the responsibility for projects onto the states and municipalities.

There was, however, a fourth serious barrier to creating a suitable unifying national experience in these societies: differing interpretations of the foundation myths and core symbols of the nation. These were tied to conceptions of group status and had implications for the current series of overlapping conflicts in these societies about the distribution of power: between different political parties and movements; between (and, in Canada, within) the 'old' core settler population and 'newer' ethnic minorities; and between European and indigenous peoples.

In Canada the idea of Confederation between two nations was invoked differently by Liberals, anxious to create a neutral Canadian identity with a new flag and bi-culturalist policies, and by Conservatives determined to retain traditional British symbols. It meant different things to English and French Canadians (who regarded the practice of confederation which had resulted in English economic and cultural hegemony as a betrayal of the original compact). Newer ethnic groups demanded a multicultural rather than a bi-cultural ethos.

In the USA the 1776 Revolution and the Constitution were invoked both by Democrat President Johnson, who justified federal activism to advance social reform by reference to its egalitarian ideals, and by Republicans who resisted Johnson in the name of states' and individual rights. Black civil rights leaders made a contrast between the original ideals of 1776 and their history of discrimination, as did American Indians, until the 1960s excluded from citizenship, who, demanding self-management of their lands, regarded European settlement as an act of conquest.

Likewise, the 1788 settlement symbolized for Liberals the centrality of Britain and the Crown in Australia, whereas, for Labour, it meant the founding of a new democratic culture which had yet to achieve true autonomy. For Australians of Anglo-Celtic stock it could symbolize their priority over the post-war European migrants who, in the name of multiculturalism, sought to change the national flag, anthem, language and immigration policies. For Aborigines, now struggling for land rights, it evoked their near genocide.

Since interpretations of founding events implied hierarchies of power, the planning agencies faced an impossible task in creating an official consensus on national symbols. Various expedients were tried, notably a horizontal approach to groups, dubbed 'tactical pluralism', that included an extension of the celebration to cover not just the founding events but the full range of the country's history in an attempt to incorporate the experiences of indigenous peoples and later arrivals (both states/provinces and peoples). But such approaches were either perceived as hypocritical by the marginalized, or, if seriously pursued, were rejected by the dominant groups. There were no neutral national symbols, and, indeed, given the political resonance of the occasion, governments in Australia and the USA were unable to resist the temptation to enforce on the agencies their ideological agenda, which in turn provoked further criticism.

After his election in 1968, Nixon gave the planning a conservative Republican thrust by pushing the ARBC to a states-centred mode that celebrated 'middle' America and was funded by private enterprise. He rejected, as redolent of the Democrat 'big government' ethos, the original conception of a federally funded renovation of the inner cities and the environment that would extend the democratic vision of the Revolution by opening opportunities for Black and other poor ethnic minorities.

This left the ARBC exposed to ideological and ethnic criticism. The first was effectively articulated by a New Left group, the People's Bicentennial Committee, who, mobilizing popular disillusionment with Nixonian republicanism over Watergate and Vietnam, argued that the lack of interest in the revolutionary nature of 1776 and the commercialization of the event exemplified the betrayal of the original American democratic vision at home and abroad by governments tied to multinational capitalism.[31] The second attack was directed at the exclusive composition of the ARBC, when, in 1972, it was disrupted by resignations from youth and other representatives who complained of the dominance of white middle-aged conservative business interests and the lack of awareness of the concerns of the young, ethnic minorities and women.[32] Indeed, radical Blacks and Indians argued for a boycott of or counter demonstrations against an event with little relevance for them.

Gathering criticisms and fears that the Watergate scandal would torpedo the whole enterprise led in 1974 to desperate efforts to secure participation by women and ethnic minorities, and to the promotion of an 'American Issues Forum' that would involve Americans in the evaluation of their historical experience, in order to defuse criticism that the Bicentennial was degenerating into a fiesta of commercialized trivia. But this opened the ARBA to attack from 'libertarian' Republicans. Concerned about the failure of the Nixon counter-revolution, they objected to a perceived leftist tone to the Forum, and, more fundamentally, to an agency which they characterized as yet another incompetent arm of Big Government, smothering by paternalist central direction what should have been a joyful celebration by and of the people.[33]

In Australia the election in 1983 of Hawke's Labour government on a republican platform (including support for a new national flag and national anthem) led to a return to the ABA's original conception, vetoed by Fraser, of a multicultural nation that would make amends for past mistreatment of the Aborigines. This entailed a future-oriented festival that downplayed the imperial and British aspects of 1788. Thus the ABA planned to substitute for a re-enactment of the landing of the First Fleet on Australia Day 1988, a parade of tall ships from different countries to symbolize Australia's multinational heritage, and proposed that the Australian Travelling Exhibition be organized round the concept of 'one nation from three (equal) waves of migrations' (Aboriginal, British, and European).[34]

But, for many, this cultural egalitarianism devalued the British contribution to the making of Australia by equating it with the brief post-war experience of European migrants, and met the response from Aborigines that '40,000 years don't make a Bicentennial'. It led to a critique from conservatives, already strongly mobilizing in 1984 against high rates of Asian migration and the Aboriginal land rights campaigns, that the ABA was subverting the core values of traditional Australia (the British heritage of monarchy, parliamentary democracy, free enterprise, the Anzac traditions) and presenting Australia as a land of incoherent diversity without unifying traditions and values.[35] At the same time, Aborigines, finding the campaign for a Treaty recognizing their prior possession as the *original* inhabitants blocked, rejected the Bicentennial as a hypocritical farce and resented its conception of them as migrants.

Alarmed at the prospect of these controversies sabotaging the Bicentennial, Hawke and the new officers of the ABA backtracked. Increasingly they promoted spectacles such as an international naval review that, by highlighting the armed services, gave comfort to the conservative lobby and gave grudging support, under pressure from public campaigns, in 1987 to the ailing First Fleet re-enactment consortium.

The Canadian case was distinctive. Because of the estrangement of the two dominant language cultures, territorially separated in large part, most of the debates took place within intergovernmental forums or the CCC rather than in the public domain. In effect, the planners 'solved' the problem of integration by bilingual fudging (saying different things to each language community) and permitting two different celebrations, one for English Canada, the other for Quebec and heavily oriented to Expo with explosive consequences.

The Consequences of the Festivals

I argued before that there was no inherent necessity for states to commemorate such moments and in such an extended fashion. But once they decided, at times of deep-seated social conflict, to give an official status and elaborate attention to these (literally) extraordinary commemorations of the national birth, they focused attention on those *transcendent* questions about the identity of the nation and the status of various groups within it, that are normally submerged beneath day-to-day issues, and they created expectations of their decisive resolution. As we noted, governments and their agencies engaged in a series of expensive initiatives to achieve certain goals, and the official nature of the festival galvanized, in turn, responses from a range of elites who sought to co-opt the occasion to advance the claims of their respective groups.

As we will see, neither governments nor, with one major exception, non-dominant groups were successful in their aims. Nevertheless, one of the major consequences of these festivals was to stimulate a wide-ranging debate about the meaning and direction of the nation among the intellectuals and elite groups who found themselves propelled into the public spotlight by the moment. Increasingly, the commemoration itself became perceived by opinion-makers not just as a means to an end but rather as *the* gauge of the national 'will'. Failure to live up to such heady hopes brought with it consequences unintended by the initiators of these festivals.

REALIZATION OF OFFICIAL GOALS

How far were the official goals of state legitimation, tourist promotion, national integration and landmark achievements realized?

With respect to the first goal, all states in securing large-scale foreign participation boosted their self-images and prestige, and reinforced links with British roots and with the homeland states of their later migrants, although the effects were uneven.

The greatest beneficiary was the USA, which, demoralized by

the slur of Watergate on its primary political institution, the Presidency, recovered some degree of self-belief in its democratic world mission as a result of the active participation in its celebrations by over a hundred countries through visits by heads of state and festivities within their territories. The *New York Times* editorial of 4 July 1976 remarked on the extraordinary outpouring of esteem from so many nations. After Watergate and Vietnam the friends who were ashamed of the USA:

> seem to be saying now that they see America's better values surviving. The oldest written constitution still in effect . . . assures this nation a solid place in the hearts that cherish the world's receding zone of freedom.[36]

Canada highlighted its credentials as an international actor from the visits of sixty heads of state. But the festival nearly led to a breakdown in relations with France as a result of de Gaulle's decision to stir up Quebec separatist sentiments during a truncated visit, and tensions with the USA over Canada's criticisms of the Vietnam War were exposed in President Johnson's surly visit. Although the Australian Bicentennial was used to emphasize the country's recently acquired status as a distinctive multicultural nation through visits from heads of state from the newer migrant countries, the year probably reinforced its reliance on British symbols, given the centrality of the royal family in the major ceremonies.

The second goal, tourist promotion, may have been achieved in the short term, but the long-term effects were questionable.

As regards the third objective, the official festival failed to achieve national cohesion in the sense it intended. As we have seen, the conceptions of national unity were politically driven, evoked bitter controversies among elites, and had an uneven appeal to the various social groups. True, there was mass attendance at the central spectacles, and, in Canada and the USA, strong local participation by many municipalities who tied their local centenaries to the national. But this outbreak of sentiment in the USA was as much a communitarian assertion of nationality independent of the federal office holders, or a product of contingency in the case of Canada.

Thus the USA Bicentennial year had a cathartic, grass-roots and nostalgic character that resulted from its following the resolution of the agonizing constitutional crisis of the Nixon presidency, during which there had been an unprecedented collapse of confidence in official institutions and a sense of helplessness before the crises of the cities and social disorders. This was expressed by the emphasis on local, small-town heritages, and a return in the eastern states to the nation's 'youthful' vigour through local re-enactments of the revolutionary past.[37]

In Canada, the Centennial functioned initially as an accidental outlet for English Canadians, imbued with an inferiority complex *vis-à-vis* their domineering southern neighbour, the USA, to express national pride. For, enjoying an economic boom and basking in international attention and praise (of the Montreal Expo), to their own surprise they had the unusual opportunity of being able to favourably compare their country's economic well-being, peace and apparent social harmony with the discomfiture of the USA, wracked by recession and mired in social discord over civil rights issues and the Vietnam War. But as we see below, the early sense of Canadian harmony was illusory, and the festival later revealed the existence of two mutually unintelligible nations and generated, during the visit of de Gaulle, a full-scale national crisis.

In Australia the attempt to create a new multicultural nation, reconciled with the Aborigines, collapsed, and fudging reached the level of bathos when Australia Day was celebrated by a procession into Sydney Harbour both of tall ships (symbolizing multiculturalism) and of a re-enactment of the First Fleet (symbolizing British origins).

CULTURAL POLITICS AND THE STATUS ORDER

If then the official nation could claim only partial success and certainly no landmark achievements, what impact did the festivals have on the intense competition for symbolic and material power in these periods? To what extent were groups able to advance their goals by participating in, co-opting, or resisting the occasion?

In concrete terms, how far were groups able to extract concessions from the federal state?

Successes of groups were very uneven, and here I wish to examine briefly two ethnic groups, alienated from the official state, whose cultural politics throw light on the problems of identity and cohesion of the immigrant nation: the Quebecois of Canada, and the indigenous peoples, in particular, the Australian Aborigines.

The success of the French-Canadians in Quebec is interesting because it shows the divisive implications of such occasions for states, when faced with an alienated ethnic minority that is strong in terms of its numbers, territorial concentration, political resources (a provincial government) and international allies (France). Thus, as a price for its participation, the Quebec government won several major symbolic and material concessions: the commitment and financial support of the federal government for Montreal's bid to mount an International Exposition in 1967; a redefinition of the Centennial as the commemoration of confederation rather than of nation; the obtaining of the largest sum of all the provinces for heritage projects which it channelled into a celebration of a specific Quebec heritage (predating that of confederation), distinct from that of English Canada; the use of Expo – identified as a provincial achievement – to pose as a quasi-independent state with its own foreign policy by effectively controlling the access by distinguished visitors such as President de Gaulle.[38]

These achievements, together with the controversy of de Gaulle's visit, served to intensify a sense of Quebec's identity and autonomy *vis-à-vis* English Canada.

Most poignant was the position of indigenous peoples, in all three countries, alienated from a nation-state built on the expropriation of their lands, which excluded them from citizenship until the 1960s and viewed with relative indifference their demoralized and impoverished status. However, the festivals were preceded in Australia (and the USA) by a politicization of these peoples, focused on rights to traditional lands and self-management. This was made possible by the emergence of an indigenous intelligentsia of lawyers and civil servants and, in Australia, by the Whitlam Labour government's creation of independent power bases in the form of the Northern Lands Council and the Department of Aboriginal Affairs and legal-aid centres. The festivals stimulated this radicalized indigenous intelligentsia to use the commemoration to strengthen their campaigns for land rights and the redress of other grievances.

Although otherwise weak in terms of numbers, organization, and access to resources (e.g. the media), these peoples possessed a symbolic power in their capacity as *indigenes* endowed with an ancient and distinctive iconography and culture. This could be used as a lever against states trying to distance themselves from their European imperial origins and active in pursuing ties with post-colonial Third World societies, for two reasons. First, native grievances, if articulated, would subvert in international eyes the celebrations of these countries as New World and multi-ethnic societies by highlighting their origins and continued basis in European racist conquest. Second, these grievances made it more difficult for political communities, searching for emblems of distinctiveness *vis-à-vis* the 'Old World', to appropriate aspects of the indigenous culture in order to lend a spurious historical depth and cultural romance to societies otherwise noted for their pragmatic materialism. In all three countries some attempt was made to fuse a sense of the primordial (the timeless land) with a futuristic ethos (e.g. the Eskimo Katimak design of the Canadian Pavilion at Expo; the use of Ayers Rock, a sacred aboriginal site, as a symbol of Australian uniqueness).

To gain their participation or, at least, acquiescence, the states felt compelled to make gestures (e.g. the handing over to Aborigines of the management of Ayers Rock) and to offer financial incentives. For their part, the indigenous peoples could use the unusual world spotlight directed at the nation-state to exert collective pressure on the governments through adverse publicity, threats of demonstrations and even violence in order to extract funding for projects specific to their needs (better water, health, and housing facilities on their reservations). The Australian Bicentennial, in particular, was significant for the employment by Aborigines of a new transnational politics, made possible by the development of links with radical anti-colonialist forums and United Nations agencies which compelled a reluctant Australian government, at that time vociferous in the anti-apartheid campaign, to concede very reluctantly in 1987 a Royal Commission into Aboriginal deaths in custody.

The achievements of such groups were, however, limited by internal weaknesses (geographical dispersal, 'tribal' divisions, poverty, lack of Western education and organizational skills) and the larger constraints on governments (the Australian government, for example, found itself faced with a conservative backlash over the issue of land rights). The major effect of the occasions may have been to accelerate the politicization of these groups.

THE NATIONALIZATION OF PUBLIC DISCOURSE

Obviously an event that foregrounds issues of national identity and future directions favours cultural producers and national intellectuals, propelled from querulous obscurity into the limelight by public expectations of their capacity to evaluate the import of the commemoration for a general audience and to affirm the distinctive creativity of the nation. Thus the occasion serves as a catalyst to emergent forces, enabling the realization of long-term cultural initiatives, previously frustrated by indifference, which now gain recognition and finance.

On the individual level, projects such as the Longreach Stockman's Hall of Fame were completed because of Bicentennial funding. In all three countries a permanent and concrete legacy was left in the huge range of heritage and cultural projects in the centres and localities that added significantly to the patrimony of the nation, financed by central, state (or provincial) and local governments and by private sponsorship. Such festivals may have a still more dramatic impact where they are preceded by a collective build-up of cultural energies. In Canada, because of the provision of commissions and exposure in the public media, an emerging national orientation among artists crystallized into a major cultural revival. This sustained itself beyond the year by forming permanent trade and professional associations that in turn helped establish the Federal Cultural Policy Review Committee to promote the development of a Canadian national culture.[39]

The major cultural effect of festivals, however, was to reinforce among elites and, to a lesser extent, the educated public the discourse of nationality as the proper idiom of political identity, by engendering over several years a series of overlapping debates about the proper forms of the festival and the historical significance of the occasion. For, by investing the commemorative year as a decisive moment for assessing the international status of the community, the continued relevance of its political legacy, and the prestige and rights of its constituent groups, they encouraged citizens to consider the problems and dilemmas of the present in terms of their relationship to the founding moment, and thereby accept the teleologies of nationalism.

Various intellectuals might agonize over the proper form of festivals, the thinness of the national cultural traditions and the lack of a genuine interest in history in comparison with other societies. But this itself encouraged comparisons between the values and practices of their community and older societies, and between past and present. Contrasts might be made, as in Stephen Alomes's polemical history, *A Nation At Last?*, aimed at the Australian popular market, between the rhetoric of authenticity and autonomy used in the Bicentennial with the realities of multinational capitalist control of the economy.[40] Such critiques, however, based on assumptions about Australian exceptionalism and the need for Australian economic autonomy, merely mirrored nationalist tenets. This process recreated and generalized the familiar conceptualizations of their society as a New World society and the tendency to analyse the problems of the present in terms of a quasi-personification of the nation as young and in need of 'maturity'.

Hence, one of the recurring themes of commentators was the representation of the occasion as a rite of passage, as an index of the 'maturity' of the young nation which was on the verge of 'coming of age' (or becoming 'a nation at last'). For example, in the USA a range of crises in the areas of the environment, education, constitution, and foreign policy, were attributed both by left and right (though in different terms) to 'arrested' development: to the unwillingness to sully the imagined innocence of youth by facing the responsibilities and complexities of modernity. Or, alternatively, others complained that the current demoralization had occurred because the USA had sacrificed its New World revolutionary mission to become a cynical great power just like the corrupt Old World imperialisms.[41] In all three countries the year itself was, therefore, to be judged by its ability to propose decisive solutions to fundamental problems.

The very expectations of social regeneration aroused by festivals doomed them to varying degrees of disillusion. Commentators in the USA increasingly looked back nostalgically to the model 1876 Centennial, which fell at an equivalent time of political corruption, economic recession and discord in the aftermath of the Civil War. With its unifying focus on the Philadelphia International Exhibition, this had allegedly rallied the nation by its triumphant demonstration of American technological prowess to achieve world economic leadership in the twentieth century.

Since these were state festivals, this sense of failure had consequences in the political arena. In Canada, the shocking eruption of English-French divisions ushered in the era of French Canadian Pierre Trudeau, who, elected in 1968 as leader of the Liberal Party and Prime Minister on a platform of national reconciliation, sought to accommodate French grievances by removing British symbols and promoting bilingualism in Canadian public life. In the USA, the Bicentennial intensified a growing reaction against the failures of 'Big Government' and the social ills of the cities in favour of a nostalgic return to a mythic nation of small-town certainties and innocence. This communitarian nationalism had long-term effects, for it was exploited successfully against the Presidential incumbent in the election of 1976 by the populist Jimmy Carter, who presented himself as the charismatic outsider who would clean out the Washington stables. Carter's presidency reinforced a suspicion of social engineering and a revival of conservative religious values. This yearning for a return to a 'traditional' America was later harnessed powerfully to a neo-liberal economic and social programme of national regeneration by Ronald Reagan, under whose folksy leadership the USA advanced in an optimistic haze towards the sunlit plains during the 1980s. In Australia, the divisive experience of 1988 may have created the groundswell to change the foundation myth itself, from one of ethnic settlement to the (more neutral) political establishment of Australia as a federal state in 1901.

Conclusions

Four main conclusions follow from the above analysis.

The first is that although the holding of these festivals indicates a measure of integration of the federal state with the civil society, the state faces considerable limitations on its attempts at nation-building for three reasons. First, in a federal system it is not able to control the actions of states or provinces which have their own agenda and whose decisions can shape the occasion. Second, such elaborate events, with their extended planning time, offer hostages to fortune (including political disasters such as Watergate, economic recessions, or immigration debates), which change the popular perceptions of these festivals in unpredictable ways. Fortune can favour the planners: the Canadian Centennial, by occurring at a time of increasing Canada–US tensions, was able to unite English Canadians against a significant other; but then came another random factor: de Gaulle. Third, there are in-built contradictions between the desires of official elites to impose a national definition and the needs of a democratic state to be able to legitimate itself to its citizenry and to the international order by claiming a broadly based participation. As we saw, the US and Australian planners initially promoted a partisan vision which they had to jettison, and, in desperation, turned to anodyne public spectacles to achieve the appearance of popular consensus.

The two preceding chapters have explored how the intrinsic

tension between ethnic identifications, which are necessarily exclusive and hierarchical, and the commitment to citizenship equality has created problems of stability both for communist and liberal-democratic states in modern Europe which are not ethnically homogeneous. It is chastening, therefore, to note a second lesson: namely, that even in New World societies with a relatively weak historical sense and without mythic claims to 'primordial' homelands, foundation myths are associated with a specific ethnic core population and with patterns of power and exclusion, and cannot easily be manipulated.

This was demonstrated when Australian planners cut against the symbolic grain of an ethnic settlement myth, identified with British Australia, by trying to convert the occasion into a festival of multiculturalism. Of course, this may show the need for a more neutral civic or political foundation myth, but the experience of Canada and the USA suggests that such myths are essentially contested in multi-ethnic societies. Indeed, such was the distaste of many Quebecois for the Canadian myth of Confederation that they converted the occasion into a celebration of the survival of a distinctive French culture. The Canadian Centenary was thus an important moment in the crystallization of a distinctive and exclusive Quebec national identity. It highlighted emphatically the deep-seated differences within Canada, that, in spite of all initiatives since 1967, may prove to be intractable.

A further fundamental challenge to the notion of a horizontal status order came in Australia and (to a lesser extent) the USA from the indigenous peoples, who not only drew attention to their history of exploitation, but also demanded recognition of themselves as founding peoples. How this can be reconciled in the long run with the essentially immigrant basis of the nation-state is unclear, despite recent land treaties in Canada and the 1992 Mabo High Court decision in Australia which recognized native land title. But in Australia at least, the international dimension of the festivals enabled Aboriginals to force their concerns on to the national agenda and strengthened the formation of an indigenous intelligentsia which made links with international organizations and their equivalents in other countries.

Similar points might be made about the Colombus Quincentennial of 1979. Originally envisaged in celebratory terms with Italian and Hispanic Americans vying for the leading role, the commemorative occasion was captured by radicals in order to highlight the grievances of indigenous peoples in both North and Latin America, and their history of oppression under the European yoke.

This discussion may lead us to argue that the image of these societies, sometimes presented as pioneers of a post-national experiment in ethnic diversity, is mythical. There is a gap between the official self-image of such multi-ethnic societies as egalitarian, and the existence of ethnically based status hierarchies. This is not to deny that these societies are much more successful than the European nation-states in coping with ethnic diversity. There is a reality to the myth just as there is to that of the ethnic nation-state in Europe. But one might regard the claims (in their different varieties) to offer futuristic models of successful living together to an increasingly interdependent world as a part of a drive for a national identity by relatively recently settled immigrant territories which have to define themselves in an international order dominated by states with claims to a long historical ancestry.

This brings us to our third conclusion: that such festivals reveal both in their idioms and ambitions the status anxieties of these countries, formulated in a language of maturation. The fact that such nations still conceptualize themselves so has its absurd side, since the USA has claims to be the oldest modern state in possessing a continuous democratic constitution since 1788. Moreover, there is a deep ambivalence among national intellectuals imbued with a 'Peter Pan' complex, for to 'come of age' is to lose one's 'youth'.[42] This ambivalence is not simply rooted in historical peculiarity but is the local expression of twin and competing impulses felt by all national elites: for their countries to be acknowledged, on the one hand, as *distinctive* (based in this case on their *new* world origins and subsequent multi-ethnic migrant character); and, on the other, to be recognized as *normal* members of the established international political and economic community, as they become world actors and as industrial development detaches them from their pioneer roots.

There is no final resolution to these competing drives, and the concept of 'maturity' that emerges out of their interplay has no objective referent: 'maturity' entails not a surrender of distinctiveness by becoming like the old European nation-states but simply the will to face the future by overcoming the problems and illusions of the past. The continued use of this idiom, however, reveals the insecurity of societies without the dignity of a *usable* 'immemorial' lineage (*pace* the indigenous cultures) which, in defining themselves in futuristic terms, feel the need of a periodic stocktaking of their achievements and weaknesses as a platform for action.

For this very reason, the US, Canadian and Australian state festivals became the focus of existential and social anxieties, and of expectations that these anxieties would be resolved in a decisive way. But because 'maturity' is subjectively defined, the festivals generated conflict as groups, in the absence of a significant other, indulged their different expectations of the occasion. They, therefore, failed to function formatively *in the sense intended* as galvanizers of a once-and-forever transition. They became landmarks, however, in another sense: because of the very conflicts they engendered. For these conflicts elaborated options in a common idiom and, by highlighting the intensity of divisions, inspired fresh initiatives of national reconciliation.

Finally, such events confirm once again nationalism as a recurring force in modern societies, one which purports to provide new direction at times when established identities and institutions are shaken by geopolitical, economic or cultural challenges. As we've observed, the commemorations gained support in all three countries from those who saw a need to redefine their political communities as international actors in the post-war period. This was most salient for the USA which, now thrust into assuming the leadership of the West against world communism, faced the problems (painfully posed in the Vietnam debacle) of reconciling an 'imperial' *Realpolitik* with its original revolutionary idealism. But influential figures in Australia and Canada, too, felt a need to construct new and autonomous identities for their societies from the 1960s onwards as the British 'Mother' country downgraded its Commonwealth links in favour of a European future. A second reason for the staging of these festivals was to restore national cohesion to societies wracked by internal conflict. In the USA there was the issue of race, in Canada the antagonisms between Quebec and English Canada, and in Australia increasing tensions over the questions of land rights, Asian immigration and multi-culturalism.

Resolutions were proposed but even had they been applied successfully, the respite would have been temporary, because of the new and often unpredictable challenges to which all societies are exposed. In recent years new demographic and immigration trends in the USA have provoked fears that by 2017 European Americans will be in a minority, and there have been prophecies of social and political instability. Whether this will come to pass remains to be seen, but such considerations do suggest the pro-visional nature of contemporary cultural and political identities and a long future for nationalism.

NOTES

INTRODUCTION

1. Hobsbawm (1990: 183).

CHAPTER I

1. Seton-Watson (1977: 15).
2. Connor (1991: 5).
3. See Deutsch (1966); Gellner (1964; 1983); Anderson (1983); Hobsbawm (1990).
4. Hobsbawm (1990: 14–20).
5. Connor (1991: 9).
6. Hobsbawm (1990: 9–10, 18–19).
7. Gellner (1973).
8. Gellner (1983; 1).
9. See McNeill (1986).
10. See Anderson (1983).
11. Gellner (1983: 141).
12. Ibid., ch. 3.
13. Deutsch (1966: ch. 1).
14. Gellner (1983: 138).
15. Breuilly (1982).
16. Their most important works are Armstrong (1982) and Smith (1986a).
17. See Barth (1969).
18. Armstrong (1982).
19. Smith (1986a: ch. 6).
20. Smith (1991: ch. 2).
21. Smith (1981a: ch. 4).
22. Smith (1986a: ch. 4).
23. Ibid., ch. 6.
24. See Smith (1989).
25. This and the following sections are indebted to the seminal articles of Walker Connor (1990; 1991).
26. See Weber (1976).
27. Hobsbawm (1990: 49–50).
28. Connor (1991: 6).
29. Quoted in Connor (1990: 98).
30. Loc. cit.
31. Ibid., 101.
32. Anderson (1983: ch. 2).
33. Hobsbawm (1984).
34. See Hroch (1984: 86–116).
35. Connor (1990: 99).
36. Gellner (1983: 1).
37. Hobsbawm (1990: 18–19).
38. Connor (1978).
39. Smith (1989).
40. Mosse (1971).
41. Smith (1986a: 208).
42. Although Gellner's interpretation first appeared in (1964: ch. 5), it is most fully presented in his (1983).
43. On this, see ch. 3.
44. See Smith (1971: ch. 6) for forceful criticisms of Gellner's model.
45. Gellner (1983: 111–22) provides an extended discussion of this issue.
46. See Hobsbawm (1990: ch. 6).
47. Loc. cit.
48. See Smith (1971: ch. 6).
49. Tilly (1975).
50. Anderson (1983: ch. 3).
51. See McNeill (1986: 33–54).
52. See Yoshino (1992: 75) for this

term, which he applies to Tilly (1975), Poggi (1978), and Breuilly (1982).

53. See Smith (1981b) for an extended analysis.
54. Smith (1986a: 197).
55. See Weber (1976).
56. The argument is presented in Howard (1976: ch. 7).
57. See the introduction in Barth (1969).
58. Smith (1986a: ch. 8).
59. Gellner (1964: 164).
60. Gellner (1983: 56).
61. See Trevor-Roper (1983).
62. See Burke (1978: 14–19).
63. Hobsbawm (1990: 10).
64. For these points in this and the subsequent paragraph, see Hobsbawm (1984).
65. Brass (1979: 38).
66. Ibid., 40–1.
67. Robinson (1979).
68. See Skinner (1974).
69. Brym has a useful discussion in his (1980: 35–6).
70. Elaborated first in Smith (1971: ch. 10).
71. Brass (1979: 38–40).
72. Explored in Smith (1986a: ch. 1, 96–8).
73. I owe this point to Diana Solano.
74. See Mayall (1990: 122–5).

CHAPTER 2

1. The major study is Ozouf (1988).
2. On this, see Gellner (1983: 1) and Hobsbawm (1990: 9).
3. Mazrui (1968: 193–4).
4. Pech (1976).
5. Rudnytsky (1977).
6. As well as being an incisive bio-

graphical study of this important Chinese figure, Levenson's (1959) is a searching study of the intellectual tensions within reformist nationalists.

7. Kedourie (1966: 9, 49–50).
8. Ibid., 58.
9. For further analysis, see Smith (1971: ch. 10).
10. On this, see Lewis (1968).
11. Herder (1968: 130).
12. Berlin (1976: 158–63).
13. Herder (1968: 50–60).
14. Brock (1976: 22).
15. Barnard (1969: 385–90).
16. Smith (1986a: 191–2).
17. Levenson (1959: 122).
18. Berlin (1976: 203–4).
19. See Argyle (1976).
20. Brass (1979: 49).
21. Pech (1976: 347).
22. Boyce (1982: 60–1).
23. Argyle (1976: 42–3).
24. See H. Kohn (1946) and Gellner (1983).
25. Kohn (1946: 3–4).
26. Ibid., 329–41.
27. Ibid., 429–30.
28. Gellner (1983: 57–61).
29. McCully (1966: ch. 5).
30. Rudnytsky (1977).
31. Brock (1976: 9–19).
32. See Heimsath (1964: ch. 7).
33. See Herder (1968: 106).
34. See Heimsath (1964: ch. 7).
35. Ibid., 331–6.
36. Ibid., 355.
37. Levenson (1959: 93–4); on Blyden, see July (1968: 215–9).
38. Levenson (1959: 103).
39. See Kopf (1969).
40. Hutchinson (1987a: 166–7).
41. Kohn (1946: 429–30).
42. See Smith (1971: ch. 10).

43. For a fuller exposition, see Hutchinson (1987b).
44. Hutchinson (1987a).
45. Ibid., ch. 3.
46. Ibid., 76–9.
47. For a fascinating study of the artistic ramifications of this revival, see Sheehy (1980).
48. Hutchinson (1987a: 94–5).
49. Ibid., 95–111.
50. Ibid., ch. 4.
51. Ibid., ch. 5.
52. Ibid., ch. 8.

CHAPTER 3

1. See Siavoshi (1990: 178).
2. For a useful survey of contemporary Islamic political movements, see Esposito (1991).
3. See the essays in Ramet (1989b).
4. For a discussion, see Mortimer (1991).
5. Siavoshi (1990: 181).
6. For an explication of these concepts and an interesting application to South Asia, see Bellah (1965).
7. For a discussion of this modernization paradigm, see Sahliyeh (1990: 3–5).
8. Siavoshi (1990: 176–7).
9. Hertzberg (1986: 89).
10. See Kedourie (1966: ch. 6; and 1970: introduction).
11. On this, see Baron (1960).
12. On England and France, see Guenée (1985: 54–8); on Russia, see McNeill (1963: 658–64); on Persia, see Savory (1992).
13. On Slovak religious movements, see Brock (1976: 7–19); on Indian, see Heimsath (1964: ch. 6).

14. See chapter 2 on Ireland; on Japanese Shintoism, see Fridall (1983).
15. Smith (1971: ch. 10), and for a further development of his thesis, see his (1981a: ch. 5).
16. On this, Smith (1984).
17. D. E. Smith (1974: 3–28).
18. D. E. Smith (1990).
19. Gellner (1992: 4–22).
20. Sahliyeh (1990: 3–10).
21. Roy (1985).
22. For a useful brief survey of Zionism up to 1945, see Hertzberg (1986) and Tessler (1990).
23. Tessler (1990: 270).
24. Davis (1987: 154).
25. Schnell (1987: 173–6).
26. Davis (1987: 153–5).
27. Schnell (1987: 173).
28. This and the following paragraph draws on Voll (1987).
29. For an important study, see Sivan (1985: ch. 3).
30. Davis (1987: 163).
31. Haddad (1991: 34).
32. See Voll (1987).
33. Haddad (1991: 9).
34. See Cantori (1990).
35. On the relationship between religious movements and the republic, see Lipsitz (1984).
36. Esposito (1991: 42).
37. Schnell (1987: 180–9).
38. On the politics of the Muslim Brotherhood in Egypt and the Sudan, see Voll (1992).
39. Cantori (1990: 192–4).
40. Voll (1992: 212–13).
41. Hunter (1990: 43).
42. Piscatori (1986: 144–5).
43. Kramer (1986: 1).
44. See Kramer's (1986) carefully documented study.

45. Siavoshi (1990: 186–8).
46. Hunter (1990: 45).
47. Piscatori (1986: 146).
48. See Voll (1992).
49. Piscatori (1986: conclusion).
50. For example, Bellah (1964).

CHAPTER 4

1. Definitions of *ethnie* vary, but 104 were listed in the Soviet census (Krejci and Velimsky, 1981: 117).
2. Rywkin (1990: 68).
3. For example, Dallin and Lapidus (1991) and Brumby (1991).
4. Szporluk (1986) discusses Richard Pipes' thesis about the imperial pattern of Russian national formation; Raeff (1971) surveys the differing modes of imperial expansion; and Seton-Watson (1986) provides a historical overview of Russian nationalism.
5. See Connor (1984: chapters 2 and 3).
6. G. Smith (1990: 4–5).
7. See Kagedan (1990).
8. For an authoritative analysis of the contradictions in this policy, see Connor (1984: ch. 8).
9. For a survey of the range of non-Russian responses to the Russians, see Bennigsen (1986).
10. See D'Encausse (1979: ch. 2).
11. Schwartz (1990: 143).
12. Mace (1990: 177).
13. Swietochowski (1990: 23, 35).
14. Bromlei (1991: 201).
15. See Ramet (1989a).
16. Swietochowski (1990: 229–32).
17. Suny (1990: 117).
18. Shanin (1989: 416–20).

19. Szporluk (1986: 168–9).
20. Mace (1990: 177–81).
21. Krejci and Velimsky (1981: 131).
22. Simon (1991: 281).
23. Ibid., 275, for a discussion of the increase in Russian influence.
24. See Sadomskaya (1990).
25. Simon (1991: 305–7).
26. Ibid., 284–5, 295.
27. Rakowski-Harmstone (1986: 248).
28. See Motyl (1987).
29. De Tocqueville (1966: 196).
30. See Simon (1991: ch. 9).
31. See Miner (1989).
32. Collins (1986: ch. 8).
33. See Schroeder (1986: 301–7).
34. On this, see Dunlop (1983).
35. Pospielovsky (1989).
36. Motyl (1987: 158).
37. Suny (1990: 122).
38. Kennedy (1989: 645).
39. Roeder (1991: 215).
40. See Simon (1991: 266). In 1959–60 506,300 non-Russians enrolled in college, whereas in 1980–81 the figure was 2,219,000. In 1959–60 502,200 were enrolled in vocational education whereas in 1980–1 the figure was 2,000,000.
41. See Roeder (1991) for an important overview.
42. Ibid., 212–14.
43. Lapidus (1991: 107).
44. Simon (1991: 283–4).
45. Roeder (1991: 219–24).
46. Pearson (1991: 100–2).
47. Suny (1991: 114).
48. Ibid., 115.
49. For a useful discussion, see Pearson (1991).
50. Schroeder (1991: 377–8).

51. See Suny (1991).
52. For example, Bennigsen (1986).
53. See Collins (1986: ch. 8).
54. See Conquest's foreword to Alexei and Wimbush (1988). Ellen Jones – not a proponent of this perspective – reports in 1985 that of the highest ranking military, Russians composed 80% and Slavs 98%. The equivalent figures for senior officers were 57% and 80%, respectively. Muslims were underrepresented but not excluded (Jones 1985: 200).
55. See essays in Alexei and Wimbush (1988).
56. D'Encausse (1979: ch. 2).
57. Ibid., ch. 8.
58. Loc. cit.; and also Alexei and Wimbush (1988: introduction).
59. See Szporluk (1986) on the state's distinctiveness, and Laitin (1991: 142–4) on its comparability with others.
60. Seton-Watson (1986: 28).
61. Gellner (1989: 26).
62. On collapse followed by uncertainty see Hroch, quoted in Hobsbawm, 'Dangerous Exit from a Stormy World', *New Statesman*, 8 November 1991.
63. Hobsbawm (1990: 173). This hydraulic thesis runs quite against the thrust of Hobsbawm's 'invention of tradition' argument in his study.
64. Besançon (1986).
65. See Sadomskaya (1990).
66. For an authoritative analysis of these contradictions, see Connor (1984: ch. 11).
67. See Roeder (1991).
68. For a similar critique of Brass's

political model discussed in chapter 1, see Robinson (1979: esp. 106–7).
69. On the Lithuanians, see Verdys (1990).
70. Duncan (1990: 106).
71. On this, see Szporluk (1991: 443).
72. Besançon (1986: 9).
73. For a survey of the range of nationalist ideas, see Szporluk (1991).
74. Ibid.
75. Laitin (1991: 142–3).
76. See Conquest's essay in Alexei and Wimbush (1988).
77. See Smith (1986a and b).

CHAPTER 5

1. For an 'internationalist' perspective, see Halliday (1988); also the recent monographs of McNeill (1986) and Hobsbawm (1990).
2. On the EC challenge to the nation-state, see Wallace (1990: chapters 2 and 6).
3. Breuilly (1982: ch. 14); also Hobsbawm (1990: ch. 6).
4. For a survey of post-1945 minority nationalisms, see the essays in Watson (1990).
5. The outstanding scholar on this is Hammar (1990).
6. Pinder (1991: 201).
7. Wallace (1990: 21–8, 49).
8. Bertram (1990: 55).
9. Pinder (1991: ch. 9).
10. For a discussion, see Wallace (1990: ch. 4) and Pinder (1991: 212–13).
11. One of the leading exponents of

this, Ernst Haas (1958), was also an important EEC official.

12. De Witte (1987: 132–4); and for an example see Bruce (1990).

13. Keohane (1991: 18).

14. Pinder (1991: 10–15, ch. 10).

15. See Keohane (1991: 21–33).

16. See de Witte (1987).

17. Notably, Wallace (1990).

18. Ibid., ch. 4.

19. See de Witte (1990).

20. Pinder (1991: ch. 1).

21. Story (1990) argues this strongly.

22. Keohane (1991: 10–12).

23. See Story (1990). On French defence policies, see Yost (1990) and on Germany, Bertram (1990).

24. Keohane (1991).

25. On some of these issues, consult Goldstein (1991).

26. See Krejci and Velimsky (1981: 77, 83).

27. Watson (1990) is useful; also Smith (1981a).

28. Beer (1977: 150–1).

29. The classic text is Hechter (1975).

30. Arlett and Sallnow (1989: 6).

31. As Nairn (1977: 200–2) observes in his criticisms of Hechter.

32. On Italian regional Leagues, see Woods (1992).

33. See Watson (1990: ch. 12).

34. Arlett and Sallnow (1989).

35. Keating (1990: 187–94).

36. Brugmans (1989) makes this point.

37. Grugel (1990: 113).

38. See Legum (1965: 38–63) and Neuberger (1976).

39. Hrbek (1987) provides an interesting analysis.

40. McNeill (1986: 1–31).

41. Ibid., 31–47.

42. Ibid., 57–85.

43. Hammar (1990: 1).

44. See Brubaker (1990).

45. McNeill (1986: 76–80).

46. Hammar (1990: ch. 6).

47. On this, see the useful collection in Sheffer (1986).

48. See Hammar (1990: ch 12).

49. Ibid., 129–30.

50. *Le Monde*, 20 May 1992.

51. Discussed in Asad (1990: 470–5).

52. Koven (1992: 25–33).

53. See the important work of Hall (1985).

54. On the role of cultural nationalism in shaping Japanese business elites, see the perceptive study of Yoshino (1992).

CHAPTER 6

1. See the discussion of the immigrant nation in Anthony Smith (1986b: 241).

2. As argued in Stephen Castles et al (1988).

3. Federal expenses specifically for the Centennial in Canada were Can.$85.5 million, given in *Canadian Centennial Commission, 6th and Final Report*, 1967–8; for the Australian Bicentennial Aus.$198 million, see Denis O'Brien (1991: 119). But there were also special initiatives, such as in Canada Expo '67 (Can.$200 million), and in Australia the construction of the New Parliament House

(Aus.$1.1 billion) and a road building programme (Aus.$2.5 billion).

4. E. J. Hobsbawm (1984: 263–80).

5. See Bothwell (1985); also American Revolution Bicentennial Authority, *The Bicentennial of the United States of America: A Final Report to the People*, vol. 1, 1977, 58.

6. Ibid., 33.

7. On these internal conflicts, see H. Tennant, 'Are we going to be late for our own birthday party?', *Maclean's Magazine*, 16 November 1964, 24; LaMarsh (1968: ch. 8).

8. In the USA, for example, there were nearly 12,000 approved projects, and a limited survey suggests that 70% of costs were financed by local government and private funds, see ARBA, ibid., 77–88.

9. See LaMarsh (1968: 184).

10. See Zelimsky (1989: ch. 2).

11. ARBA, ibid., 102.

12. National Archives of Canada, *Records of the Centennial Commission*, RG 69, vol. 39, International Development Programme, 26 January 1967.

13. ABA, 'Australian Bicentennial Celebrations', *Australian Foreign Affairs Record*, 56 (1), January 1985, 9.

14. See Zelimsky (1989: 102).

15. Quoted in *Maclean's Magazine*, 18 May 1963, 1.

16. *Canadian Centennial Commission, 3rd Annual Report*, 1964–5, 7.

17. J. Dusche, 'The American Tragicomedy', *Saturday Review*, 1 July 1972.

18. See Warhurst (1987: 8–18).

19. *IPA Review*, 30 (1), Winter 1985, 49.

20. J. Warner, 'The Rediscovery of America', *Saturday Evening Post*, April 1977.

21. *Centennial Facts: General Information on the Centennial of Canadian Confederation, 1867–1967*, Ottawa, September 1965, 38.

22. *Canadian Centennial Commission, 6th and Final Report*, 1967–8, 8.

23. See O'Brien (1991: 30, 38–9).

24. *IPA Review*, 30 (1), Winter 1985, 49–51.

25. Warhurst (1987: 13).

26. J. Michener, *New York Times*, 5 April 1975, 29.

27. *Canadian Centennial Commission, 6th and Final Report*, 1967–8, 7.

28. LaMarsh (1968: 179, 190).

29. P. Spearitt (1988: 7).

30. ARBA, ibid., vol. 2, 23.

31. J. Dusche, op. cit.

32. Ibid.

33. William Buckley Jr, 'Living up the 200th', *National Review*, 9 July 1976.

34. ABA (1985: 29).

35. Ken Baker, 'Reply to John Reid', *IPA*, 39 (1), 1985, 51–3.

36. *New York Times*, 4 July 1976.

37. On local re-enactments, see Lowenthal (1977, 253–67).

38. For the financial figures, see *Canadian Centenary Commission, 4th Annual Report*, 1965; also LaMarsh (1968: 181–3).

39. See Crean and Rioux (1983: chapters 2 and 3).

40. Alomes (1988).

41. See H. Kissinger, 'America and

the World: Principles and Pragmatism', *Time*, 27 December 1976; and the reprints of articles by Archibald Macleish and H. Commager in *Current*, 185, September 1975, 3–25.

42. See C. Van Woodward (1977).

BIBLIOGRAPHY

Alexei, A. and Wimbush, S. E. (eds) 1988 *Ethnic Minorities in the Red Army*, Boulder, Colorado: Westview Press.

Alomes, Stephen 1988 *A Nation At Last?*, North Ryde, NSW: Angus & Robertson.

Anderson, Benedict 1983 *Imagined Communities*, London: Verso.

Antoun R. T. and Hegland M. E. (eds) 1987 *Religious Resurgence: Contemporary Cases in Islam, Christianity, and Judaism*, New York: Syracuse University Press.

Argyle, W. J. 1976 'Size and Scale as Factors in the Development of Nationalist Movements', in Anthony D. Smith (ed.), *Nationalist Movements*, London: Macmillan.

Arlett, S. and Sallnow, J. 1989 'European Centres of Dissent', *Geographical Magazine*, 61, 6–9.

Armstrong, John 1982 *Nations before Nationalism*, Chapel Hill: University of North Carolina Press.

Asad T. 1990 'Multi-Culturalism and the British Identity in the Wake of the Rushdie Affair', *Politics and Society*, 18 (4), 455–80.

Barnard, F. M. 1969 'Culture and Political Development: Herder's Suggestive Insights', *American Political Science Review*, LXIV (2), 379–97.

Baron, S. W. 1960 *Modern Nationalism and Religion*, New York, Meridian Books.

Barth, Fredrik (ed.) 1969 *Ethnic Groups and Boundaries*, Boston: Little, Brown and Co.

Beer, W. 1977 'The Social Class of Ethnic Activists in Contemporary France', in M. J. Esman (ed.), *Ethnic Conflict in the Modern World*, Ithaca: Cornell University Press.

Bellah, Robert N. 1964 'Religious Evolution', *American Sociological Review*, 29, 358–74.

Bellah, Robert N. (ed.) 1965 *Religion and Progress in South Asia*, New York: Macmillan.

Bennigsen, Alexandre 1986 'Soviet Minority Nationalism in Historical Perspective', in R. Conquest (ed.), *The Last Empire*, Stanford: Hoover Press.

Berlin, Isaiah 1976 *Vico and Herder*, London: Hogarth Press.

Bertram, C. 1990 'The German Question', *Foreign Affairs*, 69 (2), 45–62.

Besançon, Alaine 1986 'Nationalism and Bolshevism in the Soviet Union', in R. Conquest (ed.), *The Last Empire*, Stanford: Hoover Press.

Bothwell, R. 1985 'Centennial Year', *The Canadian Encyclopaedia*, Edmonton: Hortig.

Boyce, D. George 1982 *Nationalism in Ireland*, London: Croom Helm.

Brass, Paul R. 1979 'Elite Groups, Symbol Manipulation, and Ethnic Identity among the Muslims of South Asia', in D. Taylor and M. Yapp (eds), *Political Identity in South Asia*, London: Curzon Press.

Breuilly, John 1982 *Nationalism and the State*, Manchester: Manchester University Press.

Brock, Peter 1976 *The Slovak National Awakening*, Toronto: East European Monographs.

Bromlei, J. B. 1991 'The Rise of Ethnic Assertiveness', in A. Brumby (ed.) *Chronicle of a Revolution*, New York: Pantheon Books.

Brubaker, W. R. 1990 'Immigration, Citizenship, and the Nation State in France and Germany: A Comparative Historical Analysis', *International Sociology*, 5 (4), 379–407.

Bruce, L. 1990 'Europe's Locomotive', *Foreign Policy*, 78, 68–90.

Brugmans, H. 1989 'Today's Nationalism: Old Forms and New', *History of European Ideas*, 11, 305–11.

Brumby A. (ed.) 1991 *Chronicle of a Revolution*, New York: Pantheon Books.

Brym, Robert J. 1980 *Intellectuals and Politics*, London, Allen & Unwin.

Burke, Peter 1978 'The Discovery of the People', in *Popular Culture in Early Modern Europe*, London: Temple Smith.

Cantori, L. J. 1990 'The Islamic Revival as Conservatism and Progress in Contemporary Egypt', in E. Sahliyeh (ed.), *Religious Resurgence and Politics in the Contemporary World*, New York: State University of New York Press.

Castles Stephen et al. 1988 *Mistaken Identity: Multi-culturalism and the Demise of Nationalism in Australia*, Sydney: Pluto Press.

Collias, K. A. 1990 'Making Soviet Citizens: Patriotic and Internationalist Education in the Formation of a Soviet State Identity', in H. R. Huttenbach (ed.), *Soviet Nationality Policies*, London: Mansell.

Collins, Randall 1986 *Weberian Sociological Theory*, Cambridge: Cambridge University Press.

Connor, Walker 1978 'A Nation is a Nation, is a State, is an Ethnic Group, is a . . . ', *Ethnic and Racial Studies*, 1 (4), 378–410.

Connor, Walker 1984 *The National Question in Marxist-Leninist Theory and Strategy*, Princeton: Princeton University Press.

Connor, Walker 1990 'When is a Nation?', *Ethnic and Racial Studies*, 13 (1), 92–103.

Connor, Walker 1991 'From Tribe to Nation?', *History of European Ideas*, 13 (1/2), 5–18.

Conquest, R. (ed), 1986 *The Last Empire*, Stanford: Hoover Press.

Crean S. M. and Rioux M. 1983 *Two Nations*, Toronto: Lorrimer.

Dallin A. and Lapidus G. W. (eds), 1991 *The Soviet System in Crisis*, Boulder, Westview Press.

Davis, E. 1987 'Religion against the State: A Political Economy of Religious Radicalism in Egypt and Israel', in R. T. Antoun and M. E. Hegland (eds), *Religious Resurgence: Contemporary Cases in Islam, Christianity, and Judaism*, New York: Syracuse University Press.

D'Encausse, H. Carrere 1979 *Decline of an Empire*, New York: Newsweek Books.

De Tocqueville, Alexis 1835 *The Ancien Régime and the French Revolution*, 1966 London: Fontana.

Deutsch, Karl 1966 *Nationalism and Social Communication*, New York: MIT Press.

De Witte, Bernard 1987 'Building Europe's Image and Identity', in A. Risksbaron et al. (eds), *Europe From a Cultural Perspective*, The Hague: UPR.

De Witte, Bernard 1990 'Cultural Linkages', in W. Wallace (ed.) *The Dynamics of European Integration*, New York: Pinder.

Duncan, Peter J. S. 1990 'Ukrainians' in G. Smith (ed), *The Nationalities Question in the Soviet Union*, London: Longman.

Dunlop, John 1983 *The Faces of Contemporary Russian Nationalism*, Princeton: Princeton University Press.

Esposito, J. L. 1991 'Trailblazers of the Islamic Resurgence', in Y. Y. Haddad, J. O. Voll and J. L. Esposito (eds), *The Contemporary Islamic Revival*, New York: Greenwood Press.

Fridall, W. 1983 'Modern Japanese Nationalism: State Structure and the Religion that was "not a Religion"', in P. H. Merkl and N. Smart (eds), *Religion and Politics in the Modern World*, New York; New York University Press.

Gellner, Ernest 1964 *Thought and Change*, London: Weidenfeld amd Nicolson.

Gellner, Ernest 1973 'Scale and Nation', *Philosophy of the Social Sciences*, 3, 1–17.

Gellner, Ernest 1983 *Nations and Nationalism*, Oxford: Blackwell.

Gellner, Ernest 1989 *Culture, Identity and Politics*, Cambridge: Cambridge University Press.

Gellner, Ernest 1992 *Postmodernism, Reason, and Religion*, London: Routledge.

Goldstein, W. 1991 'EC Eurostalling', *Foreign Policy*, 85, 129–47.

Grugel, Jean 1990 'The Basques' in M. Watson (ed.) *Contemporary Minority Nationalism*, London: Routledge.

Guenée, Bernard 1985 *States and Rulers in Later Medieval Europe*, Oxford: Blackwell.

Haas, Ernst B. 1958 *The Unity of Europe: Political, Social, and Economic Forces (1950–57)*, Stanford: Stanford University Press.

Haddad, Y. Y. 1991 'The Revivalist Literature and the

Literature on Revival' in Y. Y. Haddad, J. O. Voll and J. L. Esposito (eds), *The Contemporary Islamic Revival*, New York: Greenwood Press.

Hall, John A. 1985 *Powers and Liberties*, Oxford: Blackwell.

Hall, John A. 1988 *Liberalism*, London: Paladin.

Halliday, Fred 1988 'Three Concepts of Internationalism', *International Affairs*, 64 (2), 187–98.

Hammar, Tomas 1990 *Democracy and the Nation State*, Aldershot: Avebury.

Hechter, Michael 1975 *Internal Colonialism*, London: Routledge.

Heimsath, C. 1964 *Indian Nationalism and Hindu Social Reform*, Princeton: Princeton University Press.

Herder, J. G. 1968 *Reflections on the Philosophy of the History of Mankind*, (ed.), F. Manuel, Chicago: University of Chicago Press.

Hertzberg, A. 1986 'The Religious Right in the State of Israel', *Annals*, AAPSS, 483, 84–91.

Hobsbawm, E. J. 1984 'Mass-Producing Traditions', in E. J. Hobsbawm and T. Ranger (eds), *The Invention of Tradition*, Cambridge: Cambridge University Press.

Hobsbawm, E. J. 1990 *Nations and Nationalism since 1780*, London: Clarendon.

Howard, Michael 1976 *War in European History*, London: Oxford University Press.

Hrbek, R. 1987 'The German Länder and the European Community', *AussenPolitik*, 38, 120–33.

Hroch, M. 1984 *Social Preconditions of National Revivals in Europe*, Cambridge: Cambridge University Press.

Hunter, Shireen T. 1990 *Iran and the World*, Bloomington: Indiana University Press.

Hutchinson, John 1987a *The Dynamics of Cultural Nationalism: The Gaelic Revival and the Creation of the Irish Nation State*, London: Allen and Unwin.

Hutchinson, John 1987b 'Cultural Nationalism, Elite Mobility, and Nation-Building', *British Journal of Sociology*, XXXVIII (4), 482–501.

Jones, Ellen 1985 *The Red Army and Society*, Boston: Allen and Unwin.

July, R. W. 1968 *The Origins of Modern African Thought*, London: Faber.

Kagedan, A. 1990 'Territorial Units as Nationality Policy', in H. R. Huttenbach (ed.), *Soviet Nationality Policies*, London: Mansell.

Keating, M. 1990 'Minority Nationalism and the State: the European Case', in M. Watson (ed.) *Contemporary Minority Nationalism*, London: Routledge.

Kedourie, Elie 1966 *Nationalism*, London: Hutchinson.

Kedourie, Elie (ed.) 1970 *Nationalism in Asia and Africa*, London: Weidenfeld and Nicolson.

Kennedy, Paul 1989 *The Rise and Fall of the Great Powers*, London: Fontana.

Keohane R. 1991 'Institutional Change in Europe in the 1980s', in R. Keohane and S. Hoffman (eds), *The New European Community: Decision-Making and Institutional Change*, Boulder, Colorado: Westview Press.

Kohn, Hans 1946 *The Idea of Nationalism*, New York: Macmillan.

Kopf, David 1969 *British Orientalism and the Bengali Cultural Renaissance: The Dynamics of Indian Modernization (1773–1835)*, Berkeley: University of California Press.

Koven, R. 1992 'Muslim Immigrants and French Nationalists', *Society*, 18 (4), 25–33.

Kramer, M. 1986 *Islam Assembled: The Advent of the Muslim Congress*, New York: Columbia University Press.

Krejci, J. and Velimsky, V. 1981 *Ethnic and Political Nations in Europe*, London: Croom Helm.

Laitin, D. 1991 'The National Uprisings in the Soviet Union', *World Politics*, 44, 139–177.

LaMarsh, Judy 1968 *Memoirs of a Bird in a Golden Cage*, Toronto: McLelland and Stewart.

Lapidus, G. W. 1991 'Gorbachev's Nationalities Problem', in A. Dallin and G. W. Lapidus (eds), *The Soviet System in Crisis*, Boulder: Westview Press.

Legum, C. 1965 *PanAfricanism: A Short Political Guide*, London: Pall Mall Press.

Levenson, Joseph 1959 *Liang Ch'I Ch'ao and the Mind of Modern China*, Berkeley: University of California Press.

Lewis, Bernard 1968 *The Emergence of Modern Turkey*, London: Oxford University Press.

Lipsitz, George 1984 '"The Drum Major Instinct": American Religion since 1945', *Telos*, 58, 95–107.

Lowenthal, D. 1977 'The Bicentennial Landscape: A Mirror Held up to the Past', *The Geographical Review*, 67 (3), 253–67.

McCully, B. T. 1966 *English Education and the Origins of Indian Nationalism*, Gloucester, Mass.: Smith.

Mace, James E. 1990 'The Famine of 1932–33: A Watershed in the Study of Soviet Nationality Policy' in H. R. Huttenbach (ed.), *Soviet Nationality Policies*, London: Mansell.

McNeill, W. H. 1963 *The Rise of the West*, New York: New English Library.

McNeill, W. H. 1986 *Polyethnicity and National Unity in World History*, Toronto: Toronto University Press.

Mayall, James 1990 *Nationalism and International Society*, Cambridge: Cambridge University Press.

Mazrui, Ali 1968 'Some Socio-political Functions of English Literature in Africa', in J. A. Fishman (ed.) *Language Problems of Developing Nations*, New York: Wiley.

Miner, S. M. 1989 'Military Crisis and Social Change in Russian and Soviet History', in G. E. Hudson (ed.), *Soviet National Security Policy under Perestroika*, Boston: Unwin Hyman.

Mortimer, Edward 1991 'Christianity and Islam', *International Affairs*, 67 (1), 7–17.

Mosse, George L. 1971 'Caesarism, Circuses, amd Movements', *Journal of Contemporary History*, 6 (2), 167–82.

Motyl, A. 1987 *Will the Non-Russians Rebel?*, Ithaca: Cornell University Press.

Nairn, Tom 1977 *The Break-Up of Britain*, London: New Left Books.

Neuberger, B. 1976 'The African Concept of Balkanization', *Journal of Modern African Studies*, 14 (3), 523–9.

O'Brien, Denis 1991 *The Bicentennial Affair*, Sydney: ABC.

Ozouf, Mona 1988 *Festivals and the French Revolution*, Cambridge, Mass.: Harvard University Press.

Pearson, R. 1991 'Nationalities: Decolonizing the Last Empire' in D. K. Spring (ed), *The Impact of Gorbachev*, London: Pinter.

Pech, S. Z. 1976 'The Nationalist Movements of the Austrian Slavs in 1848: a Comparative Sociological Profile', *Social History*, IX (18), 336–56.

Pinder, John 1991 *European Community: the Building of a Union*, Oxford: Oxford University Press.

Piscatori, James P. 1986 *Islam in a World of Nation States*, Cambridge: Cambridge University Press.

Poggi, Gianfranco 1978 *The Development of the Modern State*, London: Hutchinson.

Pospielovsky, D. 1989 'The "Russian Orientation" and Orthodox Church: From the Slavophiles to the "Neo-Slavophiles"', in P. Ramet, (ed.) 1989a *Religion and Nationalism in the Soviet Union and Eastern Europe*, Durham NC, Duke University Press.

Raeff, M. 1971 'Patterns of Russian Imperial Policy Towards the Nationalities', in E. Allworth (ed.), *Soviet Nationality Problems*, New York: Columbia University Press.

Rakowska-Harmstone, Teresa 1986 'Minority Nationalism Today: An Overview', in R. Conquest (ed.), *The Last Empire*, Stanford: Hoover Press.

Ramet, P. (ed.) 1989a *Religion and Nationalism in the Soviet Union and Eastern Europe*, Durham NC, Duke University Press.

Ramet, P. 1989b 'The Interplay of Religious Policy and Nationalities Policy in the Soviet Union and Eastern Europe', in P. Ramet (ed.), *Religion and Nationalism in the Soviet Union and Eastern Europe*, Durham NC, Duke University Press.

Robinson, Francis 1979 'Islam and Muslim Separatism', in D. Taylor and M. Yapp (eds), *Political Identity in South Asia*, London: Curzon Press.

Roeder, P. G. 1991 'Soviet Federalism and Ethnic Mobilization', *World Politics*, 43, 196–232.

Roy, Oliver 1985 'Fundamentalism, Traditionalism and Islam', *Telos*, 65, 122–7.

Rudnytsky, I. L. 1977 'The Ukrainian National Movement on the Eve of the First World War', *East European Quarterly*, XI (2), 141–54.

Rywkin, M. 1990 'Searching for Soviet Nationalities Policy', in H. R. Huttenbach (ed.), *Soviet Nationality Policies*, London: Mansell.

Sadomskaya, Natalia 1990 'New Soviet Rituals and National Integration in the USSR', in H. R. Huttenbach (ed.), *Soviet Nationality Policies*, London: Mansell.

Sahliyeh, E. 1990 'Religious Resurgence and Political Modernization', in E. Sahliyeh (ed.), *Religious Resurgence and Politics in the Contemporary World*, New York: State University of New York Press.

Savory, Roger M. 1992 'Land of the Lion and the Sun', in B. Lewis (ed.), *The World of Islam*, London: Thames and Hudson.

Schnell, David J. 1987 'Religion and Political Dissent in Israel: the Case of Gush Emunim', in R. T. Antoun and M. E. Hegland (eds), *Religious Resurgence: Contemporary Cases in Islam, Christianity, and Judaism*, New York: Syracuse University Press.

Schroeder, G. E. 1986 'Social and Economic Aspects of the Nationality Problem', in R. Conquest (ed.), *The Last Empire*, Stanford: Hoover Press.

Schroeder, G. E. 1991 'The Soviet Economy on a Treadmill of *Perestroika*: Gorbachev's First Five Years', in A. Dallin and G. W. Lapidus (eds), *The Soviet System in Crisis*, Boulder: Westview Press.

Schwartz, Lee 1990 'Regional Population Distribution and National Homelands', in H. R. Huttenbach, (ed.), *Soviet Nationality Policies*, London: Mansell.

Seton-Watson, Hugh 1977 *Nations and States*, London: Methuen.

Seton-Watson, Hugh 1986 'Russian Nationalism in Historical Perspective', in R. Conquest, (ed), *The Last Empire*, Stanford: Hoover Press.

Shanin, Teodor 1989 'Ethnicity in the Soviet Union: Analytical Perception and Political Strategies', *Comparative Studies in Society and History*, 31, 409–24.

Sheehy, Jean 1980 *The Rediscovery of Ireland's Past: The Celtic Revival (1830–1930)*, London: Thames and Hudson.

Sheffer, G. (ed.) 1986 *Modern Diasporas in International Politics*, London: Croom Helm.

Siavoshi, Susan 1990 *Liberal Nationalism in Iran*, Boulder, Colorado, Westview Press.

Simon, G. 1991 *Nationalism and Policy Towards the Nationalities in the Soviet Union*, Boulder, Colorado: Westview Press.

Sivan, Emmanuel 1985 *Radical Islam*, New Haven: Yale University Press.

Skinner, Quentin 1974 'Some Problems in the Analysis of Political Thought and Action', *Political Theory* 2 (3), 277–303.

Smith, Anthony D. 1971 *Theories of Nationalism*, London: Duckworth.

Smith, Anthony D. 1981a *The Ethnic Revival in the Modern World*, Cambridge: Cambridge University Press.

Smith, Anthony D. 1981b 'War and Ethnicity: the Role of Warfare in the Formation, Self-Images, and Cohesion of Ethnic Communities', *Ethnic and Racial Studies*, 4 (4), 375–97.

Smith, Anthony D. 1984 'National Identity and Myths of Ethnic Descent', *Research in Social Movements, Conflict, and Change*, 7, 95–130.

Smith, Anthony D. 1986a *The Ethnic Origins of Nations*, Oxford: Blackwell.

Smith, Anthony D. 1986b 'State-making and Nation-building', in John Hall (ed.), *States in History*, Oxford: Blackwell.

Smith, Anthony D. 1989 'The Origins of Nations', *Ethnic and Racial Studies*, 12 (3), 340–67.

Smith, Anthony D. 1991 *National Identity*, Harmondsworth, Middlesex: Penguin.

Smith, D. E. (ed.) 1974 *Religion and Political Modernization*, New Haven: Yale University Press.

Smith, D. E. 1990 'The Limits of Religious Resurgence' in E. Sahliyeh (ed.), *Religious Resurgence and Politics in the Contemporary World*, New York: State University of New York Press.

Smith, Graham 1990 'Nationalities Policy from Lenin to Gorbachev', in G. Smith (ed), *The Nationalities Question in the Soviet Union*, London: Longman.

Spearitt, P. 1988 'Celebration of a Nation', *Australian Historical Studies*, 23 (91), 3–20.

Story, Jonathan 1990 'Europe's Future: Western Union or Common Home?', in C. Crouch and D. Marquand (eds), *The Politics of 1992: Beyond the Single Market*, London: Blackwell.

Suny, R. G. 1990 'Nationalities and Nationalism', in A. Brumby (ed.) *Chronicle of a Revolution*, New York: Pantheon Books.

Suny, R. G. 1991 'Incomplete Revolution: National Movements and the Collapse of the Soviet Union', *New Left Review*, 189, 111–124.

Swietochowski, T. 1990 'Islam and Nationality in Tsarist Russia and the Soviet Union', in H. R. Huttenbach, (ed.), *Soviet Nationality Policies*, London: Mansell.

Szporluk, Roman 1986 'The Ukraine and Russia', in R. Conquest, (ed), *The Last Empire*, Stanford: Hoover Press.

Szporluk, Roman 1991 'Dilemmas of Russian Nationalism', in A. Dallin and G. W. Lapidus (eds), *The Soviet System in Crisis*, Boulder: Westview Press.

Tessler, Mark 1990 'Religion and Politics in the Jewish State of Israel', in E. Sahliyeh (ed.), *Religious Resurgence and Politics in the Contemporary World*, New York: State University of New York Press.

Tilly, Charles (ed.) 1975 *The Formation of National States in Western Europe*, Princeton: Princeton University Press.

Trevor-Roper, Hugh 1983 'The Invention of Tradition: the Highland Tradition of Scotland', in E. J. Hobsbawm and T. Ranger (eds), *The Invention of Tradition*, Cambridge: Cambridge University Press.

Van Woodward, C. 'The Ageing of America', *American Historical Review*, 83, 1977, 583–94.

Verdys, V. Stanley 1990 'Lithuanians', in G. Smith (ed), *The*

Nationalities Question in the Soviet Union, London: Longman.

Voll, J. O. 1987 'Islamic Renewal and the "Failure of the West"' in R. T. Antoun and M. E. Hegland (eds), *Religious Resurgence: Contemporary Cases in Islam, Christianity, and Judaism*, New York: Syracuse University Press.

Voll, J. O. 1992 'Religion and Politics in Islamic Africa', in M. C. Moen and L. S. Gustafson (eds), *The Religious Challenge to the State*, Philadelphia: Temple University Press.

Wallace, William 1990 *The Transformation of Western Europe*, London: Pinter.

Warhurst, J. 1987 'The Politics and Management of Australia's Bicentennial Year', *Politics*, 22 (1), May, 1987, 8–18.

Watson, M. 1990 *Contemporary Minority Nationalism*, London: Routledge.

Weber, Eugene 1976 *Peasants into Frenchmen: the Modernization of Rural France (1870–1914)*, Stanford: Stanford University Press.

Woods, Dwayne 1992 'The Rise of Regional Leagues in Italian Politics', *West European Politics*, 15 (2), 56–76.

Yoshino, Kosaku 1992 *Cultural Nationalism in Contemporary Japan*, London: Routledge.

Yost, David S. 1990 'France in the New Europe', *Foreign Affairs*, 69 (5), 107–28.

Zelimsky, Wilbur 1989 *Nation into State*, Chapel Hill: University of North Carolina.

INDEX

Fontana History of Germany

The Divided Nation
1918–1990

Mary Fulbrook

Division has been the touchstone of German history since 1918: from the self-destructive Weimar Republic, through the extremes of the Nazi era to the political fragmentation of the nation after 1945. The Federal Republic of Germany and the German Democratic Republic appeared – in very different ways – to represent remarkably stable, successful solutions to the problems of Germany history; yet they too were based on shifting ground, on political uncertainties and self-doubt, in the shadow of the Holocaust. And with the gentle revolution of autumn 1989 and the breathtakingly rapid unification of the two Germanies in 1990, new divisions between past and present, and within and between the Germans of East and West, ran through the complexities of political and economic reconstruction.

May Fulbrook recounts the tortuous historical narrative, of revolutions and reaction, of continuities and change, of prosperity and deprivation, with precision and clarity. In a powerful new interpretation of the dynamics of German history since 1918, she focuses particularly on the role of elites, and the implications of political dissent and opposition, under changing socio-economic conditions and international circumstances. *The Divided Nation* – an accessible, persuasive study which treats of twentieth-century history as a whole, from the perspective of reunification – is essential reading for all who seek answers to the fundamental questions of modern German history.

ISBN 0 00 686111 3

Fontana Press